A Passion for God's Story

A Passion for God's Story

Discovering Your Place in
God's Strategic Plan

Philip Greenslade

PATERNOSTER PRESS

First published in 2002 by Paternoster Press

08 07 06 05 04 03 02   7 6 5 4 3 2 1

Paternoster Press is an imprint of Authentic Media,
P.O. Box 300, Carlisle, Cumbria, CA3 0QS, UK
and
P.O. Box 1047, Waynesboro, GA 30830-2047, USA

Website: www.paternoster-publishing.com

British Library Cataloguing in Publication Data
A catalogue record for this book is available from the British Library

ISBN 1-84227-094-X

Cover Design by FourNineZero
Typeset by WestKey Ltd, Falmouth, Cornwall
Printed in Great Britain by Cox & Wyman Ltd, Reading, Berkshire

Contents

Preface

This book is a modest exercise in biblical theology. Its aim is the ambitious one of seeking to outline the big story of God's redemptive plan in Scripture, largely by tracing the covenantal commitments God has made in furtherance of that plan.

'God's Story' first emerged as the basic structure of a one-year, day-release, training course that I taught at Waverley Abbey House under the auspices of CWR. The material was subsequently reformatted as weekend and evening classes and, latterly, as a seminar series for presentation at various locations. The kind reception it has received has encouraged me to present it in book form.

Having taught the Bible for over thirty years, I have often encountered the comment that, although engaged with the many disparate and important themes of Scripture or topics of Christian truth, many Christians lacked any idea of the big picture, of what the Bible as a whole was about – hence *A Passion for God's Story*.

- I have a passion for God's story because I recognise that it is in story form that the Bible has chiefly come to us and that God has chosen to reveal himself to us.
- I have a passion for God's Story because I believe it to be the essence of what the apostles preached as gospel

and the shape into which they sought to pastor the
churches in their care.
- I have a passion for God's story because I sense that
such an approach fits the Church's current context in a
post-modern world that is suspicious of all overarching
accounts of reality.
- I have a passion for God's story, not least because
I believe that Jesus did, and that when teaching his
disciples, he endorsed the narrative approach taken
here.

In the layout of the book, the first section gently probes
the narrative approach to understanding Scripture,
believing that it derives, essentially, from Jesus himself.
The second section paints with a broad brush the 'big
picture' of what Scripture tells us God is doing to fulfil his
redemptive plan. It does this by tracing the covenantal
connections that culminate in Jesus. The final part offers
some reflections on how we might relate our small
stories to the larger story, and may prove helpful to those
evangelists, pastors, ethicists, and story-tellers, seeking
fresh ways of shaping people's lives to the gospel.

Given the developing nature of a story, each move that
is made, inevitably, builds on and develops earlier stages
in God's revelation. For this reason, the careful reader
will meet repetition of major themes and key phrases,
but this is deliberate and, like the recurring motif of a
symphony, will, I trust, enhance the intended *cumulative*
impact of the whole story. For best effect, therefore, the
chapters should be read in their stated sequence and,
preferably, with an open Bible to hand.[1]

Given the scale of the subject and the size of this book,
the material is inevitably compressed. It presents, in *concentrated* form, the distilled findings of my own reading
and reflection and of the more wide-ranging research of

others. With this in mind, endnotes have been added, not out of pretensions to scholarship, but to help those who might want to dig deeper than this overview allows.

Whatever else this project has been, I have found it an exhilarating experience to overhear the echoes, make the connections and trace the trajectories in the Bible's myriad-voiced and messily human, but, nonetheless, coherent story-line. As Karl Barth observed, 'A quite specific astonishment stands at the beginning of every theological perception, inquiry and thought ...'.[2] And if such a wondering 'fear of the Lord' is the beginning of the search for Scriptural wisdom, then abounding joy is surely the result!

It will be obvious that in everything I have discovered, I owe much to those 'bravehearts' – William Dumbrell, Graeme Goldsworthy and Christopher J. Wright among others – who have swum against a fashionable tide in asserting the essential unity within diversity of the Scriptures.

Throughout the text, it is clear, too, how much I have gained from the stirring work Dr Tom Wright is doing. Thanks are also due to CWR who first allowed me to give this material an airing and in particular to Selwyn Hughes (founder of CWR), Trevor Partridge, Sean Gubb, and Paul Grant. Beth Davies deserves a mention for so cheerfully administrating so much of what I have taught in the last decade.

My primary debt, however, is owed to my wife, Mary. Only she knows what a triumph of love and grace it is to live with me. She has contributed so much to my learning curve by so eagerly joining me on it and I love her the more for doing so. Scarcely any word has not passed through our often-animated conversations about truth or has evaded her keen proofreader's eye. Her fuelling of our shared enthusiasm for choral music has simply been the latest way in which she continues to enrich my life and thinking.

I am grateful also to our dear friends Alan and Kathy Overton for their loving encouragement over several years, and to all the members of my Prayer Support Group, including, especially, Ros Trembath, and Ken and Jean Kinnear.

No one could be more blessed than I am in having two such staunch friends as Trevor Martin and Stuart Reid who continue to lighten my darker days with warmth, wit and steadfast brotherly love.

There it is. The mistakes are entirely mine. But as American comedienne, Gracie Allen once said: 'They laughed at Joan of Arc, but she went right ahead and built that boat anyhow!'

I am heartened – and sobered, too – to recall that an amateur built the ark and professionals the Titanic.

I am strengthened even more by sharing the confidence of Peter Taylor Forsyth when he said: 'I sink under what has to be done for the world, 'til I realise it is all *less than what has been done* and put into the charge of our faith and word. The world's aweful need is less than Christ's aweful victory. And the devils we meet were all foredamned in the Satan he ruined.'[3]

I wish you joy on your journey as you rediscover, as I trust you will, both for yourself and for others, the God-given narrative-shape of our lives.

Yours in the grip of passionate grace.

Philip Greenslade
Lent 2001

Notes

[1] For a version of this theme presented as a year's daily reading programme with devotional notes by Selwyn Hughes, see my *Cover to Cover, God's Story* published by CWR, 2001. For further information visit the website: www.cover2cover.org.

[2] Karl Barth, *Evangelical Theology*, 64.

[3] Peter T. Forsyth, *Missions in State and Church*, 16.

Previewing the Story

1

Opening the Final Chapter!

Luke 24:13–49

Noah and his ark, Joseph and his 'technicolour dream-coat', Moses ('Prince of Egypt'), David and Goliath, Daniel in the lions' den – I am of a generation that grew up familiar with the fascinating stories in the Bible. Being familiar with Bible stories is one thing: *knowing the Bible's story* is another altogether. Elizabeth Achtemeier picks up this point and challenges preachers to 'tell the story of the whole Bible, with God as the subject, in a twenty-minute sermon'.[1] The fragmentation in modern society has affected the church: truth is increasingly atomised and teaching is becoming randomly topical. Achtemeier goes on to observe that 'most of our people never learn how the whole canon hangs together. They do not know the continuous story, and they do not know the overarching theme of the whole canon'.[2]

This was brought home to me recently as I picked up my newspapers in my local 24-hour convenience store. The funky background music faded and a voice invited us to 'Take part in our Trivia Quiz. Yesterday's question was: "which biblical character was hidden in bulrushes as a baby?" ' By the time I reached the checkout, the music having come and gone again, the answer was announced: 'Of course, it was Moses'. 'Imagine that,' I thought, 'Moses reduced to a trivia quiz question!' Try telling that to Jesus or any Jew for that matter. Far from being trivial, Moses' story was the start of a whole nation's liberation that was to have world-shaking and long-term consequences! Diminish Moses and, in a strange way, I felt like saying, you diminish *me*. For, as we shall discover, investing ourselves in these larger stories is precisely what gives *our* lives meaning and significance. Trivialise these stories and we trivialise our dreams and destiny, our history and our hopes.

Hope does not easily die, but when it does, it is destructive. Hope is the oxygen of the soul. To lose hope is to leak life, to close the door on the future and reach a dead end. It seemed a dead end for two followers of Jesus trudging disconsolately back to their home village of Emmaus in the bitter aftermath of his crucifixion. Their personal correspondence with Jesus was now closed; the great adventure was over: 'we had hoped that he was the one who was going to redeem Israel' (Lk. 24:21). 'We had hoped ...' sums up their disillusionment.

There was nothing wrong with their dream. It was a noble one and had been cherished in various forms within Israel for over five hundred years, ever since the exiles had returned from Babylonian captivity. These two followers of Jesus, like so many Israelites before them, had hoped for someone to 'redeem Israel' (Lk. 24:21) from its deeper exile in alienation from God so that they were no longer under his judgment. These two men had pinned their hopes on Jesus, this carpenter from Nazareth. They thought they could get Jesus elected Messiah, but the block-votes of the powerful institutions had gone against him and his cause. Perhaps these followers had surmised that this was their moment of destiny, the time to engage with the cogs of history's big wheel. Like the students on the barricades in *Les Miserables*, they had felt sure that 'There is a life about to start when tomorrow comes'. But when 'tomorrow' came it was Good Friday. The death of Jesus had slammed shut the door of hope for these two followers.

Dulled by despair and preoccupied with grief, these men forget that Jesus had said there *was* a key to death's door, a key that he alone held. The two travellers fail to recognise the stranger who falls in with them on the road because they are so depressed! Emmaus is where we all tend to go at such times. Frederick Buechner puts it well:

> Emmaus is whatever we do or wherever we go to make ourselves forget that the world holds nothing sacred; that even the wisest and bravest and loveliest decay and die; that even the noblest ideas that men have had – ideas about love and justice and freedom – have always in time been twisted out of shape by selfish men for selfish ends. Emmaus is where we go to forget.[3]

At the start of the twenty-first century we can celebrate the gift of God's creativity to his human partners; we can applaud and enjoy the fruits of that creativity in art and music, science and technology. I suspect that no one alive today would prefer to have lived during the Middle Ages – at least not in Britain where life expectancy was around forty years of age. For people then 'life begins at forty' was an idle dream and not a cynical cliché. On the other hand, as the twenty-first century unfolds, we moderns cling to our own broken dreams. We had hoped to see a better world, one free of disease, poverty and injustice. However, we are far less confident after the Gulag, the Holocaust and two world-engulfing wars; it's as if the century we have left behind has drained us of energy for the future; we are left world-weary and have a shrug-the-shoulder mentality. In Robert Jenson's words:

> Modernity's hope was in progress: the model of this hope was biblical hope in God as the Coming One, the *Eschatos*. Modernity cannot hope in the biblical God, founded as it is in a declaration of independence from him. Therefore, when hope in progress has been discredited, modernity has no resource either for renewing it or for acquiring any other sort of hope. The mere negation of faith in progress is sheer lack of hope; and hopelessness is the very definition of post-modernism.[4]

It is precisely in this context and mood that Easter is good news. There is a stranger who falls in beside us on the uncertain road ahead to surprise us with hope. There is something that makes all the difference in the world: there is someone who makes all the difference to the world! We celebrate the good news of Jesus Christ's resurrection from the dead.

At the outset of the third millennium, as at the start of the first millennium, it is the resurrection of Jesus Christ that opens the doorway into God's new creation and leaves a gaping hole in all failed, alternative versions of reality. His resurrection is the foundation of our faith and our gospel. Without it, as Paul reminded the Corinthians, we have nothing and are nothing (1 Cor. 15). The resurrection is not some happy ending tacked on to the Jesus story because without it the gospel of Jesus Christ is no gospel at all. We should not be deterred by critics who say that resurrection is too incredible to fit with the modern way of looking at the world. As Lesslie Newbigin said so well: 'The resurrection cannot be accommodated in any way of understanding the world *except one of which it is the starting-point* ... the starting-point of a whole new way of understanding the cosmos and the human situation in the cosmos'.[5]

The resurrection of Jesus is the ultimate postmodern event! It was this radical new way of viewing the world, opened up by the resurrection of Jesus, which was about to dawn on the two Emmaus-bound travellers. It is resurrection reality that now breaks through to these two dispirited followers of Jesus and opens everything up for them.

Opening Day

Luke uses the Greek verb *dianoigō* ('to open') on three occasions in this passage to describe the impact of the resurrection on the two followers.

1. Notice how *their eyes are opened*. At the heart of the narrative is a wonderful recognition scene that grips the imagination, as it has for many great artists, notably, Rembrandt. As evening approaches, Jesus seems intent on moving on, but the two followers urge him, 'Stay with us … When he was at table with them, he took bread, gave thanks, broke it, and began to give it to them. Then their eyes were opened and they recognised him' (Lk. 24:29–31). Their eyes, which had been mysteriously closed to Jesus (perhaps by disappointment), were opened and they realised he was alive. The fact of resurrection is brought home to them in a very personal way.

   Each of us experiences this 'recognition' in different ways, but happen it must and every true believer can witness to a sudden or growing realisation that Jesus Christ is alive and facing us, as it were, across the table! To meet Jesus in this way is unforgettable and though we walk the long road of faith, not sight, we meet him again and again (perhaps as bread is broken) and taste his presence as the living Christ.

2. All the more remarkable then is the two Emmaus-bound travellers' reflection on their encounter with Jesus: 'Were not our hearts burning within us while he talked with us on the road and *opened the Scriptures to us?*' (Lk. 24:32). This explains why, for me, Luke 24 is almost holy ground. Here is the 'Burning-heart Bible School' we would all like to attend!

   The conjunction of events is striking and very revealing. Jesus opened the Scriptures to these two followers and set their hearts on fire with the breath-taking purposes of God. Beginning with Moses, sweeping through the prophets and culminating in his own suffering and glory as Israel's representative – the anointed king – Jesus showed them the big picture from Scripture (Lk. 24: 27). Then, while breaking bread over supper, the followers' eyes were opened and they recognised the risen Jesus.

3. This is mirrored by subsequent events in Jerusalem, when Jesus joins the larger group of disciples (Lk. 24:33–49). Luke tells us that *Jesus opened the disciples' minds so they could understand the Scriptures* (Lk. 24:44–45) after he had appeared to them and convinced them that he was alive.

   We praise God that, in our day, the Holy Spirit is opening more and more eyes to the truth of the gospel and the reality of the risen Jesus. Yet this, I dare to suggest, sets the stage for a sharp learning curve, which is similar to the one the two Emmaus-bound followers were on. It was those whose eyes were being opened to Jesus' personal, living presence – who subsequently 'see' him in a fresh way – who were being enrolled in his 'Burning-heart Bible School'. Having a remarkable, personal experience of the living Christ, however sensational, was not, apparently, enough in itself. It was also vital that these same people, hearts on fire and eyes wide open to the risen Christ, should have their minds opened to understand the Scriptures – and this wasn't just 'post-conversion', this was 'post-Resurrection'! Conversely, those who are well grounded in the Bible as the book of truth, need their eyes and minds opened by personal encounter with Jesus if they are to grasp its abiding significance for them and their world.

In the end, it scarcely matters in what sequence these twin disclosures occur, but occur they must if Jesus is to be truly known. Under the heading 'Walking to Emmaus in a Post-modern World', Tom Wright observes:

> The heart is warmed, says Luke, when Scripture is expounded so as to bring out the true story; and the Lord is known in the breaking of the bread. The two belong together, interpreting each other, and together pointing to the new world, the new vocation, the kingdom of God, and above all, to Jesus himself as the climax of Israel's history and now the Lord of the world.[6]

Resurrection Priorities

Needless to say, Jesus' sense of priorities at this point is extraordinary. After all, what would any one of us have done immediately after being raised from the dead and vindicated as Messiah? What might Jesus have been expected to do? Empty all the sick beds in Israel, perhaps? Not so it seems. Throw himself off the pinnacle of the Temple to prove his divinity? No, he had faced that one before. Embark for Rome to unseat Caesar as Lord of the world? No, that was his for the asking. Jesus' priority is different and very striking. He spends much of those priceless forty days before his ascension in Bible teaching, explaining the Scriptures to his disciples.

What was Jesus doing when he opened the Scriptures to them? He was explaining how the Old Testament finds its climax in him. 'And beginning with Moses and all the prophets, he explained to them what was said in *all the Scriptures concerning himself'* (Lk. 24:27). 'Everything must be fulfilled that is *written about me* in the Law of Moses, the prophets, and the Psalms' (Lk. 24:44). The Old Testament makes no final sense *without Jesus*, nor can we fully grasp who Jesus is without the Old Testament. In Chris Wright's words, Jesus' 'personal identity, the shape of his mission and the pattern of his life are all, so to speak, programmed by the spiral patterns of a genetic code provided by the Old Testament scriptures'.[7] In a discussion of the hermeneutical importance of the journey to Emmaus for seeing Christ as the key to Scripture, R.W. Moberley argues that 'as Jesus cannot be understood apart from Jewish scripture, Jewish scripture cannot be understood apart from Jesus; what is needed is an interpretation which relates the two – and it is this that Jesus provides (Lk. 24:27)'.[8]

Seeing how the whole Old Testament story reaches its climax in Jesus is not simply a matter of finding scattered proof-texts that somehow anticipate him. It's not a case of ferreting out isolated prophetic predictions that somehow apply to him. The picture is much bigger than that. The language of 'must' and 'be fulfilled' implies a coherent thread of divine intention and purpose. I believe Jesus showed his 'students' how familiar Bible stories were connected as parts of the one big story of what God was doing. Jesus was, in effect, drawing onto himself the whole story told in the Old Testament, as he brought the long-term strategy of God to its successful conclusion. Jesus was showing the disciples the *big picture* and how central he was to the successful outworking of God's strategic plan.

- *God's pledge to Noah*, which preserves this first creation until God's redemptive work is done and he can bring in a new creation, has now reached its climax in Jesus' death on a cross and his subsequent resurrection. Easter is the point of convergence where the sin and mortality of the old fallen creation are dealt with by Jesus' death; it is where the one creator God re-affirms, through the resurrection, the goodness of his first creation, even as he re-launches it as a new creation.
- *God's promise to bless all nations through Abraham* sets in motion the long story of faith, which now finds its fulfilment in Jesus, the true seed of Abraham, who turns God's original judgmental curse on our original sin into blessing for the world.
- *As messianic king*, Jesus embodies Israel's role as God's obedient son, faithful covenant partner and servant for the sake of the world. He completes what Israel was meant to achieve, but had left undone; he successfully re-enacts what Israel was summoned to be, but had failed to realise. In him, Israel's destiny is being brought to its intended goal.
- *The trajectory of kingship* launched with David, by which Israel's anointed Messiah and king was destined to be Lord of the world (though much discredited over five centuries by faithless kings) finally comes good in Jesus!
- *The prophetic vision* of salvation beyond exile, which envisaged God returning as king to restore his people on the other side of death and resurrection, is concentrated and clarified in Jesus. His blood is the blood of

the new covenant shed for many. His resurrection is the glory of his people Israel and the light of revelation to the Gentiles.

Every covenantal connection leads, eventually, to Jesus. Every tributary of truth flows into his river. Every promise of God finds its 'yes' and 'amen' in him. Each aspect of God's big strategy is focused and filled-full in him. *This* is what Jesus wanted the disciples to grasp.

The way Jesus opens up the themes and traces the threads of God's strategy in the story of the Scriptures 'warms the heart' – hearts that have iced-up with despair or frozen over with false views of reality are thawed out with truth. A lost passion is rekindled as Jesus opens up the book, as only he can. As the apostle John saw through his tears of relief, no one is worthy to open the scroll of God's purposes for history except this Lamb of God, who was once slain but now stands alive as Israel's king and the Lord of the world (cf. Rev. 5 and 6).

Open Minds

For this our eyes have been opened: for this *our minds need to be opened* (Lk. 24:45).

The limits set by materialism, unbelief and the seeming finality of death close modern minds. Resurrection opens the rationalist's closed system to a sparkling new world of possibilities and potential. Our minds run on pre-determined tracks and are closed to the strange story of the Bible. Like these first disciples, we are slow of heart to believe the paradoxical message of the prophets. But what was it they were 'slow' to grasp? Where are the obvious Old Testament prophecies of suffering *and* glory? Might it not be that Jesus was alerting them to a larger lesson, one that only Israel's whole history could teach. Indeed, Israel's entire story, from the Exodus to the Exile, is one of repeated suffering and rescue. They were slow to see that the pattern of Israel's rejection and vindication is a pattern of suffering and glory that devolves onto her anointed king. We are slow to see the strange calling of servanthood as the way to recover our lost dominion. We are slow to grasp that losing one's life is the way to find it! Our minds need to be opened to see all this otherwise we may misread the path of discipleship as being too hard and consequently step off the narrow way that leads to life.

It is entirely natural, as some in Israel did, to join Jesus on his journey in the hope of coming glory and to walk with him as far as the cross. But to balk at the cross is to miss the whole reason for his living and loving because his real glory is achieved only through suffering. It is perfectly possible to journey with Jesus, even after his resurrection, and walk – as it were – in parallel with him, as though he is an unrecognised stranger, one who is peripheral to our vision or the direction our lives are taking. (But since resurrection is so beyond the parameters of our normal perception perhaps even this is excusable.) It is even possible to meet the risen Christ in an incandescent moment of real disclosure and to remain in the dark about his real significance as the central character in God's big story, which alone explains him as the only true reading of reality, as verified by his resurrection.

We will only 'know the truth' of the big story that explains Jesus when we have met the risen Christ and heard him unfold it. But we must also join the community of other bemused disciples who are obediently attempting to 'live out the story', empowered by the Spirit, and are finding its truth joyfully confirmed. As Joel Green puts it, the risen Lord 'ensures that the disciples grasp fully how the past, present and future of God's activity belong to one great mural of salvation'.[9] We need our minds expanded to take in the worldwide implications of this Christ-event and the gospel that is entrusted to us. We need our minds opened to see that it goes beyond private faith and personal experience into the realm of *public truth*. 'And repentance and forgiveness of sins will be preached in his name to all nations, beginning at Jerusalem' (Lk. 24:47).

Wide-open World

The gospel is a call to the nations to lay down their arms and surrender cherished ideologies such as the 'American dream' or 'the British way of life'. The gospel issues a challenging invitation to everyone, whatever their race, skin-colour or social status, to tear up the script of their own self-made stories and to enlist with a clean start in God's big drama of redemption. The resurrection of Jesus Christ is the real climax to the earlier parts of the story. The suffering Messiah is gloriously vindicated. In Jesus, Israel's exilic 'death' is overturned. Through Jesus, Adam's defeat is reversed. Because of Jesus, the material creation is not 'written off' but redeemed as the new creation.

Commenting on the Jerusalem-based disciples, Chesterton said:

> On the third day the friends of Christ coming at daybreak to the place found the grave empty and the stone rolled away. In varying ways they realised the new wonder; but even they hardly realised that the world had died in the night. What they were looking at was the first day of a new creation, with

a new heaven and a new earth; and in the semblance of the gardener God walked again in the garden, in the cool not of the evening but of the dawn.[10]

That life 'about to start when tomorrow comes' has, for us, begun. If that tomorrow is not fully or finally here, we are sure it has clearly and conclusively dawned. Jesus' resurrection means we now live 'between the times'. Knowing this helps us accept our limitations and incompleteness without despair. The 'now-but-not-yet', which now characterises our lives, encourages realism and inspires hope: 'what we will be has not yet been made known. But when we see him we shall be like him' (1 Jn. 3:2). Life in the 'middle' need not be life in a muddle. The best is yet to be because the best has already come. Hope is reawakened. As with the Emmaus two, our stories are redeemed from despair and meaninglessness by being reattached to God's big story of salvation for the world! Because the End has already dwelt among us we can be sure we are in a story, one that has a good beginning and will have a redeemed and satisfactory conclusion.

Since this is all God's work, we can only open our lives again and again to the incoming power of the Holy Spirit (Lk. 24:48–49). God creates and redeems. God summons and saves. God works out his long-term covenantal purpose through the painfully human story of Israel. God brings that purpose to its climax in the cross of his Son, Jesus. God raises Jesus from the dead, vindicating him as the Messiah of Israel and Lord of the world. As the head of a great family bestowing blessing on his children, or as a priest pronouncing a lasting and life-giving benediction on the worshippers, so the risen Lord blesses his witnessing disciples with the creative potential of resurrection life.

It is this God who, in Jesus Christ, opens the book for us, opens our eyes to see a new vision of Jesus and opens our minds to begin to grasp his amazing purposes in Scripture. It is his Spirit who lights a fire in our hearts that the cold water of a sceptical world cannot quench. It is this God who sends us out in his world with a message of meaning, hope and renewal; he is the one who gives us his blessing, his power, and his very own Spirit. *Who could ask for a better story to be part of than this?*

Notes

1. Elizabeth Achtemeier, 'The Canon as the Voice of the Living God' in C.E. Braaten & R.W. Jenson (eds.), *Reclaiming the Bible for the Church*, 128.
2. Ibid.
3. Frederick Buechner, *The Magnificent Defeat*, 85.
4. Robert W. Jenson, 'How the World Lost its Story' in *First Things* 38 (October 1993), 19–24.
5. Lesslie Newbigin, *Truth to Tell*, 11.
6. N.T. Wright, *The Challenge of Jesus*, 127–8.
7. Christopher J.H. Wright, *Knowing Jesus Through the Old Testament: Rediscovering the Roots of Our Faith*, 110. If I had read Chris' superb book before developing the teaching series on which this present book is based, I would not have felt the need to write it at all! This would be top of my recommended reading list!
8. R.W.L. Moberley, *The Bible, Theology and Faith: A Study of Abraham and Jesus*, 51.
9. Joel B. Green, *The Gospel of Luke*, 856.
10. G.K. Chesterton, *The Everlasting Man*, 247.

2

Seeing the Big Picture

The starting-point for our journey of discovery is the fresh realisation that *the Bible is essentially God's story*. God is the chief character in the drama that unfolds through the Bible. God makes himself known to us through God's participation in the story. 'We are forever getting confused into thinking that Scripture is mainly about what *we* are supposed to do, rather than a picture of *who God is*.'[1] We, of course, get to know one another by telling our stories. When I meet a stranger I identify myself by giving them a brief glimpse of my personal story, I do not introduce myself by listing my height, weight and personal statistics.

God has made himself known to us in a similar way. The word 'god' is simply a generic term for 'a deity'. The identity of the real 'God' will only be disclosed as we follow the unfolding story of what he says, feels, plans and does through interaction with events and people. As Stanley Hauerwas has reminded us: 'There is no more fundamental way to talk of God than in a story'.[2] This should shape our approach to the Bible.

- The Bible is sometimes treated as a cookery book that is full of enticing spiritual recipes. It's left to the individual reader to pic 'n' mix and concoct whatever dish takes the fancy.

• The Bible can be misused – almost as some people use a horoscope – to provide a daily dip into devotional serendipity.

• The Bible is sometimes approached as if it were an elaborate code full of occult meanings – decipherable only by those with a special brand of insight or esoteric skill.

• We often succumb to over-simplifying and sloganeering because of the pressure to achieve 'relevance' and 'application'. All too frequently, we drain the Bible of its colour; squeezing the life out of it and thereby rendering it a 'flat' book. We then content ourselves by extracting passionless 'principles' from the biblical drama, distilling bland abstract 'truths' from richly textured narrative and mining complex sections of Scripture for facile, moralistic 'character studies', which Aesop's fables would have sourced just as well.

• The Bible has all too often been treated as the 'Yellow Pages' of theology, even within impeccably orthodox Christian circles. It has been used like a compendium of proof-texts, which are meant to give answers to all the questions we deem urgent.[3] More often than not, at least in my experience, it refuses to yield such answers and instead, puts us on the spot by posing awkward questions of its own!

Narrative Shape

The Bible, of course, has not come to us in any of these forms. In approaching Scripture we need to keep in mind that it has largely been given in the form of *narrative*, it is a story. This significant fact should begin to condition our approach to the Bible. Eugene Peterson reminds us:

Nothing comes to us apart from the form. And we cannot change or discard the form without changing or distorting the content. The *way* the Bible is written is every bit as important as *what* is written in it. Narrative – this huge, capacious story that pulls us into its plot and shows us our place in its development from beginning to ending. It takes the whole Bible to read any part of the Bible.[4]

This does not imply a downgrading of the authoritative substance of the Bible. An emphasis on the narrative of Scripture can only strengthen our confidence in the Bible as utterly true and trustworthy. Indeed, a renewed appreciation of the narrative quality of Scripture may free us from inflexible and inerrant dogmas, and allow us to enjoy a fresh encounter with the Word of God in all its vivid and dramatic power.

For the benefit of those who may be nervous at this approach, it is worth stressing that the use of the imagery of 'story' is not incompatible with convictions about the underlying historical reliability of the biblical account. It does not threaten the evangelical commitment to the propositional aspect of truth. As Gabriel Fackre says of the Bible story, 'while imaginatively portrayed, it is no fictive account, having to do with turning points that have "taken place" and will take place, a *news story* traced by canonical hand'. Fackre goes on to say that the Bible's ' "*good* news" is about events in meaningful sequence, unrepeatable occasions with a cumulative significance internal to their narration …'.[5] Alister McGrath states:

> Recognising the narrative quality of Scripture allows the full-ness of biblical revelation to be recovered … Narratives are based in history, in actions, enabling us to avoid thinking of Christianity in terms of universal abstractions, and instead to ground it in the contingencies of our historical existence.[6]

Traditionally, evangelical believers have also expended much ink and energy on emphasising that God is the *author* of the biblical story, and rightly so. However, Brent Curtis and John Eldredge raise the intriguing question 'what if? Just what if we saw God not as Author, the cosmic mastermind behind all human experience, but as the central character *in* the larger story? What could we learn about his heart?'[7] Discovering this is precisely the aim of this journey through God's story. Richard Lints encourages this quest when he writes:

> God acts in and through history. He is not simply the grand professor at the head of the class who stands and lectures. He is integrally involved in human history, serving not only as the author of the 'story' of redemption but also as a genuine character in the story.[8]

To see the world through God's eyes is to see it as the stage for the greatest story ever told; it is to see history as the unfolding of a great drama in which *God is the chief actor*.

Of course, not every part of the Bible is 'narrative' in a literary sense – Scripture includes laws, songs and words of wisdom. But, as Peterson says:

> Sometimes we are told that the Bible is a library made up of many kinds of writing: poems and hymns, sermons and letters, visions and dreams, genealogical lists and historical chronicles, moral teaching and admonition and proverbs. And, of course, story. But that is not so. It is all story.[9]

It could be argued that even the 'non-narrative' parts of the Bible – like the Wisdom literature – presuppose the particular storyline of the one creator God and his people, Israel. The 'non-narrative' parts were treasured and preserved within a believing community that was shaped by this story and sustained in its true identity by the memories and hope the story inspired.

'Story' is therefore not inferior to 'doctrine', as if the matter could be better told in theological concepts. Doctrines are essentially only shorthand ways of defining the terms in which we retell the story – it can also be powerfully retold in other ways, for example liturgy and, not least, through discipleship. The Christian doctrine of God as Trinity is a case in point. It may have been refined by the early Church Fathers who used Greek metaphysical categories, but the doctrine that emerged was an inevitable outcome of the story the New Testament told. Apostles, heirs to the Jewish Old Testament relationship with the one creator God, encountered Jesus who reintroduced them to God as his and their Father. These first Christians, through their experience of the Spirit of God as the personal Spirit of Jesus, included Jesus in the same categories normally reserved for the one creator God, without dissolving the unique 'oneness' of God! The story they lived was the 'raw' material for the finished confession. The truth of the Trinity is not only a doctrine to be believed, it is also a drama we are drawn into by grace.

Gripping Stories

Calvin Miller says, as Christians 'we have our story. Once upon a time, Jesus; once upon a time a cross, a tomb. Once upon a time, Easter.'[10] The features common to all gripping stories are present in the biblical story.

- There is a *dramatic beginning*, like the rousing overture to a stirring symphony. The opening narrative usually determines the shape of the plot. Clues, which will only progressively be developed, are sown. It is said that 'bringing the riderless horse home with blood on the saddle in the first paragraph' is the recipe for launching an intriguing mystery story.

- In every great story there is a *catastrophe*, a disaster, a fall. The basis of life is tragedy. All life is played out in its shadow. The best humour gains in poignancy from a touch of pathos. The sad clown is funniest. Romance is heroic and self-sacrificing. Unrequited love is the order of the day.

- *The rescue mission* grips the readers or in the Bible's case engages the hearers in redemption. In all the world's literature this typically involves either a battle or a journey before the rescue is achieved.

- *Character development* usually determines the quality of the story being told. Thin characterisation means a pot-boiler bought at an airport bookstall to help time fly. Depth of characterisation, on the other hand, usually spells a classic story. It is worth noting at this point that Bible characters should not be isolated from their context – as preachers are prone to do – and presented as lessons for faith or morals. Bible characters find their meaning only in their contribution to and connection with the overall drama of redemption. The story of Jesus can only be properly understood as the re-running of the story of Israel and, through it, as the revelation of the story of God.

James McClendon is among those who have pointed out that in order for character formation to take place it must be set firmly in a narrative understanding of life that provides a measure of connectedness and continuity. 'Virtues', he writes, 'cannot be mere episodes; practical intentions cannot be mere whims; the practices of morality require the coherence of a single story, the story of our lives'.[11]

- The best stories have a satisfactory *ending*. They don't leave the plot hanging in the air, but provide a denouement, a fitting resolution of the drama. In Calvin Miller's words,

  > Completion is the finest answer we can give to our search for meaning. There is something in us that resents the unfinished novels of symphonies of life. We all want settled conclusions to critical issues. We want stories … to end with recognisable conclusions of hope.[12]

To use the theologian's language, the best stories are 'eschatological'; they end well.

- Above all, stories are *enthralling*. They have the capacity to get behind our mental defences by drawing us into the tale they are telling before we have time to resist. This is even more the case with the Story, and stories, the Bible is telling. 'Ultimate stories tell life truths, truths that are so filled with universal meaning that they can speak to the smaller, particular truths of our own hearts'.[13] Since the Bible's stories dress its 'universal truths' in very particular, historical garb, their impact is even more keenly felt. What happens here utterly refutes the tired scepticism of the philosopher Lessing when he spoke of the 'ugly ditch of history' and argued that 'eternal truths cannot be contingent on mere historical events'. But they are, and yesterday's stories change people in today's world. We may justifiably share Calvin Miller's confidence that

  > with this studied story, we shall advance on the knowing world. In the wake of Christ's great 'once upon a time', no man or woman will be left the same. Earth will be made better, heaven will be populated by his story, and glory of glory, we are called to be its tellers. We shall be heralds of

hope in a day of cultural desperation, sentinels who reply to the emptiness of our time.[14]

The Grand Narrative

This is an appropriate point to note contemporary objections to the narrative approach being taken here. Postmodernism is as slippery a concept to grasp as a bar of wet soap in a bath. But if it presupposes anything it is a deep distrust of any overarching scheme that seeks to explain all of reality. In the oft-quoted words of Jean Francois Lyotard, writing in 1984 when pressed to define the postmodern condition: 'simplifying in the extreme, I define postmodern as incredulity towards metanarratives'.[15] This attack on all 'big stories' to explain the world, whether offered by the Enlightenment's faith in science and rationality or by the Church's faith in God, is typically the reaction of Marxist intellectuals whose dreams bit the dust with the demise of worldwide communism. All we are left with is consumer capitalism, which some pundits have construed as the end of history. At a popular level, fewer and fewer people look to any coherent, linear narrative to give them meaning and fall back on fragmented and idiosyncratic stories and sensations. It has been said of my generation that where we sought a career and our children sought an education, our grandchildren seek experiences – either through music or backpacking around the world. Whether at an elitist or popular level, all master stories are to be rejected in favour of a host of local, particular and self-made stories.

One major reason often offered for the intellectual rejection of metanarratives is that they were construed as inherently oppressive and totalising. The contention is that such overarching interpretations of the world have been used by the 'powers-that-be' to buttress their power-base and suppress dissent. Richard Middleton and Brian Walsh have ably answered this charge, at least where it might be aimed at the biblical narrative we are attempting to describe. They do this by pointing out that the story told in the Bible contains at least *two* clear counter-ideological dimensions or anti-totalising factors.

> The first of these dimensions consists in a *radical sensitivity to suffering* which pervades the biblical narrative from the exodus to the cross. The second consists in the rooting of the story in *God's overarching creational intent* which delegitimates any narrow, partisan use of the story.[16]

Nowhere is the irony of this felt more keenly than in the story of Jesus.

> The very one who discerned the anti-ideological thrust of the canonical story, that Israel is God's servant to bring blessing to the nations (including the Romans), and who attempted to restore Israel to that vocation, is sacrificed on the altar of Roman and Jewish self-protective ideology. Jesus quite literally suffers for the sins of the (Jewish and Gentile) world.[17]

More of this later, but suffice to say here that, undeterred, we *affirm* what postmodernity *denies*: there is a *masterstory* – an overarching metanarrative that makes sense of all reality. It is the strategic plan of God revealed in the Bible. At the same time, we *supply* what postmoderns *demand*: we offer a *truly local and particular story*, in this case, the very localised and historically-conditioned story of the one creator God's involvement with one people, Israel, and their Messiah, Jesus of Nazareth who represents what has been called the 'scandal of particularity'!

The 'Olympic Rings'

In exploring our theme further, I want to suggest that the Bible may be viewed as five overlapping, interlocking stories:[18]

- The story of God.
- The story of God's world.
- The story of Israel in the Old Testament.
- The central story of Jesus as gathering in all the other stories.
- Our story as the people of God, including your story and mine as personal, believing participants in the 'big story'.

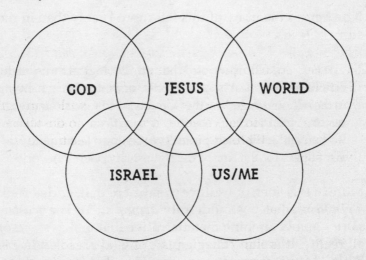

As an example of how these stories interact we can take Paul's brilliant summary statement in Romans 15:8–9, which encapsulates the whole biblical story: 'For I tell you that Christ has become a servant to the Jews on behalf of God's truth to confirm the promises made to the patriarchs so that the Gentiles may glorify God for his mercy.'

Here the *Jesus-story* is viewed as the culmination of the *Israel-story* among whom he comes as the Jewish Messiah (Christ) bringing to fruition God's promises to Abraham and the fathers with the result that blessing reaches the whole *gentile world*. In this way the *story is told of a truthful and merciful God*. This story, in turn, has become the Romans' story and by grace it becomes *our story too*. Like the Roman Christians, we too are called to indwell this story and invited to live it out by accepting one another in the church and glorifying God together!

The Five Lenses

These stories then serve as *five lenses through which to view the Bible*.[19] Like lenses on a camera, all are eventually needed to give clarity and depth of focus as we move from the long-range view of God and his world through Israel and Jesus to the close-up application to ourselves.

To bring the Bible into focus we need to see through all five lenses.

1. The God lens

Looking through this lens we 'read' the Bible *theologically*, with a *God-oriented* stance, seeking to discover first of all, who God is, what God is saying, feeling, doing and planning. We seek to respect the *givenness* of the Bible, to receive it as *revelation from God*, to be confronted by its truth. Our approach is *doxological* in that we recognise that 'from him and through him and to him are all things' and all things are 'to the praise of his grace and glory'.

2. *The world lens*

Looking with this wide-angle lens we see that the Bible moves from *first creation to new creation*, addressing the concerns of the whole earth and all humankind. *The story of Adam, of Israel – called to renew humanity – and Jesus are directly linked.* We will not limit the Bible to private devotional exercises. Rather, we will relish its power to speak truthfully, from within the community of faith, across the whole range of human affairs, e.g. international politics, economics, social justice as well as Christian living in the world of business and the home. While not giving us answers to every question we might ask, this approach offers us a true vantage point on reality. This *creational* approach will save us from a 'gnostic' devaluation of the material and physical realm in favour of the 'spiritual' realm. Hopefully, it will incite our thinking to a *worldview* and our mission to *world-vision*.

3. *The history lens*

This lens will help us pay close attention to the story of Israel in the Old Testament – that of the particular people through whom the one creator God brings to fulfilment his saving plan for all people. In the New Testament we will look to discern the Old Testament roots of the apostolic gospel and message of Jesus, listening out for the 'echoes of Scripture in Paul' and the other writers. We will acknowledge that these ancient texts were not addressed *to* us in the first place but to another people in another time and place, but that in the continuity of faith we can take these texts as written *for* us (e.g. Rom. 4:32; 1 Cor. 10:1ff.). From within the Old Testament we can trace the trajectories of promise that climax in Jesus and shape still our future hope. What theologians call 'eschatology' ('study of the last things') is simply the recognition that history is *purpose-driven* and not random. The historic story has a beginning, middle and *an end*.

4. The Jesus lens

By taking a *Jesus-centred* view of the Bible – a *Christological* approach as scholars call it – we will see the Lord Jesus Christ as the key figure around which everything revolves and onto whom all devolves. We will not understand him without acknowledging that the Old Testament leads up to him. Neither can we understand the Old Testament without seeing it in the light of its completion in him. The Pharisees were diligent in Bible study, and although they were keen students, they refused to acknowledge Jesus and deprived themselves of the life-changing effects of God's Word (Jn. 5:39). However, as the Samaritan woman said to Jesus: 'I do know that the Messiah is coming. When he arrives, we'll get the whole story' (Jn. 4:25, *The Message*). In him, the 'Final Word made flesh' (Jn. 1:14; Heb.1:1), the story of Israel is successfully re-written, the story of God is fully revealed, and the story of the world redeemingly redrawn.

5. *The contemporary lens*

Through this lens we can take the Word '*personally*' and '*corporately*'. We 'envisage' ourselves living within the world of the biblical text. As Lesslie Newbigin taught us so well, we seek to '*indwell*' the story so that, with new eyes, we learn to look out from *within the biblical world* and on to the world in which we live. In this way we re-imagine our postmodern lives as part of God's story in Christ and begin to live in the light of that cross and resurrection-shaped story.[20] Faith comes by this kind of hearing so that we trade in the dog-eared, self-written script of our own autonomous lives in order to be written into the larger saving script of God's big story. At once *my* story becomes *our* story as we are joined to a community of faith, to God's one covenant family. At once, we gain a new history and a new future. To the strange new world of the Bible we come, in David Wells' words, 'to take meaning; we come to give up the narrative of our own life with its parables of self-constructed meaning in order to find the truth that God has given in his own narrative'.[21] In the church we become new chapters written by the Spirit into the script of the ongoing story.

Short Stories, Long View

We can anticipate a number of findings by the following considerations. First, as we have seen, *all parts of Scripture are not narrative but all are narrative-based*.

- The Old Testament is the unfolding story of God's often emotional resolve to be with Abraham and the sons of Jacob, the chosen people Israel – a presence which, as we shall discover, is turned into a partnership *by God's covenant commitments.*

- The story of the one God is 'told' through the story of Israel.

- The historical books (the prophetic history of Joshua to Samuel) tell how the post-Deuteronomic generation fared. They re-evaluate the story at the time of the Babylonian exile – they probe the reasons for it (1 and 2 Kgs.) and, after the exile, ask if there is hope for the future (1 and 2 Chr.). The prophets recall the kings and people to the vocation at the heart of their story. Singers and psalmists sing the story because liturgy exists to tell the 'old, old story' of Yahweh and his love.

- The New Testament is the unfolding of the gospel as the decisive account of God's action in and through the life, death and resurrection of Jesus. Each of the Gospel writers, however distinctive their picture, follows this same basic outline of the Jesus story, with particular emphasis on the intensity of action leading up to the cross.

- The apostles have already told this same story as 'gospel'.

- Even in the Epistles – sometimes regarded as conceptual – Paul is summarising the story as he does to the Corinthians (1 Cor. 15:3–11). His thinking and writing come out of a Jewish 'narrative thought world'.[22] Richard Hays has shrewdly suggested that the problems Paul addresses arise because the church – or a group within that church – has 'lost the plot' and placed themselves in a wrong part of the storyline.[23] For example, the Corinthians have 'got ahead of themselves', being tempted to pre-empt the end of the story. The Galatians, on the other hand, are under pressure to regress and re-locate themselves in an earlier, outdated, pre-Christian phase of God's unfolding narrative.

- In all his letters, in one form or another, Paul recasts the old story of Israel and her God to show how Jesus embodies the destiny of the one and incarnates the reality of the other. In one striking instance, Paul expands Israel's basic credal confession (the *shema*) to include Jesus – and all in the cause of arguing for the oneness of God (1 Cor. 8:6)! In re-working Israel's story, Paul finds himself rewriting the story of Adam and humankind (e.g. Rom. 5; Phil. 2:5–11) and, again, redrawing the picture of God.[24]

Secondly, it can be said that all *smaller units of stories gain their significance from being seen as compatible – or indeed sometimes in tension – with the overall narrative of God*.

- To underline what has been said previously, the use of 'Bible characters' solely to draw moral or psychological or even spiritual 'lessons' is hazardous unless we take the trouble to 'place' these characters in the story and to show how integral they are to it. In fact, many biblical characters make dubious moral examples. It is far better to see them as stories about how often unlikely people can by grace be grafted onto God's story.
- Ruth is a shining exception to the dubious examples, but even this charming story of a young widow and the redemptive friendships that change her life, gains added significance from its position in the canon of Scripture. Placed where it is, Ruth's story highlights the darkness of the days of the Judges and forges another link with the future king David (Ruth 1:1; 4:13–22). In short, Ruth serves to offset the terrible trilogy of 'Bethlehem' stories of Judges 18–21 and anticipates both the model Davidic king and the messianic Davidic king who shared the same birthplace.

The third consideration is that *major segments gather up, and enlarge upon earlier aspects of the story.*

• What we experience as we live through the narrative is the *cumulative impact* of the story. In a real sense, Noah recapitulates Adam's story. Israel recapitulates both Noah and Adam's story. The king in Israel incorporates the destiny of his people. Jesus recapitulates Israel's and Adam's story. His story will be seen to gather up and make sense of all the others. By faith and baptism Christians enter into and, in their own dying and rising, recapitulate the Jesus story. We feel too the *expansive force* of the story. Jesus emphasised that 'salvation is from the Jews' (Jn. 4:22) to the woman at the well in Samaria. In other words, the Messiah is a Jew *and* the whole previous revelation God gave to Israel is the matrix for the world's salvation. Israel was made steward of the human vocation to glorify God on earth and entrusted with his word for his world so that no one would live by bread alone. Israel was thus fated to bear – through both her faithfulness and failure – the strange burden of the world's hopes. The story unfolds cumulatively and expands along the way. Only by being exclusively Jewish can it transcend all cultures. The specifically Jewish Messiah comes to slake the thirst of all so that no longer need anyone drink at Jacob's well or any other. This Jewish Messiah leads all lost worshippers home to the Father to worship God 'in Spirit and in truth', not on the Samaritan mountain or in the Jerusalem Temple. Salvation, for Samaritans, Jews and all of us, is truly 'from the Jews' because, from them and their history, comes the 'Saviour of the world' (Jn. 4:42).[25]

Plot Line

I am arguing that the narrative approach to Scripture, compared to other more systematic approaches, is more appropriate to the progressive nature of God's revelation and its cumulative impact in Christ. 'By this model the story the Bible tells is God's own story, told in *the way God pleases to tell it*.'[26]

Our next move is to ask *what is the plot of the biblical story?* Has God, in fact, got *a 'plan', a purpose* or is he simply seen as reacting to events in a random way? Does God merely have a 'devotional' relationship with believers or has God a plan for human history and for his creation? The approach taken here assumes that God has a plan, that the intelligent creator entertains redemptive aims for his unredeemed creation. In fact, a story, by definition, *implies intentional behaviour that is purposeful but not determined*.[27]

The whole Bible presupposes this to be true of God and of his will in the world. It is often made explicit. The psalmist, for example, celebrates the way in which the word of the Lord launched creation and shapes history: 'The LORD foils the plans of the nations; he thwarts the purposes of the peoples. But the plans of the LORD stand firm forever; the purposes of his heart through all generations' (Ps. 33:10–11). These plans are implemented by God's *covenant* word, which demonstrates to his people that he is 'faithful in all he does' (Ps. 33:4) just as his *creative* word sustains the natural world (Ps. 33:6–9). His uttered word is effective in carrying out his plans, which shape the way the world is going. 'No king is saved by the size of his army' so that, despite appearances to the contrary, military hardware does not determines the outcome of history (Ps. 33:16). 'The eyes of the LORD' oversee the outworking of his plans and watch over his people

(Ps. 33:18–19). The righteous are promised, not success and prosperity, but covenant love that will not let them go (Ps. 33:18–19) – even in famine and death.

The power that made the world, the plans that steer it to its intended goal and the caring providence that supervises the process all are stamped with God's 'unfailing love', which, with the psalmist, we dare to hope will prove to be the last reality in the universe. The prophet Isaiah announces the uniqueness of Yahweh who alone can say: 'My purpose will stand, and I will do all that I please. What I have said, that will I bring about; what I have planned, that will I do' (Is. 46:10–11). The prophet is seeking to enlarge the vision of the exiles in Babylon, confined as they are by Babylonian definitions of what is true. Nebo, one of the gods of Babylon mentioned by Isaiah (Is. 46:1), was reputed 'to write on tables of destiny the fates decreed by the gods for the coming year'.[28] But God's plans are sovereign and rooted in a long history of sustaining his people from 'birth to old age and grey hairs' (Is. 46:4). Our memory of God's 'proven track record' plays no tricks. But he moves in 'mysterious ways his wonders to perform' – few more mysterious than his summoning of a 'bird of prey' from the East, the pagan Medo-Persian warlord, Cyrus to be the agent of deliverance for God's people from Babylon! Isaiah evokes a vivid image of the Babylonians, now refugees themselves, weighed down by the burden of their gods as they seek to flee captivity (Is. 46:1–2). This encapsulates Isaiah's message. There is all the difference in the world between a god whom you carry and *a God who carries you*, between a god whom you have hastily to accommodate to your plans and a God who majestically includes you in his plans!

As we will see later, the apostle Paul, celebrates how Christian believers have been let in on the secret of God's strategy: 'He set it all out before us in Christ, *a long-range plan* in which everything would be brought together and summed up in him, everything in deepest heaven, everything on planet earth' (Eph. 1:9–10, *The Message*).[29]

Promise Plan

We can gain more purchase on what this 'plan' entails by adopting Walter Kaiser's designation of it as the 'promise-plan of God'.[30] He argues, 'The New Testament writers named this single plan of God the "Promise". About forty passages may be cited from almost every part of the New Testament which contain the word "promise" as the quintessence of the Old Testament teaching.'[31]

As has been pointed out, the category of *promise* is especially helpful because 'it embraces both the initiative of the promiser and the need for acceptance of it, with truth and full knowledge inseparable from future developments'.[32] Promise, in other words, encapsulates the sovereign grace in which the promise is made and the free response invited by it. It implies openness to a future that alone will bring into experience the full reality of who the promiser is and what the promise entails. Promise is not inexorable law, because it cannot be abstracted from the God who promises and keeps faith. Jürgen Moltmann in his classic discussion of the power of promise, points out that 'the fulfilments can very well contain an element of newness and surprise over against the promise as it was received'.[33]

Kaiser maintains that as far as the Bible is concerned, 'there is only one promise; it is a single plan'.[34] Paul reminds us that all the promises of God find their 'yes' in Jesus (cf. 2 Cor. 1:20), but this does not mean they are rubber-stamped by him in some random way. It means, instead, that all the promises of God converge on Jesus as the focal point of a coherent plan that occasion them all. Paul's defence before Agrippa illustrates the point: 'And now I stand to be judged for the hope of the promise made to our fathers' (Acts 26:6; cf. 13:32). 'Paul's confidence, then, rested on a single promise, not a prediction, nor a number of scattered prognostications. It was a definite singular plan of God to benefit one man and through him to bless the whole world.'[35] The 'promise-plan' Paul has in mind, as we shall discover, is essentially enshrined in the promises God gave Abraham (Gen. 12:1–3). For the moment, however, we simply stress the *singleness* of the promise.

Kingdom and Covenant

We can bring the promise-plan of God into even sharper focus by employing two key categories: *the kingdom of God* and the *concept of covenant*. This does not mean we imprison the Bible in a rigid grid, or overlook the diverse, and even dissenting, voices within the one story the Bible tells. The terms 'kingdom' and 'covenant' are two among others that help us get a handle on the big story. Kenneth Barker has put it well: 'It seems clear that though there are several great theological themes in Scripture, the central focus of biblical theology is the *rule of God, the kingdom of God*, or the interlocking concepts of *kingdom and covenant*'.[36]

The kingdom of God is the overarching theme, viewed as God's sovereign rule over creation, manifested in Israel's vocation, decisively established in Jesus, anticipated in the church by the presence of the Holy Spirit, and looked for as the hope of his coming. This will keep

our horizon large and lifted to the ends – and the end – of
the world!

> When we privatise Scripture we embezzle the common
> currency of God's revelation. But Scripture is never that – the
> revelation draws us out of ourselves, out of our fiercely
> guarded individualities into the world of responsibility
> and community and God's sovereignty – 'kingdom' is the
> primary biblical metaphor for it.[37]

The Concept of Covenant

Covenant spells relationship and mutual agreement.
William Dyrness defines covenant as 'a solemn promise
made binding by an oath'[38] often accompanied by signs
whether verbal or symbolic. Ancient covenant ceremonies were often sealed by ritual bloodletting. It used to be
held that the Hebrew word for 'covenant' (*berith*) implied
'cutting a covenant', but etymologically this is doubtful.
Be that as it may, an association with shedding of blood is
well founded. In O. Palmer Robertson's words, 'a covenant is a bond-in-blood sovereignly administered'.[39] The
bloodletting was not so much a symbolic mingling of life
forces but a self-directed curse: 'death be to me if I do not
keep faith with you my covenant partner'! Covenants
were made in the ancient world between individuals, as
in the biblical case of David and Jonathan, Saul's son.
Our aim, however, will be to trace the covenantal
arrangements *God* makes with individuals and the nation
of Israel in furtherance of his sovereign promise-plan of
salvation. 'Redemption does not happen all at once, nor
does it evolve uniformly. Rather, it develops with strange
twists and turns in separate but related epochs. These
epochs are demarcated by God's acts and redemptive

covenants.'[40] We shall note at one key point how Israel's life is shaped by covenant.

The Torah as a whole, and Deuteronomy in particular, is broadly similar in form to the covenant agreements made in the ancient world between lords and their subjects (especially conquered subjects), which scholars term 'suzerain-vassal treaties'. So, covenant almost invariably implies kingship. Honouring the king and owning his story – in biblical terms 'worship' – is the first obligation of a covenant people. It will be important to remember this as most of our focus will be on the covenantal thread in Scripture. This is always in the service of the larger, longer-term goals of God's kingdom. The biblical story then can be seen in the broadest way as the implementing of *God's kingdom rule* in history through a series of *covenantal arrangements* – all in pursuit of a coherent goal.

The approach adopted here can be pictured as a viaduct supported by five major Old Testament covenants, across which the promise-plan of God makes its way to Christ. He takes the weight of all the previous covenant commitments of God, launching the worldwide promised blessings and inaugurating the still future kingdom.

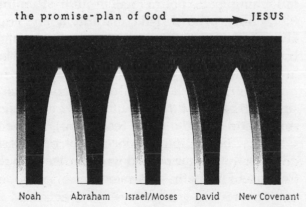

the promise-plan of God ⟶ JESUS

Covenant with   Noah   Abraham   Israel/Moses   David   New Covenant

This figure of course unduly smoothes the progress of God's plan through history. It reflects little of the astonishing ways in which God makes himself vulnerable and lays himself open to rebuff. It also conceals God's willingness to enter into dialogue with his human partners and the frequent, strange intercessory negotiations from the human side.[41] Neither does it convey the immense persistence of God in the teeth of international imperial designs or the covenantal unfaithfulness of his own people.

However, what it does show, in Bill Dumbrell's words, is that 'there could only be one biblical covenant of which the later biblical covenants must be sub-sets'.[42] Paul talks intriguingly of the 'covenants of the promise' (Eph. 2:12). This clue shows that there are several covenants (in the plural) all of which serve the one singular promise-plan of God. As Tom McComiskey's put it, 'The unity of grace throughout redemptive history is a covenant unity. It is the promise covenant, the force of which never fails'.[43]

As has already been indicated (and again anticipating later discussion) it is worth saying at this point that at the heart of God's promise-plan is undoubtedly the promises and *covenant made with Abraham*. Genesis 12:1–3 is the launching pad for the redemptive story in Scripture. Abraham is promised descendants, a land and a relationship with God characterised by blessing. And the bottom-line of his promise, later guaranteed by covenant, is God's intention to bring *blessing to all the nations of the world*. As Dumbrell shows, 'the Abrahamic covenant continues to be seen throughout the Old Testament' (and we might add into the New Testament) 'as the framework within which all other concepts of relationships which concern the people of God would arise'.[44] In the words of Paul and Elizabeth Achtemeier:

With the promise made to Abraham, probably in the eighteenth century BC, God the Lord of the universe and the ruler of history, has spoken a word into the life of mankind. But this is no idle word. It is the affirmation of the Bible that God's word is an active power. It is a power which shapes the course of history. It is a power which moves history forward and brings about events.[45]

The goal of the promise-plan of God entrusted to Abraham is nothing less than the establishment of the kingdom of God on a global scale. The exclusive relationship with Abraham and his descendants, in other words tokens the commitment of the one creator God to redeem the whole of his creation. Which is why our story will begin with Noah!

Our Story

Before we continue, we need to embrace the fact that *the Bible is our story too*. To accept the gift of life is to acknowledge the call to participate in the flawed but glorious human story. To accept the call of grace is to accept the call to join the divine story, the redemptive, covenantal story of the kingdom of God and to gain the recovery of our true humanness.

Abraham's faith was not that of a man seeking to fit God into his world, to make God useful to his success or family or even retirement. Abraham – whose faith-footsteps we all follow in – was seduced from his culture by the glimpse of God's glory, lifted out of 'his world' to be fitted amazingly and riskily into God's world and into God's adventure story. In Stanley Grenz's words:

The central purpose of this story is to be the Spirit's instru-
mentality in bringing sinful humans to change direction.
This change occurs as they re-interpret their own life narrative in terms of the categories of that story and to link their
personal stories with the story of God through connections
with the story of the people of God. As we proclaim the 'old,
old story', the Holy Spirit calls its hearers into the family of
God and assists them in viewing all of life from the perspective of that story.[46]

We encounter the real God, get to know his character and
find out what he's really like through *hearing God's story*:
we re-live God's story with him and in so doing find our
true selves shaped by it. We discover the majesty of the
overarching meaning without draining colour from the
separate stories: we learn to listen to the one continuous
word of the Lord without drowning out the disparate,
sometimes dissenting voices in dialogue with it. We grow
to appreciate the satisfying unity of Scripture while
enjoying the fascinating diversity: we follow the sweeping contours of the metanarrative while feeling the sharp
edges of the individual contexts and particular stories.
We also embrace universality and coherence without
reading the Bible mechanically or history fatalistically.

Through *believing the story*, we are drawn into the action
and find ourselves caught up in the saving movement of
God. We learn to 'indwell' the story so looking out from
within the biblical world with new eyes onto our
postmodern lives and world: we stop trying to make the
Bible relevant to our lives and instead begin to find
ourselves being made relevant to the Bible. We give up the
clumsy attempt to wrench the ancient text into our
contemporary world and instead bring our world back
into collision with, and cleansing by, the strange new
world of the Bible. Through believing the story, we allow

our minds to be continuously renewed by the normative narrative of God.

By *living out the story together,* we make church as 'that covenant community that has a story powerful enough to bond people together in the corporate and personal effort to find purposes for their lives which are part of the purposes of God'.[47] We are changed that together we may change the world.

The call is to be history-makers. To this end Christ 'ruined many careers'! He diverted would-be followers from fishing for fish in the nearby lake to fishing for people in a worldwide ocean. So, he calls all his disciples away from a faith in which God is available to bless their business into a faith in which disciples are available to God to be part of his business. And God's business is a multi-national company with branches everywhere!

> To be redeemed is nothing less than to learn to place ourselves in God's history, to be part of God's people. Personal experiences of salvation cannot in themselves be substitutes for learning to find the significance of our lives only in God's ongoing journey with creation.'[48]

As we immerse ourselves in this story, we begin to realise that the destination matters more than the emotions. What we are feeling at any one moment is less important than where we are going.[49] We 'plunge' first of all – if that's not an inappropriate word – into the story of Noah!

Notes

[1] Stanley Hauerwas & William Willimon, *Resident Aliens: A Provocative Christian Assessment of Culture and Ministry for People Who Know That Something is Wrong*, 85.

[2] Stanley Hauerwas, *The Peaceable Kingdom: A Primer in Christian Ethics*, 25. Cf. Stanley Hauerwas, *Truthfulness and Tragedy: Further Investigations in Christian Ethics*, 71–81. A modern pioneer in the evangelical use of the narrative approach has been Gabriel Fackre, see *The Christian Story: A Pastoral Systematics*; Dorothy and Gabriel Fackre, *Christian Basics: A Primer for Pilgrims*; and, more weightily, in relation to the way in which God has been revealed to us, Gabriel Fackre, *The Doctrine of Revelation: A Narrative Interpretation*.

[3] Cf. Richard Lints, *The Fabric of Theology: A Prolegomenon to Evangelical Theology*, 269.

[4] Eugene Peterson, 'Eat This Book: The Holy Community at the Table of the Holy Scripture' in *Theology Today* 56.1 (April, 1999), 13–4.

[5] Fackre, *Doctrine of Revelation*, 3. He contrasts this with myth where uniqueness is dissolved in favour of what is always and everywhere the case. In my view, evangelicals have been too ready to respond to the supposed Enlightenment demand to 'prove the Bible true' from sources outside the Bible itself. One small benefit of the emerging postmodern condition may be to alleviate this pressure a little and allow us to see and present the Bible on its own, authoritative and narrative terms. I concur with Fackre's judgement that to recognise the imaginative role of the narrator 'does not preclude the historical core of the account'. See 20, n.8.

[6] Alister E. McGrath, *A Passion for Truth: The Intellectual Coherence of Evangelicalism*, 107–9. For further confirmation that the narrative approach enhances evangelical convictions, see also the stimulating work of Harold H. Knight III, *A Future for Truth: Evangelical Theology in a Postmodern World*, especially chapter six.

[7] Brent Curtis & John Eldredge, *The Sacred Romance*, 72.

[8] Lints, *Fabric of Theology*, 263.

[9] Peterson, 'Eat This Book', 13.

[10] Calvin Miller, *Spirit, Word and Story: A Philosophy of Preaching*, 173. Miller has enriched the church as a master story-teller by practising what he preaches, starting with his wonderful allegory of Jesus as *The Singer* which I first read to a church congregation twenty-five years ago. See Calvin Miller, *The Singer*.

[11] James Wm. McClendon, *Systematic Theology* Vol. 1 – *Ethics*, 171.

[12] Miller, *Spirit, Word and Story*, 159.

[13] Ibid., 158.

[14] Ibid., 193.

[15] Jean Francois Lyotard, *The Postmodern Condition: A Report on Knowledge*, xxiv. I cite this from the brilliant analysis of J. Richard

Middleton and Brian J. Walsh, *Truth is Stranger Than It Used To Be: Biblical Faith in a Postmodern Age*, 70. Middleton and Walsh helpfully summarise their viewpoint in 'Facing the Postmodern Scalpel: Can the Christian Faith Withstand Deconstruction', in Timothy R. Phillips & Dennis L. Okholm (eds.), *Christian Apologetics in the Postmodern World*, chapter 7.

[16] Middleton and Walsh, 'Facing the Postmodern Scalpel', 142.

[17] Ibid., 152–3.

[18] After developing this theme, I have lately come across heavyweight scholarly support for it, utilising almost identical language, in Ben Witherington, *The Paul Quest: The Renewed Search for the Jew of Tarsus*, 237.

[19] Confirmation of this metaphor for how the Bible may be understood is offered by Christian ethicist, Bernard Adeney who goes so far as to say: 'The primary way we learn goodness from the Bible is by making the story of the Bible the interpretive lens through which we view all of life. This approach does not deny that we learn propositions or doctrines from the Scriptures. But ... we do not view these doctrines as propositions that we learn and then apply to various contexts. Rather, they are lenses through which we see reality. They help us to see the truth. The lens is not the truth, but helps us describe what is true.' *Strange Virtues: Ethics in a Multicultural World*, 85. Caution needs to be exercised not to offset concept and imagery unnecessarily, but I am broadly sympathetic to Adeney's stance.

[20] Lesslie Newbigin, *A Word in Season: Perspectives on Christian World Missions*, 89, is a characteristic statement.

[21] David F. Wells, *No Place for Truth: The Reality of Truth in a World of Fading Dreams*, 279.

[22] Richard Hays, *Echoes of Scripture in Paul*; N.T. Wright, *The Climax of the Covenant: Christ and the Law in Pauline Theology*; and Ben Witherington, *Paul's Narrative Thought World: The Tapestry of Tragedy and Triumph* – whose description this is.

[23] Richard Hays, *Pauline Theology* Vol. 1, 235.

[24] Discovering how the Old and New Testament phases of God's self-revelation are connected is exciting and profitable. It can be done in two broad ways. (1) At the 'macro' level by comparing the larger repeated patterns of God's workings in the actual events of history in an exercise that is us usually termed 'typology'. For very helpful description of typology – distinguishing it from allegory – see Wright, *Knowing Jesus*, 107–16. (2) At the 'micro' level, it can take a

more detailed and nuanced form as in what Richard Hays calls 'inter-textuality' where the text is listened to for 'echoes' of and allusion to previous scriptural passages. On this see Hays, *Echoes of Scripture*. I have found two works, which employ both methods, to be extremely enriching: Sylvia C. Keesmat, *Paul and his Story: (Re)interpreting the Exodus Tradition* and William G. Webb, *Returning Home: New Covenant and Second Exodus as the Context for 2 Corinthians 6:14 – 7:1*.

[25] For a superb study of the covenantal shape of the whole of John's Gospel see John W. Pryor, *John, Evangelist of the Covenant People: The Narratives and Themes of the Fourth Gospel*.

[26] McClendon, *Systematic Theology*, Vol. 2 – *Doctrine*, 476. Italics mine.

[27] Hauerwas, *Truthfulness and Tragedy*, 76.

[28] Barry Webb, *The Message of Isaiah*, 187.

[29] For ideas on how an appreciation of God's plan might be applied to various theological and pastoral disciplines, see the discussion by Graeme Goldsworthy, Peter Jenson, Barry Webb and others in R.J. Gibson (ed.), *Interpreting God's Plan: Biblical Theology and the Pastor*.

[30] Walter C. Kaiser Jnr., *Toward Rediscovering the Old Testament*, 83–100.

[31] Walter C. Kaiser Jnr., *Toward an Old Testament Theology*, 264.

[32] Frances Young and David Ford, *Meaning and Truth in 2 Corinthians*, 238.

[33] Jürgen Moltmann, *Theology of Hope: On the Ground and the Implications of a Christian Eschatology*, 102–6.

[34] Kaiser, *Toward an Old Testament Theology*, 264.

[35] Ibid., 264.

[36] From his foreword to Roy Zuck (ed.), *A Biblical Theology of the Old Testament*.

[37] Eugene Peterson 'Eat This Book', 13.

[38] William A. Dyrness, *Themes in Old Testament Theology*, 113.

[39] O. Palmer Robertson, *The Christ of the Covenants*, 15.

[40] Lints, *Fabric of Theology*, 263. Lints notes that 'normally one of two errors is committed by modern evangelical interpreters who take this route. Some overstress the continuity between the epochs (as in theonomy); others overstress the discontinuity of the epochs (as in dispensationalism)'. Lints concurs with Edmund Clowney's observation that 'modern dispensationalism rightly recognises that there are great divisions in the history of redemption; it errs in failing to grasp the organic relation of these successive eras, as developing manifestations of one gracious design', 278. Lints is citing Clowney's, *Preaching and Biblical Theology*, 15.

[41] See chapter 11 – 'Meet the God of the Story'.

[42] William Dumbrell, *Covenant and Creation: A Theology of the Old Testaments Covenants*, 43. It will be obvious that I am everywhere indebted to this insightful work. I am glad to see Dumbrell's work receive more recent endorsement from Greg Beale in his contribution to the symposium 'The Eschatological Conception of New Testament Theology' in K.E. Brower and M.W. Elliott (eds.), *The Reader Must Understand – Eschatology in Bible and Theology*, 22. It is equally heartening to see that Paternoster Press have re-issued Dumbrell's work in low-price format. Another work of Dumbrell's that has shaped my thinking is his *The End of the Beginning: Revelation 21 – 22 and the Old Testament*. Also influential for me, at an early stage in my thinking, was Willem A. VanGemeren, *The Progress of Redemption: The Story of Salvation from Creation to the New Jerusalem*. A pioneer among evangelicals in establishing the covenantal dimension of Scripture was Meredith G. Kline, especially in *The Structure of Biblical Authority*. Mention also ought to be made of the long-standing contribution to biblical theology of the distinguished mainline Old Testament scholar, Bernhard W. Anderson who has particulaly maintained the connection between creation and covenant in *Creation Versus Chaos: The Reinterpretation of Mythical Symbolism in the Bible*; *From Creation to New Creation: Old Testament Perspectives* – which has an essay on the Noahic Covenant; and *Contours of Old Testament Theology*, which surveys the role of God's covenants in the Old Testament.

[43] Thomas E. McComiskey, *The Covenants of Promise: A Theology of the Old Testament Covenants*, 141.

[44] Dumbrell, *Covenant and Creation*, 78.

[45] Paul and Elizabeth Achtemeier, *The Old Testament Roots of Our Faith*, 21.

[46] Stanley Grenz, *Theology for the Community of God*, 508.

[47] James Fowler, *Faith Development and Pastoral Care*, 27.

[48] Hauerwas, *Peaceable Kingdom*, 33.

[49] Tom Smail, *Reflected Glory: The Spirit in Christ and Christians*, 11.

Pursuing the Story

3

God is Committed to
Preserving the Earth for God's Future

Noah's voyage
Genesis 6:5–9:17; 2 Peter 3:1–18

One Small Step for Noah, One Giant Leap for Humankind

Stepping out of the ark has always seemed to me as big an act of faith as stepping into it. When Noah entered the ark he was not embarking on an escapist trip to a fantasy world. But the salvation never is. It is not like climbing aboard the Eurostar express in London, entering the rail tunnel beneath the waters of the English Channel and being disgorged into Paris Disneyworld! For Noah, boarding the ark was more like entering a space module to venture to a whole new planet, which was why getting out of the ark was a very big step of faith.

Noah's step of faith was also 'a giant leap for human-kind'. He was the focal point in God's strategic plan to preserve the world for redemption. Noah is the new Adam. Jewish and Christian commentators point to the many echoes of Genesis 1–3.[1] The first point to notice is that Noah's high-calling as a new Adam is foreshadowed in the name given him by his father, Lamech: 'He named him "Noah" saying: "Out of the ground that the LORD has cursed this one will bring us comfort from our painful toil" ' (Gen. 5:29; NRSV adapted). Noah's name is not derived from the Hebrew word for 'rest' (*nwh*), but – by a bit of word play – from the word *nhm*, which means 'comfort'. Noah is a gift to the world from the 'God of all comfort' (cf. Is. 40:1ff; 2 Cor. 1:3). Lamech's prophetic announcement amounts to a reversal of Genesis 3:17 where the earth is 'cursed' and made the scene of Adam's 'painful labour'. And there is almost something incarnational in the hint that it will be out of the cursed ground that the comforter will come!

The Pathos of God

Our next point of reference for Noah is Genesis 6:6–8 where we see how a father's wish for his child becomes, in time, God's calling on the man. Noah's interest in the drama derives precisely from God's deeper involvement in his creation. The text highlights what God saw, felt, and decided.

1. 'The LORD saw' (Gen. 6:5)

God sees the mounting evil and wickedness that has disfigured his earth since the Fall. He sees how his untrusting human partners have succumbed to demonic seduction. He sees the subsequent bitter recriminations and how they accuse and make each other the scapegoat. He watches as anger provokes fratricide and revenge leads to murder and mayhem, culminating in a mysterious and illicit involvement of humans with angelic-beings.

God doesn't just look at the outward appearances; he also looks deep into the human heart out of which, Jesus was to say, comes all manner of evils. Fantasies that rise in the mind in the hotel bedroom conjure up the pornography and adultery that follow. A radical dream of social engineering birthed in the darkened imagination of Pol Pot and his fellow Paris-educated comrades, spawns the nightmare of the 'killing fields' of Cambodia. Ideas always have consequences. The Lord sees it all.

2. 'The LORD felt' (Gen. 6:6)

God sees the deep crisis at the heart of the world's betrayal of his trust. He was grieved and his heart was filled with pain. The text uses strong language to describe God's intense emotions. He felt 'a mixture of rage and bitter anguish ... the anger of someone who loves deeply'.[2] This is an extraordinary invitation to step up close and feel the pain in the heart of God. Biblically, God is changeless, incapable of being controlled by external pressures and unwavering in his sovereignty. However, the Bible also teaches that God is not distant, aloof, remote and unfeeling; he is sharply impacted by the pain, suffering and rebellion of his world.[3] Here we get a glimpse of the deep pathos in God. God is profoundly affected by the human condition. The narrative does not emphasise the severe judgment of God by centring on the flood alone; it focuses on the deep feelings of God, as if to anticipate his mercy and grace. He knows our hearts, better than we know ourselves, but as the apostle John says, 'God is greater than our hearts, and in this our hearts find rest' (1 Jn. 3:20). The prophet Hosea matches this moving glimpse into the emotions of God when he poignantly describes the turmoil in God's heart over a recalcitrant Israel (Hos. 11:1ff). We begin to see that when evil is finally routed it will involve God becoming vulnerable to the pain and wickedness of his fallen world, and in some strange way taking it upon himself.

'The LORD decided' (Gen. 6:7)

'The LORD said, "I will blot out from the earth the human beings I have created …" ' (Gen. 6:7, NRSV). God decides for justice. Once he had looked on his creation and seen that it was 'good' (Gen. 1:31); now he sees only corruption and violence. God resolves to act judgmentally and destructively to bring everything to an end (Gen. 6:13, 17). He decides on the Flood! This is the finale of the grand creation experiment. This is the final curtain. Or is it?

Suddenly the text interrupts itself: 'But Noah found favour in the eyes of the LORD' (Gen. 6:8). This appears in the text like a pinprick of light on a pitch-dark night. The narrative gravitates to it eagerly. Suddenly, Noah starts to become a significant figure, and because of God's grace there is hope. Noah finds favour from God and with it the human race finds a future.

Strange Grace

But what a strange grace it is! It is a strange grace that makes you the sole survivor of a universal catastrophe. To receive this grace is to be lifted into the drama of God; it is learning to look at the world through God's eyes and to see what he sees; it is to be made conscious of God's deep feelings and, although the text does not explicitly say Noah was aware of them, to begin to feel what God feels. To receive this grace is to be made party to God's awesome secrets. It is to be burdened with the daring dreams of God and be drawn into his redemptive activity. This is what grace does to you.

Noah found grace to walk with God in paths of righteousness through the maze of unrighteousness and corruption. This same grace empowers him to obey God and to embrace the scary challenge of being the hinge of a very big door. Grace is about to launch Noah and his family as fully paid-up crewmembers of 'Faith-ship Enterprise' so that they can redemptively and boldly go where no man has been before! This is a crucial turning point.

We are beginning to learn from the text that judgment is not God's final word. It's becoming clear that plans are afoot that provide hope. We begin to see that God has a redemptive purpose.

And it is helpful at this point to distinguish two strands to this purpose.

1. A Family Preserved

God preserves a family for the sake of the world. God takes Noah into his confidence (Gen. 6:13, 17) about the destructive judgment he is about to unleash on the earth. As with Abraham later in the story (Gen. 18), Noah is entrusted with a terrible secret. God acts as if he would rather not bear the burden alone, preferring instead to take Noah into his confidence. The command to make the ark – complete with detailed instructions – arouses all my DIY, self-assembly insecurities! Thankfully, as Walter Brueggemann puts it, Noah 'regards God's commands as promises of life'.[4]

Not for the last time, everything hangs on 'one man's obedience'. Not for the last time, when the storm winds of divine judgment beat upon the house and rain floods down, the man whose house survives is the one who hears the word of God and does it. Noah obeyed consistently (Gen. 6:22; 7:5). He is, in William Brown's words, 'a constructionist in a world on the brink of deconstruction'.[5] The letter to the Hebrews reflects that Noah did this with a sense of 'holy fear', knowing that by his action the world stood condemned for its unbelief (Heb. 11:7).

There is another dramatic turning point in the story. God promises to establish his covenant with Noah (Gen. 6:18). The God who sees, grieves, judges, confides and commands now makes a solemn promise and binding commitment to Noah. 'But' – over against the dark threat of destruction (Gen. 6:17) – 'I will establish my covenant with you' (Gen. 6:18). This is the vital hope. This is the bridge across which all God's creative intentions will pass into fulfilment in the future. On this God stakes his redemptive dreams.

Decreation

Meanwhile there must be judgment. It is important to notice that the flood is described as the unravelling of God's creative work. The fountains of the deep burst forth and the windows of the heavens are opened to drown the world in judgment (Gen. 7:11). These terms mirror Genesis 1:2, 7. The flood represents a reversal of creation. It's as if God presses the rewind button and his created order reverts to the original watery chaos out of which it had been formed. In effect, the flood is an act of decreation! This is a key point to grasp. Throughout the Bible, from here on, God's acts of judgment within history are often described metaphorically in decreation language (e.g. Is. 9–10; Jer. 4:23–28). 'End-of-the-world' language is used to give ultimate significance and theological weight to historical events that might otherwise be regarded as random or accidental. In this way, these events within history do, in fact, become parables, and portents, of the final end of history. It was with just such language that Jesus spoke of the imminent destruction of Jerusalem and the Temple as establishing his vindication in glory as the Son of Man (Mt. 24:29–31). Unsurprisingly, God's salvation is characteristically described as an act of new creation (e.g. Is. 41:17–20; 43:18–21; 65:17; 2 Cor. 5:17).

So Noah is shut inside this strange vessel by the Lord and is, therefore, shut in to God's mercy and grace as his only hope (Gen. 7:16). Noah and his entourage sit out the flood as the sole survivors (Gen. 7:23). It has to be said – from Noah's point of view – that entering the ark and sharing your living space is all very well as an ecological gesture but it sure makes life difficult. Somewhat light-heartedly, I once set a group of students the task of scripting an interview with Mrs Noah entitled 'Domestic Management and Hygiene in the Ark!' for *Hello* magazine. Presumably the Noah clan found grace for this too. More seriously, how burdened was Noah by the weight of responsibility on him? Afloat amidst death and destruction 'is a tiny ship at sea, containing the culture of life'.[6] But the text does not recount one word from Noah on all of this!

God Remembers

What matters above all to the narrator is what God is thinking and doing (Gen. 8:1). 'But God remembered Noah….' and is merciful and causes the flood to abate and the earth to dry out. 'Noah and the animals in the ark constitute a link between the old and the new creations, between remembrance and promise, the dialectic of covenant'.[7] God cannot forget the first week or blot out the

prospect of the final day. When Noah emerges from the
ark (Gen. 8:15) he receives the great creation commission
once given to Adam and Eve, 'be fruitful and multiply'
(Gen. 8:17). Noah steps out of the ark and takes a giant
leap for humankind. Standing upon a new earth as a
new Adam, Noah receives the blessing of God as at the
beginning (Gen. 9:1).

Of course, the clock cannot be turned back. The only
way is forward to cross and resurrection. The old creation
is not being reinstated. Instead, we are heading for a new
creation. Reality intrudes. There is no longer a state of
Edenic innocence. Paradise cannot be regained. Things
are different now. Our relationship with the animal world
is now shadowed with fear. Our human calling to exercise dominion over nature becomes fraught with risk and
demands delicate skill if it is not to despoil and desecrate
the earth.

Three directives are added in the post-flood situation.
Paradoxically, the effect of each of them is to safeguard
and enhance the dignity of being human.

1. Meat eating is now sanctioned (Gen. 9:3). Though this
   may be viewed as a concession to human sinfulness,
   the text also stands against any ideological attempt to
   place animal rights higher than human life.
2. There should be reverence for all 'lifeblood'. This
   increases respect for all life forms but chiefly serves to
   emphasise the value of human life so that murder is
   construed as an attack on God in whose image humans
   are made (Gen. 9:4–6).
3. God reiterates his desire to see the world populated
   (Gen. 9:7). This is remarkable in view of the universal
   lawlessness that has just incurred his judgment and
   apparently remains unaltered after the flood (Gen.
   8:21b).

The text is probably a direct contradiction of Meso-potamian flood stories where the gods grow irritated with humans for being too numerous and too noisy! The gods act to cull the human race and set up permanent measures to endorse infanticide and childlessness. By way of contrast, the one creator God apparently loves making people too much to abort his creative experiment forever. Even much modern research grudgingly admits that over-population is not the world's greatest problem. Rather, the real issue is the unequal distribution of resources and unwise use of earth's limited supply. A lack of resources is not our inevitable destiny because God pledges 'I give you everything' (Gen. 9:3c).

The world becomes a tougher place in which to be human, but evangelism and ecology can bear joint witness that this flawed world has a redeemable future. God refuses to hand in his resignation, and nor need we! God is certainly no defeatist. Noah carries the future of this creation with him. As the representative man and head of a new human family, he now stands on new ground. In Michael Fishbane's words, 'As a cosmos in miniature, the ark providentially survives the universal destruction, so that its inhabitants can serve as the nucleus for a renewed world'.[8] God has preserved a family for the sake of the world!

2. God's World Preserved

The second major strand in God's strategic plan as it affects Noah now comes into focus. God preserves the world for the sake of his future, which is redemption (Gen. 9:8–17). Noah is portrayed as a new Adam and the world as a renewed creation. The flood was viewed as a judgmental act of decreation, a reversion to the watery chaos from which the earth was formed. So, the receding of the floodwaters is tantamount to a new start for the earth. The creative Spirit-wind of God – his *ruach*, which swept across the primeval chaos to bring shape and form to the first creation – blows again over the waters to dry out the earth (Gen. 8:1). And just as his life-giving word spoke wonders at the beginning so now the earth reverberates with the hope-charged words of a great divine pledge: 'Never again …' (Gen. 8:21).

Despite everything, it seems, the human heart remains unchanged, set in its evil ways. The floodwaters of judgment have abated but the tide of evil has not. Remarkably, it is God who freely chooses to change! In Walter Brueggemann's bold words:

> God resolves that he will stay with and sustain his world. He will not let the rebellion of humankind sway him from his grand dream of creation. The flood has affected no change in humankind. But it has effected an irreversible change in God, who will now approach his creation with unlimited patience and forbearance.[9]

In the face of continuing human rebellion, God intensifies his commitment to his creation. At whatever cost, it seems, he will see it through to its successful conclusion. In every subsequent generation he will have ample reason for destroying the earth and its inhabitants, but he pledges not to do so. God's 'never again' changes the picture to one where 'grace reigns'.

Whereas in judgment God made the world a dysfunctional scene of chaos and abandonment, he now pledges to maintain the regularity of the seasons and the stability of the created order: 'As long as the earth endures, seedtime and harvest, cold and heat, summer and winter, day and night, will never cease' (Gen. 8:22). All life and all science depends on this stability. Great is God's faithfulness indeed! So the climax of this part of the story is reached: 'I will establish my covenant with you ... and with your descendants ... and with every living creature ... and [this is remarkable] with the earth' (Gen. 9:9, 10, 13).

We have to turn to the New Testament and the apostle Peter, for the clue as to 'why' God pledges to the human and animal family that he will keep faith with his creation. Writing to Christians who are being mocked by unbelievers for the seeming delay of the Parousia, Peter reminds them of the creation and the flood (2 Pet. 3:4–6). When the present creation is brought to an end, Peter says, it will not be 'by water': God's 'never again' guarantees that. But the day will come when the elements of this old order are reconstituted by fire (2 Pet. 3:7). We are destined for 'new heavens and new earth in which righteousness dwells' (2 Pet. 3:13). Until then do we conclude, puzzled by the delay, that God is slow or forgetful? No, he is patient because he does 'not want anyone to perish, but everyone to come to repentance' (2 Pet. 3:9). Here is the clue as to why God still sustains this old world, even in its sin: under the terms of this Noahic covenant, God has promised to preserve the earth until his redemptive purposes are completed.

In covenanting with Noah and the earth, God is making a redemptive commitment. Genesis marks this by telling us that God has given a permanent sign of his intention to preserve in order to redeem. The sign God has given is 'the rainbow' (Gen. 9:12–17). Just as God's sign of covenant with Abraham will be 'circumcision' and with Israel 'the Sabbath', so with Noah it is the 'rainbow in the clouds'. With the rainbow God has slapped a 'preservation-order' on this decaying but still elegant old 'house'.

Having expended his arrows of judgment, God now hangs his 'war-bow' in the sky as a sign of peace, a visual symbol of his gracious 'never again'. Just as God's original 'Sabbath-rest' was the sure sign that his creation work was completed, so the war-bow at 'rest' is the sign that his decreation work is suspended.

Rainbow Reminder

Remarkably, the 'bow' is not there so much to remind us as to remind God (Gen. 9:15–16). When God sees the outer and inner wickedness of our human condition – as he still surely does – he also sees his rainbow-sign in the sky and remembers his covenant. God's 'remembering' is our salvation, just as – in its own way – is his forgetting (Ps. 105:8–9; Jer. 31:34; Is. 43:25).

When the prophets of the Babylonian exile groped for an analogy to the judgment that had engulfed the nation, they harked back to the flood to find it. Jeremiah pictured the impending Babylonian invasion as so devastating a catastrophe that only the language of decreation could do justice to it (Jer. 4:19–28). So severe is the current crisis that not even Noah, Ezekiel feared, could have made any difference (Ezek. 14:12–20). But it was precisely at this point that recollections of Noah give cause for hope. For Isaiah, God's covenant commitment to Noah not only guarantees creation, it also becomes a promise of God's renewing work after exile. 'To me this is like the days of Noah, when I swore that the waters of Noah would never again cover the earth. So now I have sworn not to be angry with you, never to rebuke you again' (Is. 54:9). God will never loosen the grip of his covenant-love on his people again. The prophet describes God's pledge of enduring relationship a 'covenant of peace' (Is. 54:10) in

which the one creator God resolves to be an untiring
redeemer. Chris Wright comments:

> Christian thinking about the earth far too readily jumps on
> the bandwagon of gloom and doom, as if the fate of the entire
> cosmos depended on which deodorant spray to use. That is
> to ignore the tremendous significance of the covenant with
> Noah. We live not only in a cursed earth, but also in a cove-
> nanted earth, and we have to cope with the tension. It is
> tragic that the rainbow has been hijacked as the New Age
> symbol when it could and should be the symbol of positive,
> hope-filled Christian affirmation about our world'.[10]

God preserves his world for redemption through his covenants with Noah and the earth. Like Noah we too 'are
saved through water' (1 Pet. 3:21). Drawn by faith-
baptism 'into Christ – into his dying and rising – we pass
through the waters of judgment, leaving behind our old
selves and world, to emerge as part of the 'new creation'
(2 Cor. 5:17). With Noah, we can draw breath at the heart-
stopping prospect of a 'thornless world' that we look on.
With him, we can stake all on the covenant faithfulness of
this tough and tender God. We can, in faith, take our
stand with Noah as samples of a new humanity and harbingers of a new springtime yet to dawn upon the 'new
heavens and new earth'. Like Noah, we can be 'preachers
of righteousness', not a self-righteousness that condemns
but a saving righteousness that through the cross offers
hope of redemption.

In this hope, we refuse to call down floods of wrath
upon the heads of sinners and can instead bend to wash
their dusty feet. With the blind poet-preacher, George
Matheson, we can celebrate the covenant-love that 'will
not let us go'. Opening our hearts to the joy that seeks us
even through pain, we 'trace the rainbow through the

rain and find the promise is not vain, that morn shall tearless be'. In this faith, we too take those small steps of faith
and obedience that can truly make a difference to our
world beyond our wildest dreams.

As far as we can tell, Jesus mentioned Noah only once,
but when he did, he issued a two-fold warning – 'stay
awake' and 'do not speculate'. 'As it was in the days
of Noah, so it will be at the coming of the Son of Man'
(Mt. 24:37). As it was in Noah's day, we can succumb to
'sleeping sickness'. We can become so pre-occupied with
the everyday affairs of earning a living and running a
family that we forget the larger drama we are involved in.
But unlike Rip Van Winkle, we Christians cannot afford
to 'sleep through the revolution'; we must 'stay spiritually awake'.

The opposite danger to spiritual sleepiness is the
fevered speculation of armchair experts on the second
coming. In support of its theory of the 'rapture', one
brand of pop-prophecy among evangelicals harks back
to those verses (Mt. 24:40–41), which speak of those
'taken' and those 'left behind'. This point of view, well
represented by a best-selling Christian work of fiction,
assumes that those 'taken' are believers and those 'left
behind' are unbelievers. In fact, in context, the exact
opposite is likely to be the case! Those 'taken' are those
who, as in the flood (Mt. 24:39), are 'taken away' by
judgment, while those 'left behind' are God's vindicated
people! Our confidence in God's overall strategy should
never make us wiser than Jesus or the apostles about
exactly when and how the story ends, the timing of
which can be safely left in the Father's hands! Staying
awake (being spiritually aware) is evidently not something to lose sleep over, by making it a worrying obsession! As in the days of Noah, faith remains a passionate
trust in God as we walk with him into an unknown, but

not uncertain, future looking for the full glory of the new creation.

Notes

[1] For example, Michael Fishbane, *Biblical Text and Texture: A Literary Reading of Selected Texts*, 31; Victor. P. Hamilton, *The Book of Genesis 1 – 17*, 313.

[2] Gordon Wenham, *Genesis 1 – 15*, 144, 147.

[3] Walter Brueggemann, *Genesis*, 77–8.

[4] Ibid., 80.

[5] William P. Brown, *The Ethos of the Cosmos: The Genesis of Moral Imagination in the Bible*, 55.

[6] Ibid., 55.

[7] Ibid.

[8] Fishbane, *Biblical Text*, 30.

[9] Brueggemann, *Genesis*, 81.

[10] Christopher J.H. Wright, *Walking in the Ways of the Lord: The Ethical Authority of the Old Testament*, 187.

God is Committed to
Blessing Every Nation on the Planet

Abraham's adventure
Genesis 12–22; Galatians 3

What makes a seventy-five year old man uproot from a comfortable lifestyle to set out across the desert for an unknown destination? The man is *Abram*; the trek is northwest from Ur of the Chaldees in Babylonia to a place called Haran; the destination is the land of Canaan. What makes him relinquish his grip on all earthly securities, turn his back on the past and decide to grasp a new future? What makes him, as someone has said, 'take off his slippers and put on his walking shoes' to embark on such a risky adventure? Put simply, it was the *sight and sound of God* (Gen. 12:1).

The challenge to this idol-worshipper came in a stunning encounter with the reality of the one true God, Yahweh. The first Christian martyr, Stephen, reviewing Israel's history, concluded that, 'The God of glory appeared to our father Abraham while he was still in Mesopotamia and told him to leave his country for the land God would show him' (Acts 7:2). No wonder Abram loses his taste for the impressive surroundings of the advanced civilisation he lives in. No wonder he stops being seduced by the Babylonian version of truth. Abram is dazzled by a greater glory and stirred by a more commanding voice than anything he has seen or heard before. God's revelation breaks open Abram's closed world. There is no question of trying to contain this God, of inducing him to adorn Abram's plans or bless his agenda. Rather, Abram is catapulted out of his small world into God's big world; he is caught up in God's vaster dreams and designs. God's glory unsettles Abram and disenchants him of his Babylonian culture; God's word cuts him loose from his social moorings and launches him on the flowing tide of faith in search of an alternative.

When this seventy-five-year old set out from Haran nearly four thousand years ago, he set in motion a train of events that would, eventually, bring Jesus to the world, through whom would come the lasting blessings of eternal salvation, for all of us in every nation! Paul realised that God announced 'the gospel in advance' when he gave Abram this amazing promise of blessing for the nations. 'The Scripture foresaw that God would justify the Gentiles by faith, and announced the gospel in advance to Abraham, saying: "all nations will be blessed through you" ' (Gal. 3:8). The divine initiatives that grip Abram make him a pivotal figure in the whole of Scripture; he is central to our understanding of the big redemptive story told there.

God makes *five major moves*. All are crucial to the future of his redemptive purposes and Abram is summoned to respond to each of them:

1. God *calls and promises*: Abram *trusts and obeys* (Gen. 12:1–9).

2. God *re-assures* Abram and *credits him with righteous-ness*: Abram *believes* (Gen. 15:1–6).
3. God *makes covenant* with Abram while Abram *sleeps* (Gen. 15:7–21).
4. God *reaffirms* his covenant and *commands circumcision*: Abraham *circumcises* (Gen. 17:1–27).
5. God *tests his covenant partner* and *swears an oath*: Abraham *trusts and obeys again* (Gen. 22).

God Calls and Promises: Abram Trusts and Obeys (Gen. 12:1–9)

There are three strands to this:

1. God promises Abram land (Gen. 12:1, 7)

At first, God pledges to merely 'show' Abram the land (Gen. 12:1). The offer only becomes a 'gift' when Abram makes the journey to this unknown destination. In this way, the land of Canaan becomes the *Promised Land*. Abram must 'leave and let go' of his old homeland to receive this new land. The challenge moves up the scale of emotional intensity from the less personal 'your coun-try', through the more personal 'your kindred', to the most personal 'your father's house'.

There is a tension between promise and fulfilment, which the text heightens by picturing Abram as a stranger wandering through, but not settling in, the Promised Land. This becomes a recurring pattern in the Abraham stories in Genesis. No sooner does Abram arrive, then he moves through the land to the Negev (Gen. 12:9). Even when Abram returns, after famine has driven him into Egypt, he is a 'resident alien', pacing up and down the length and breadth of the land as if laying claim to it but, oddly, never putting down roots (Gen. 13:17). By the story's end Abram owns nothing of the land except the burial place for which he has paid good money so he can bury his beloved Sarah (Gen. 23:4–20)!

Abram serves to symbolise God's grace. He exists as a man who has nothing, yet possesses all things and a man who is given a homeland, but continues to live a semi-nomadic existence. The lesson was clear for his descendants who took possession of the land: never take it for granted; it is pure gift, respect the gift and the giver or it will be lost; never stake everything on occupying the land! The writer of Hebrews learnt the lesson well:

> By faith Abraham, when called to go to a place he would later receive as his inheritance, obeyed and went, even though he did not know where he was going. By faith he made his home in the promised land like a stranger in a foreign country; he lived in tents, as did Isaac and Jacob, heirs with him of the same promise (Heb. 11:8–9).

In Genesis, Abram's actions are contrasted with the builders of the Tower of Babel. 'Come let us build ourselves a city' (Gen. 11:4) sets the limit of the Babylonians' horizon. Abram makes a radical counter-cultural statement in leaving this society. He turns his back on the visible, tangible city that *man* is building for the city that *God* is building for his eternal glory, a city which is invisible except to faith. Abram refused to sink his roots into that man-made city because, in the words of Hebrews again, he was 'looking forward to the city with foundations whose architect and builder is God' (Heb. 11:10).

2. *God promises Abram descendants (Gen. 12:2)*

'I will make you a great nation' is bold talk to a childless man whose wife is barren beyond the age of childbearing. Dramatic tension is once more built into the narrative It mounts as God speaks of offspring that will be as numerous as dust of the ground and the stars in the sky (Gen. 13:16; 15:5), while the reality of Abram and Sarah's condition becomes laughable (Gen. 17:17). This question hangs in the air for over twenty-five years – will there be a son? The suspense is maintained, even when the miracle child arrives, because in Genesis 22 we are left wondering whether he will survive the sacrificial knife? Will Ishmael and Isaac survive each other's jealousy?

The later chapters raise doubts about the fulfilment of the promise by developing what has been called the 'ancestress in danger' theme as Rebekah (Gen. 25:21) and then Rachel (Gen. 29:31) are found to be barren. These stories will, in time, remind the 'great nation' Israel that it exists solely from God's grace and not on its own merit. Israel is an impossibility that exists only because God wills and works miracles of grace.

3. God promises Abram blessing (Gen. 12:2–3)

Blessing, in Old Testament terms, is a dynamic concept and not an empty gesture of goodwill. To bless someone is to speak a highly charged word that transmits happiness and material success, which Abram enjoyed in abundance (e.g. Gen. 24:1, 35). At a deeper level, blessing connects the recipient with God's original empowerment of humankind. God's 'I will bless you' is therefore doubly significant because it aligns Abram with future prosperity and links him back through Noah and Adam to God's original creation blessing and mandate (Gen. 9:1; 1:26). In other words, the narrative presents Abram, like Noah before him, as a 'new Adam', the progenitor of a new humanity. But whereas God's covenant with Noah was largely preservative, maintaining the earth as a settled environment for human beings in general, his promise to Abram launches his specific redemptive programme for blessing the human race. With this in mind, it is intriguing that the five references to 'blessing' here mirror the five-fold curse in Genesis 1–11 (Gen. 3:14, 17; 4:11; 5:29; 9:25). This reinforces the view that Abram's call is crucial if the universal curse is to be converted to a universal blessing.

Royal prospects

'I will make your name great' almost certainly implies royal status – a suggestion soon made explicit by the promise 'kings will come from you' (Gen. 17:6, 16). This connects Abram directly to Israel's future kings, especially David – to whose line the same pledge is made (2 Sam. 7:9). Abram's projected royal future is set in sharp contrast to the men of Babel whose stated aim was to make a name for themselves (Gen. 11:4). Clearly, Abram's fame and destiny lie firmly in God's hands. Abram will owe his place in history to God alone!

Furthermore, Abram will make his reputation by being made the means of blessing to others. The range of this is astonishing. By God's choice, Abram and his descendants – insignificant players though they seem to be on the world stage – will be the touchstone by which all nations are measured. 'I will bless those who bless you and curse those who curse you' (Gen. 12:3). The destiny of all nations will be critically bound up with the future of Abram's descendants. God's ultimate intention is that 'in you all the nations of the earth will be blessed' (Gen. 12:3b). This is the bottom line of the promise plan. Abram and the nation of Israel, which comes from him, are called into being and blessed for the sake of the world.

By cherishing these stories about Abram, Israel could embrace the challenge to remain sharply different from other nations, without becoming exclusive or self-serving. To be '*in* the world but not *of* the world', yet *for* the world, would be Israel's demanding calling – the prophets strove bravely to remind the Israelites of this. Sadly, throughout the story, Abram's 'great nation', Israel, diminishes her greatness and betrays her vocation to the extent that her sense of being a special nation degenerates into an introspective nationalism. Tragically, Israel, entrusted with blessing for the world, would not be ready to receive the blessing for herself when it was offered through her own Messiah and his apostles, as emphasised in Peter's speech in the immediate aftermath of Pentecost, when he pleaded with the people of God not to disown their ancient destiny. See Acts 3:25). The apostle Paul strove to convince his fellow countrymen, inside and outside the church, that Gentile acceptance of God's salvation in Christ was exactly what God had envisaged in the promise plan announced to Abram (Gal. 3:8).

God Re-assures Abram and Credits Him With Righteousness: Abram Believes (Gen. 15:1–6)

Genesis 15 recounts God's next major move and Abram's reaction to it. God's prophetic word to Abram amounts, say the scholars, to an 'oracle of assurance'. Abram's response was trust and obedience. 'After this, the word of the LORD came to Abram in a vision: "Do not be afraid, Abram. I am your shield, your very great reward" (Gen. 15:1). Quite why Abram was fearful, a feeling that was assuaged with direct words from God, is not made clear in the text. 'After this' is indeterminate, but if it is intended to forge a close link with the events described in Genesis 14 then the context of God's reassurance of

Abram is a dramatic one. Abram might well have been physically and emotionally tired after what he has just been through and so likely to fall prey to anxiety. A 150-mile route march and a night battle against superior forces are taxing enough for an eighty-five-year old man. In addition, Abram has had a close encounter of a strange kind with a mysterious, almost supernatural, royal figure called Melchizedek. Feeling inferior, Abram pays tithes to Melchizedek and receives a blessing from him! Abram has also, uncharacteristically we might assume, turned down the king of Sodom's offer to make him a rich man! Later, as the cold desert wind seeps in through the tent flaps, the chill of fear begins to settle on Abram. In the aftermath of great events the human spirit is often low and vulnerable to negative emotions like fear and self-doubt. Will Kedorlaomer and his alliance of kings return to seek revenge? Had Abram been imprudent – a rash move for such a shrewd business operator – in rejecting the king of Sodom's generous financial package? Can God be trusted in the end? After all, it's a decade on and still God's promise of a son and heir seems no nearer fulfilment.

Sensing Abram's mood, God reassures him with a prophetic vision. Abram sees a dramatised word: it looks like an ancient covenant ceremony in which a king rewards the conquering hero by symbolically handing over to him the king's own weaponry as a sign of his binding pledge of protection and friendship. As far as Abram is concerned, it is as if God were saying to him, 'Everything I have is at your disposal. I am committed to being at your side to protect you. Your battles are my battles; my victories are your victories'. This is the familiar stuff of covenant agreements in the ancient world (cf. David's covenant with Jonathan, 1 Sam. 20:16ff.). Already, it seems, there's a covenantal gleam in God's eye.

Abram replies with a classic 'Yes ... but' response – he is reassured but he still has two urgent questions with God.

1. *Abram presses God about the promise of children: 'O Sovereign LORD, what can you give me since I remain childless ...?' (Gen. 15:2).*

This is bold talk from Abraham. It's as if he is saying 'You can be my benefactor, Lord; you can be my shield and reward but what I really want is the child you promised me'. Since no child has materialised, Abram even offers to help God out by suggesting that he adopt Eliezer his servant as legal heir. God's rebuttal is swift and emphatic: Eliezer 'will not be your heir but a son coming from your own body will be your heir' (Gen. 15:4). Given Abram and Sarah's condition, nothing short of a miracle will bring this about and God seems committed to acting supernaturally to make good his promise. God has already promised descendants as numerous as the dust of the ground (Gen. 13:16). Now, under the night sky, God 'ups the stakes' further by taking Abram outside and saying, 'Look up at the night sky and count the stars – if indeed you can count them ... So shall your offspring be' (Gen. 15:5). In effect, God is encouraging Abram to look up to the one who made the stars, a promise-keeping, miracle working God and not look around or down for any half-baked alternative solution. Abram is gently reminded that God is the one who promises children and bestows righteous status.

Abram's response is striking and extremely important in the rest of the unfolding story of the Bible. He takes God at his word in a moment of faith. *'Abram believed God and he credited it to him as righteousness'* (Gen. 15:6). These are momentous words in the story. What do they imply?

In the Old Testament, 'righteousness' is essentially a
relational term. In Genesis 15 Abram is granted 'right
relationship with God' – one shortly to be sealed by covenant. Clearly, this is not reckoned to Abram because he
keeps religious observances or matches up to ethical
demands. He does not immediately become noticeably
more ethical as a result of this. Rather, righteousness is
counted to him on the basis of his *faith alone!* This is earth
shattering and revolutionary. Just as blessing is more
original than sin, so grace comes before law. Long before
the Torah was given, even before circumcision, Abram is
credited with covenant relationship.

No statement is more foundational than this to a biblical view of how God relates to people. It becomes central
to the apostles' understanding of how God's grace operates in the gospel (Rom. 4:3; Gal. 3:6). In the New Testament, 'justification' and 'righteousness' are synonymous
terms and translations of the same Greek word. They are
attained by faith alone! Paul can argue that this has been
the case right from the beginning: it is not the 'works' of
the Torah but the 'faith story' of Abram, as told in the
Torah, which provides the key to a true relationship with
God.

2. *Emboldened, Abram then boldly asks a second question, this
   time about the promise of land: 'O Sovereign LORD, how can
   I know that I shall gain possession of it?' (Gen. 15:8).*

This question prompts God to his next major move. What
he does is crucial for Abram and foundational to the
outworking of his redemptive purposes for the rest of
human history.

God Makes Covenant With Abram While Abram Sleeps (Gen. 15:7–21)

At God's command, Abram kills a heifer, a goat and a ram, cuts them in half and arranges the split carcasses on the ground in two parallel lines with a bird at the end of each line. As the day wears on, Abram beats off marauding birds of prey, perhaps symbolically rebuffing his enemies. At sunset, he falls into a deep stupor and a thick and terrible darkness envelopes him. While Abram is asleep, he is shown that his descendants will be enslaved in a strange country but will be freed after four hundred years. In addition, Abram is reassured about the peaceful end to his life.

As far as we can tell, ancient covenant ritual envisaged each party walking between and around the pieces in a figure-of-eight manner to settle their agreement. The shedding of the substitute blood probably means that the covenant was a maledictory oath (i.e. one in which each party swore death to itself if it defaulted on the arrangement). It is, however, striking that God alone passes between the pieces, in the form of fire. Theologically, this is immensely significant because it shows that this is not a negotiated settlement but an amazingly one-sided commitment on God's part – what is technically called a 'monergistic' arrangement ('on that day the Lord made covenant with Abram', Gen. 15:18). Abram does not respond because he is fast asleep! In this state, Abram can only be on the receiving end of the sovereign grace of God. God is acting unilaterally. God alone, by the blood of covenant, seals his commitment to fulfil the promise plan to bless Abram and the nation that comes from him as the means of blessing all the nations of the world. No wonder this covenant with Abram has been called 'the backbone' of the Bible,[1] 'God's permanent way of dealing with man'.[2] This promise plan, sealed in covenant with Abram, determines the future of God's dealings with his world. This is confirmed almost immediately by the text as the story of Abram unfolds.

God Reaffirms His Covenant and Commands Circumcision: Abraham Circumcises (Gen. 17:1–27)

The terminology of 'covenant' saturates Genesis 17 underlining why it is set to become 'the primary metaphor for understanding Israel's life with God'.[3]

At this point in the narrative, Abram once again stands in need of God's reassurance. On this occasion, the reason is the thirteen-year-old boy standing beside him! Thirteen years earlier Abram had finally lost patience with this dilatory God who keeps making 'promises, promises'. At Sarah's suggestion, Abram had gone to her maid, Hagar, and fathered Ishmael. Ishmael's presence is a standing indictment of every attempt to force God's hand, to short cut his promises or speed up his workings by taking things into our own hands. It was a false move, a terrible mistake. Abram has stepped outside of God's will for his life. But has he blown his chances for good? Has God written him off?

Now aged ninety-nine, Abram is in dire need of further reassurance. As before, God's reassurance takes the form of a covenant commitment (Gen. 17:2), but it is now taken to an even deeper level. Whereas the agreement described in Genesis 15 revolved around the first two components of God's original promise-plan (the issues of 'seed' and 'land'), here the focus is on the third and more international, dimension of that promise – the pledge that Abram will be a 'blessing for all nations'.[4]

First, God speaks to Abram with a *new name:* 'I am El Shaddai, God Almighty' (Gen. 17:1). Is this comfort or rebuke? Perhaps it is both. 'I am the Almighty, I am full of resources, I can cope with impossible situations, and I can do this on my own, thank you very much. I don't need your misguided efforts to help me out, I can make this promise-plan and covenant work'.

Secondly, God offers Abram a *new challenge*: 'Walk before me and be blameless' (Gen. 17:1). Is God laying down a condition or extending an invitation to experience his on-going presence? Again, perhaps both apply. It is tempting to see beyond a legalistic demand to a tender assurance of God's presence and the blessing of walking in the light of his countenance as a child takes its first steps under the watchful eye of a concerned but proud parent.

Thirdly, God gives Abram *new hope*: 'I will confirm my covenant with you and make you fruitful' (Gen. 17:2). Abram is suitably abashed. Overwhelmed by grace he prostrates himself before God, who reaffirms his covenant and spells out the mutual obligations of the agreement. The covenant deepens and relationship becomes partnership. There is also an exchange of vows: 'As for me' (Gen. 17:4) and 'as for you' (Gen. 17:9; cf. vv.15, 20).

God, *for his part*, re-emphasises the strategic role Abram plays on the world scene by endorsing him as the father of many nations (Gen. 17:4). This represents a significant upgrading of the original promise that Abram would produce a great nation. As we saw, Abram had foregone the right to make a name for himself; unlike the men of Babel, he trusted God to do it for him. Now God rewards that faith by changing Abram's name, which means 'exalted father', to *Abraham*, 'father of many' (Gen. 17:5). From our vantage point, we can see that God's commitments to Abraham establish important connections, *backwards* and *forwards*, with all the key covenantal developments in the unfolding of his saving purposes.

God promises to make him fruitful and to increase his numbers (Gen. 17:2, 6). This connects Abraham with the earlier story of Noah and through him *back* to Adam (Gen. 1:26f.; 9:1ff.). Abraham represents another fresh start for the whole of humanity, the first fruit of new creation. We can also trace the trajectory *forward*, as Genesis 12 – 50 does, to the descendants of Abraham multiplying in Egypt (Ex. 1:6) and to the formation of 'a great nation' when Israel settled in the land (Gen. 17:8). God promises kings (Gen. 17:6), thus projecting even further to the Davidic kingship in Israel.

God binds himself to be known as the God of Abraham and his descendants, which includes *Sarah* fully in these sweeping promises (Gen. 17:15–16). God's promise to be the God of his descendants (Gen. 17:7–8) anticipates the heart of Israel's covenant identity (Ex. 6:7; 29:45; etc.) and points *forward* to the ultimate new covenant which promises a deep sense of security that God is our God and we are his people (Jer. 33:31; Ezek. 36:28; Rev. 21:3).

As for Abraham, he must commit himself to practise circumcision (Gen. 17:9–14), a familiar ritual in the ancient world. This was to become the key 'identity marker' for Israel and God was saying three things by requiring it. First, 'I want your whole body, Abraham'. Marked 'in the flesh' (Gen. 17:13) 'you henceforth belong to me'. Secondly, 'I want your whole family. By the mark in your reproductive organ, I lay claim to your seed, your descendants, your children'. Above all, Abraham 'I want your whole heart'. Circumcision is to be the symbol of inner covenant loyalty (Deut. 30:6), not outward conformity.

Abraham falls on his face again, with the laughter which says: 'this is too good to be true' (Gen. 17:7).

Incredulously, Abraham asks again 'Will a son be born to a man 100 years old and to his wife 90 years old?' Then, even more astonishingly, Abraham has the nerve to ask if there's anything in this for Ishmael! God is equal to it all. It's as if he says, 'Watch my lips, Abraham, let me spell it out for you: by this time next year Sarah will be the mother of this child' (Gen. 17:19, 21).

As for Ishmael, he will prosper as part of the wider blessing on the Adamic race but, says, God 'I will establish my covenant with Isaac' (Gen. 17:21). Mysteriously, although Ishmael will be blessed, he will not be in the line of the covenant. God's covenant purposes will progress through Isaac's seed alone. This strange selectivity of grace has reverberated down through history so that the sons of Ishmael (Arabs) and the sons of Isaac and Jacob (Jews) have not been reconciled, outside of the gospel, to each other or to God's will.

So, Abraham circumcises the male members of his household including, a year later, the eight-day old miracle child, named, appropriately enough, 'laughter' – though, for all Abraham and Sarah's amazed amusement, it is God, with the birth of the boy, who has the last laugh.

God Tests His Covenant Partner and Swears an Oath: Abraham Trusts and Obeys Again (Gen. 22)

Our final move in this sequence is to the taut but tense narrative of Genesis 22 where God is said to have 'tested' Abraham. It is an extraordinary story that sounds harsh and incomprehensible to modern ears. Abraham is asked to take the miracle child on whom the whole promise plan hangs and to offer him up in sacrifice to God who has invested so much in him. Child sacrifice, though practised in the ancient world, is condemned in Scripture and, as we know, Abraham is prevented from going through with it. So was the implicit challenge for Abraham to show as much devotion to El Shaddai as pagans did to their gods?

The text is spare and poignant in its detail: 'Take now your son' (does God really mean the miracle child of promise?), 'your only son' ('only'? but what about Ishmael?), 'whom you love' (what an understatement! In the ancient near east sacrificing your firstborn was sacrificing lineage and future). To his credit, Abraham doesn't dismiss this as a bad dream but seems able to discern the voice of God. Rising early, in prompt obedience, with preparations well made, Abraham sets out for Moriah with Isaac, by now a young adult, carrying the wood for the sacrifice.

Threefold trust

Along the way, Abraham makes three great statements of faith.

1. *'We will worship'* (Gen. 22:5a) – shows the value Abraham places on his God. For Abraham, God is the supreme good, the giver worthy of receiving back the best of his gifts to us. Here is worship that offers the most treasured love to God.
2. *'We will return'* (Gen. 22:5b) – the text does not elaborate what exactly Abraham means by this. The New Testament writer to the Hebrews is in no doubt as he reflects on this story. With evident admiration, he reads Abraham's words as expressing faith in the resurrection power of God.

    By faith, Abraham, when God tested him, offered Isaac as a sacrifice. He who had received the promises was about to sacrifice his one and only son, even though God had said to him: 'It is through Isaac that your offspring will be reckoned'. Abraham reasoned that God could raise the dead, and figuratively speaking, he did receive Isaac back from death' (Heb. 11:17–19).

3. *'God will provide'* (Gen. 22:8) – such is Abraham's faith and so it proves to be. God does provide. An angel stays Abraham's hand and Isaac is spared the knife. They do return. In this is deep reassurance for Abraham. God has reassured him before when he was afraid (Gen. 15) and a seeming failure (Gen. 17). But there is a deeper reassurance from God that comes only to those prepared to risk everything. George Mueller, in nineteenth-century England, famously believed that God would provide for his orphanage, but he could only know this with the deepest assurance by taking in the orphans.

Abraham is, of course, a test case. We are not asked to sacrifice our children in this way. However, we are challenged to love God before anything else and, indeed, shelter the children if God asks us to. Abraham's faith stood the test. He is the prototype of faith. Faith with this quality is now up and flying, able to withstand the strain and pressure without breaking. The covenant holds and so does faith. Abraham passed the test of faith. He believed that God would give him a son, that a sacrificial lamb would be provided and that there would be a supernatural resurrection.

It is, therefore no surprise when Paul sees in Abraham the model for saving faith in the great provision of the gospel of Jesus Christ. The great contrast is, of course, that where Isaac was spared, Jesus was not. 'He who did not spare his own Son, but gave him up for us all how will

he not also, along with him, graciously give us all things?'
(Rom. 8:32). This is the extent to which God will go as the
'God who provides'. Is this what God was committing
himself to nearly four thousand years ago? Remarkably,
in the aftermath of the dramatic events of Moriah, it is
God who makes the big response:

> 'I swear by myself' says the Lord, 'that because you have
> done this and have not withheld your son, your only son, I
> will surely bless you and make your descendants as numer-
> ous as the stars in the sky and as the sand on the seashore.
> Your descendants will take possession of the cities of their
> enemies, and through your offspring all nations on earth will
> be blessed because you have obeyed me' (Gen. 22:16–18).

Is God demonstrating his willingness to match Abraham
in offering up his only and beloved son by swearing this
oath? This is the theological time bomb buried in the
Abraham stories. Is God committing himself to do whatever it takes, to pay any price, to bring his redemptive
plan to fruition? This is the revolutionary twist to the
Abraham narrative. God returns our sacrifices to us! The
place where God seems to demand most is the place
where he gives most. Already we begin to realise that *God
will not be outdone in sacrifice by any of his creatures.* Already
we hear the gospel 'in advance': *God is not a God who
demands sacrifice but a God who makes sacrifice.* Our salvation lies not in the sacrifices we make but in the sacrifice
we trust. Now we really do know that *God will provide.*

God provides for all nations on the planet. This is the
gospel Paul argues for in his letter to the Galatians. The
particular question he pursues with them is: *'who are the
true sons of Abraham?'* Paul's conclusion is that all who
believe in Christ, whether Jew or Gentile, are sons of God
and offspring of Abraham (Gal. 3:26–29). This global

community of faith was always envisaged in God's original promise to Abraham (Gal. 3:8). 'Just as', according to Genesis 15.6, 'Abraham believed God and it was reckoned to him as righteousness', so, Paul argues, 'so those who have faith are blessed along with Abraham' (Gal. 3:9).

We have seen in Genesis 15 that Abraham's relationship was soon defined in covenantal terms. Thereafter in the Old Testament 'to be righteous' was not so much an indication of moral character as of covenant status and identity. Similarly, referring to the 'righteousness of God' – as the Psalms and Isaiah particularly do – speaks primarily of God's own *covenant faithfulness which prompts him to saving action.*

It is with this in view that Paul seizes on Genesis 15:6. He does so not because he needs a quick proof text but because he is tracing the trajectory of faith right back to its Abrahamic launching pad. He is not looking for a mere illustration. Paul is convinced that Christian believers stand in unbroken continuity – stretching back to the patriarch, Abraham – with God's covenant people. Just as Abraham received covenant membership *by faith alone,* long before the giving of the Law and even prior to circumcision, so *all who now believe* enter covenant relationship with God. This has been achieved through the death of Jesus and the outpouring of the Spirit. Jesus hangs on the cross under a curse (Gal. 3:13; cf. Deut. 21:23). Israel, unfaithful to covenant and therefore unable to live out its vocation to be an agent of blessing for all the nations, would incur the curses of God culminating in *exile from the land.* (Deut. 28:63; 29:25–28). Jesus, 'the faithful Israel', the true covenant partner of God, dies this cursed death instead of Israel. Dying as an exile, an alien and outcast, he absorbs and exhausts the curse of judgment and so the blessing promised to Abraham can now flow out to the whole world by the gift of the Spirit (Gal. 3:13–14).

By faith in the faithful Jesus Christ, the *one*, singular 'seed' of Abraham, the *one* covenant people of the *one* God is formed (Gal. 3:16, 20, 28). Torah is seen to have been a gracious but temporary and parenthetical provision *until* Christ should come in the 'fullness of time' (Gal. 3:19, 23, 24; 4:1–4). What the Law can never do, Christ and the Spirit can now produce, achieving in 'crucified' believers that quality of life expected of God's covenant people (cf. 5:16–26). This is the gospel – it is theology and ethics; preached and lived.

Father Abraham

Writing to the Romans, Paul asks, 'What then shall we say? "Have we found Abraham to be our forefather according to the flesh?" ' (Rom. 4:1). In expecting the answer 'no', Paul is able to advance his earlier argument that God has never been the God of the Jews alone (Rom. 3:27–31). It is true that Jews have never relied for their status on physical descent from Abraham. The gospel of grace that Paul preaches, therefore, upholds, rather than contradicts, the Law (Rom. 3:31) – that is, if we view Torah rightly as embracing the narratives in Genesis to which Paul is appealing. Within Torah itself it is clear that, as Paul reminds the Romans, God always intended a worldwide family of faith. Through Christ, Abraham is now set to inherit not only the land of Canaan but also the entire earth (Rom. 4:13).

What kind of faith is Abrahamic faith? It is faith that, as in Isaac's case, believes in a God who can raise the dead. Even a 'dead' Israel can be brought back to life. And faith, as in Sarah's case, believes that the God who at creation called 'into existence that things that do not exist' can do so again so that even Gentiles, who were regarded as non-existent 'no-people' (cf. Rom. 9:25–26) in covenant terms (cf. Rom. 9:25–26), are included through Christ in the one people of God. Appropriately, covenant membership comes by grace through faith to those who believe in him who raised Jesus from the dead (Rom. 4:25).

No wonder Abraham is regarded as 'the father of all who believe' and his adventure as telling the 'gospel in advance'.

Notes

[1] Don Richardson, *Eternity in their Hearts*, 163.
[2] Leon Morris, *The Apostolic Preaching of the Cross*, 94.
[3] Brueggemann, *Genesis*, 154.
[4] Paul R. Williamson, 'Promise and Fulfilment: The territorial inheritance', in Philip Johnston and Peter Walker (eds.), *The Land of Promise: Biblical, Theological and Contemporary Perspectives*, 15–34. Williamson's research findings on which his article is based can be found in *Abraham, Israel and the Nations: The Patriarchal Promise and its Covenantal Development in Genesis*.

5

God is Committed to
Calling a People for His Own Glory

Israel's vocation
Exodus 2:24; 19:1–6

'God so Loved the World That He Chose Israel'[1]

Chris Wright's adaptation of a well-loved text takes us to the heart of this next stage of the unfolding story. The intriguing question which lies close to the centre of the mystery of God's strategic plan is, why Israel? Deuteronomy leaves us in no doubt:

> The LORD did not set his affection on you and choose you because you were more numerous than other peoples, for you were the fewest of all peoples. But it was because the LORD *loved* you and kept the oath he swore to your forefathers that he brought you out with a mighty hand and redeemed you from the land of slavery, from the power of Pharaoh king of Egypt. Know therefore that the LORD your God is God: he is the faithful God, keeping his *covenant of love* to a thousand generations of those who love him and keep his commandments (Deut. 7:7–9).

Why did God love Israel? Answer – because he loved Israel! What kind of answer is that? The only kind of answer love can give as to why it is selective at all – the heart has its reasons. Whatever else we know about God's involvement with Israel, we know this: it is unquestionably a great *love-story!* However, the summary given in Deuteronomy points back to the harsh realities of the slave labour camps of Egypt where Israel's part in the story begins and God becomes observably involved.

The book of Exodus opens with a concise summary of the last half of Genesis. Fraternal jealousy among the sons of Jacob and life-threatening famine combine with the mysterious working of God to bring the descendants of Abraham into Egypt. Even after the death of Joseph, under the patronage of a favourable Pharaoh, Abraham's descendants are fruitful and multiply greatly (Gen. 17:6). The use of language from the original creation account implies that Pharaoh is portrayed in direct opposition to the one creator God and represents the forces of chaos over against creation.

However, God's quarrel is not with an ethnic group or nation but with the false gods of Egypt (Ex. 12:12). In the plagues that devastate Egypt, God demonstrates *his* control over the forces of creation in the face of flagrant rebellion. Meanwhile, Pharaoh's fear mounts and, in the stock reaction of authoritarian regimes, he persecutes the minority deemed a threat to his power base, enslaving the Israelites in the brickyards of Egypt (Ex. 1:6–14).

> The Israelites groaned in their slavery and cried out, and their cry for help because of their slavery went up to God. God heard their groaning and he remembered his covenant with Abraham and with Isaac and with Jacob. So God looked on the Israelites and was concerned about them' (Ex. 2:23–25).

This highlights two marks of God's love:

- It is *a listening love*: God heard the groaning cries for help of an oppressed people.
- It is *a loyal love*: God remembered his covenant promises to the patriarchs.

God's love is a compassionate love that responds to a present crisis and a covenant love which reaffirms its previous commitments. Both dimensions are vital to a correct view of the 'big picture'.

We noted in the introduction that in the postmodern world all 'big pictures' are regarded as intrinsically oppressive and hostile to human freedom. All the more reason, then, to remember that Israel's story begins with the cries of the oppressed for freedom – a fact which Israel was intended never to forget (cf. Deut. 5:15; 6:21–25), not least so that she would always be sympathetic and generous to the poor, the alien and the stranger among her.

Israel was not chosen to be a dominant nation – she was too small and had been saved from a powerful nation. She was chosen to be God's servant nation, embodying the truly human vocation by giving leadership on the world stage. God set his love on Israel to continue and to extend his earlier promises to Abraham, who was called for the sake of the whole world.

When God committed himself to choosing *one* nation for his own he implemented the next stage of his over-arching promise-plan to bring the blessings of salvation to *all nations* on the earth. This is precisely why the Torah prefaces the stories of Abraham and Israel with the stories of creation and the nations (see Gen. 1–11). Israel was not chosen to fill a niche in the god-market by worshipping a local, ethnic or even national deity. Israel was chosen to proclaim the revelation of the one creator God and be the bearer of his enlightening word and redemptive plan to the whole world!

Prince of Egypt

Characteristically, God starts with one man. He singles out Moses to be the agent of Israel's deliverance. Moses' part in the story illustrates just how vulnerable God seems to be in risking his plans to fallible human hands. His saving purposes once again hang on the slender thread of what happens to one child. The action is indebted to quick-witted and resourceful women – in this case Moses' mother and sister, aided and abetted even by Pharaoh's daughter who defies her father's murderous decree. These women are pro-life in a culture of death. They vote for tenderness in a climate of violence and God is with them. Their 'motherly' instincts are as crucial to the story as God's parental attitudes. Like Noah, Moses is threatened with 'drowning' (Ex. 1:22), is entrusted to an 'ark' (Ex. 2:3 where the same word as sin is used as in the Noah story) and is drawn from the waters of death (Ex. 2:10). The threat hanging over 'all the sons of Israel' (Ex. 1:1f.), then all the male sons, (Ex. 1:16) is now concentrated in one son who will, eventually, lead Israel to freedom as the 'firstborn son of God' (Ex. 4:22–24).

The irony of God's working is delicious – a member of Pharaoh's own family saves Moses. This 'Prince of Egypt' is educated in the skills of leadership and diplomacy, all expenses paid, courtesy of the very regime God will use him to undermine! Preserved as a child and called after serious adult failure, Moses is eventually brought to a burning bush where he encounters God. There, Moses learns God's name: 'I am what I am' (Ex. 3:14; translated as 'Yahweh' by the Jerusalem Bible and capitalised as

LORD in most modern English versions). Yahweh is essentially God's personal covenant name, not so much in the metaphysical sense of entire self-sufficiency, true though that is, but in the much more personal and existential sense of 'I will always be what I will be to you and with you'.

God commits himself in all his divine resourcefulness to be all that Israel needs him to be. The extraordinary implication of this is that God chooses to reveal his divine nature to the world progressively in and through the turbulent history of his involvement with this privileged but stubborn people. God can only be known through his self-revelation and he chooses to be known through Israel. By implication, too, it is Israel's own experience with God that fully unveils the meaning of his name. God's people will have to trust and travel with him to find out who he really is.

Israel, son of God

Fortified by knowing the personal name of the one creator God, Moses is meant to confront Pharaoh. The Israelites are Pharaoh's slaves, but they are also God's son. Moses is to press God's claim on Pharaoh: 'Then say to Pharaoh, "This is what the LORD says; Israel is *my first born-son*" and I told you, "Let my son go, so that he may worship me. But you refused to let him go and so I will kill your firstborn" ' (Ex. 4:22–23). God's words are crucial for the unfolding of the rest of the biblical story. They immediately connect to the death of the firstborn in Egypt and to the later consecration of the Israelite firstborn to the LORD. Beyond this, God's words shape the role of the king in Israel; he will be called God's 'son' because he will represent both God and the people.

Moses is initially too frightened to accept his commission
and the Israelites too depressed to believe it. He cannot
find enough faith to withstand the doubts of the people
and overcome his own fears. 'Faith' only comes when
God impresses on Moses the part he will play in the big
picture.

Tragically, Yahweh's dire warning goes unheeded by
the Egyptian hierarchy. Pharaoh reacts arrogantly and
dismissively to the claims of a god he doesn't recognise
(Ex. 5:2). But, not surprisingly, it is economics and not
theology that preoccupies Pharaoh, worried as he is at
the loss of his slave labour force (Ex. 5:5). Once more
reacting in a way typical of dictators, Pharaoh stereo-
types the people he is oppressing as 'lazy' and acts to
intensify their misery by making their work impossibly
arduous. His behaviour sharpens the conflict as a clash of
gods. Pharaoh forces the issue: don't worship your god,
work for me. Ironically he asks the right question: 'Who is
the LORD that I should obey him?' (Ex. 5:2). Who indeed?
This is the issue right through this gripping story. Who
will Israel serve, Pharaoh or God? Whose interests will
God's people serve; God's or an idolatrous economic
system?

Much like the Flood, the plagues inflicted on Egypt
are, in effect, reversals of creation that paradoxically
demonstrate God's mastery over the natural world. 'God
battles Egypt by controlling creation; it does his bid-
ding'.[2] One-by-one the plagues 'display Pharaoh's impotence, despite his grandiose self-image, and Yahweh's
unquestionable and unconquerable might'.[3] But when
these afflictions fail to move Pharaoh (whose heart is
increasingly and judgmentally hardened by God) God
unleashes the final devastating assault on the regime in
Egypt and the idolatrous worship that buttressed it – the
death of all firstborn.

Great Escape

In the midst of death, however, God preserves and saves his people. Each Israelite household is told to take an unblemished lamb, kill it and daub its blood on the lintels and doorposts of their homes. That same night they are to roast and eat the lamb with bread made without yeast (unleavened bread), all the while dressed ready to leave in a hurry! Moses is promised:

> On that night I will pass through Egypt and strike down every firstborn – and I will bring judgment on all the gods of Egypt. I am the LORD. The blood will be a sign for you on your house where you are: and when I see the blood I will pass over you (Ex. 12:12–13).

By following these simple instructions, Israel is spared the judgment of God. Israel's life begins again with an act of deliverance and redemption. The children of Israel are preserved, literally saved from death. Together they experience the merciful and saving God who made himself personally known to Moses. God establishes a ceremonial meal, called the great Feast of Passover, to commemorate this great act of deliverance (12:14–23). The day when the avenging angel of death *passed over* their ancestors' homes continues to be commemorated to this day by devout Jews. Whenever children ask what the ceremony of Passover means, the answer will be, 'Let me tell you a story, *the* story of how God kept faith with our forefather Abraham, held firm to his covenant promises, heeded our cries for freedom and brought us out of slavery in Egypt …'.

The exodus or 'Great Escape' – the release from the tyrant's grip, the parting of the Red Sea, the saving exodus, the mighty act of redemption, of setting free –

defines Israel's identity as the 'redeemed people of God'. Celebrated in exultant song and exuberant dance (Ex. 15), it is the foundational event of Israel's life and the fountainhead of all her responses to God. Just as the one-time sacrifice of the 'Passover lamb' was perpetually re-enacted in the institutionalised sacrificial system, so the exodus was formative for all Israel's subsequent praise and worship. Herbert Butterfield, the notable Cambridge historian, once said of Israel's praise,

> I know of no other case in history where gratitude was carried so far, no other case where gratitude proved to be such a generative thing. Their God had stepped into history and kept his ancient promise, bringing them to freedom and the promised land, and they simply could not get over it.[4]

From now on Israel, once among the world's *Les Miserables*, will sing 'the music of a people who will not be slaves again'. Even when they borrowed rites and ceremonies from the cyclic round of the natural seasons, they turned them into commemorations of historical and redemptive events. Each of the three major festivals was, at the same time, a harvest thanksgiving and a redemptive celebration. We might expect little else of a people redeemed to worship the Creator and Redeemer – two dimensions of the one God that can never be separated.

Israel's Vocation

In Exodus 19 – the focal point of this act in the drama – we find this motley collection of ex-slaves camped at the foot of Mount Sinai, three months after leaving Egypt. There they encounter, on a larger scale, God speaking from the fire – the same God who Moses had met at the burning bush. God makes covenant with them, his mediating nation in the world, and they are forged into his people.

> Then Moses went up to God and the LORD called to him from the mountain and said: 'This is what you are to say to the house of Jacob and what you are to tell the people of Israel: You yourselves have seen what I did to Egypt, and how I carried you on eagles' wings and brought you to myself. Now if you obey me fully and keep my covenant, then out of all nations you will be my treasured possession. Although the whole earth is mine, you will be for me a kingdom of priests and a holy nation'. These are the words you are to speak to the Israelites (Ex. 19:3–6).

By calling it 'my covenant', God not only claims exclusive ownership of the arrangement but also reminds Moses that it had existed prior to this meeting at Sinai. We have already seen how God's specific bond with Israel is linked with God's previous commitments to the patriarchs, Abraham, Isaac and Jacob (Ex. 2:24; 3:15; 6:1–8). God aims to move this commitment on a stage further. One Old Testament scholar sums up the significance of this: 'The covenant at Sinai is a specific covenant within the context of the Abrahamic covenant'.[5] Furthermore, the text reasserts (and it is vital to take this to heart) that the basis of God's covenant with Israel is grace and redemption.

This is emphasised by the concise summary of the action so far in Exodus 19:4, 'What I did to the Egyptians' sums up God's judgments on Israel's oppressors and the Red Sea deliverance. 'How I carried you on eagles' wings' poetically describes the gracious action of God as he picks up his people and transports them through the wilderness so far. And how God brought Israel to himself reflects his intention to bring his people to the appointed place of worship and revelation (cf. God's earlier pledge to Moses, Ex. 3:12).

This grace is not cheap. It does not preclude obedience. Israel exists as a 'commanded people'. But what does it mean for Israel to be the chosen, covenanted, commanded people of God? The text informs us by describing Israel's threefold calling:

1. God calls Israel his *treasured possession* (Ex. 19:5). The Hebrew term *segullah* suggests Israel is God's personal property. The idea of value may also be present. God regards Israel as especially valuable and precious. She is the 'jewel in his crown' (cf. Mal. 3:17).

2. Israel is designated *a kingdom of priests* (Ex. 19:6). Should this be construed as a *royal priesthood* or a *priestly kingdom?* The latter probably serves best as it implies, in John Durham's words, 'a kingdom run not by politicians depending upon strength and connivance but by priests depending on faith in Yahweh'.[6] As a priestly kingdom, Israel is called to mediate the blessings and revelation of God to the rest of the world. Through faithful obedience to God alone, Israel is to be the intercessory, the go-between people. (It is this element in Israel's calling that was most corrupted by the monarchy which arose in Israel. The kings, almost without exception, set aside trust in God in favour of political power games, intrigues and alliances.)

The priestly mission inevitably flows in the reverse direction as well – it is not only from God to the world but from the world to God. Here we are on the edge of mystery: Israel, in some strange way, is called to intercede for a sinful world and, even stranger, somehow to draw to herself the world's sin and suffering on God's behalf. In the end, only one Israelite, the final priestly king, was up to doing this job.

3. Israel is called to be *a holy nation* (Ex. 19:6b). The concept of 'holiness', pervasive in the Old Testament, conveys something of the flavour of 'separateness' – in particular, the setting of something apart for God's exclusive use. At Sinai the world is being presented with a nation uniquely sanctified to God's holy purpose. Israel was to be a sample nation, a model of the holiness that God intends to re-establish in the whole of his sin-spoiled creation. Israel is to be a showcase nation in whom the original human vocation of being 'image-bearers' is restored. 'Be holy as I am holy' is the charter of Israel's national identity. It is repeatedly spelt out in Leviticus. Israel is commited to the *imitatio dei* (the 'imitation of God'). Just as Adam and Eve were placed on the earth to reflect God's image, so Israel is, as it were, a new prototype humanity, called once more to reflect the glory of God's life and love to the rest of creation.

Dare to be Different

Israel's original calling only serves to highlight the particular tragedy of the period of the Judges, which covers her initial centuries in the Promised Land. During that time, Israel failed to live under the blessing of God's rule; as a consequence, her life degenerated into appalling immorality and apostasy. Lacking an authoritarian figure who could restore order to the chaos, the people of Israel asked the prophet Samuel for a king, ironically so as to be, they said, 'like every other nation', which was a direct contradiction of Israel's unique vocation and destiny! No wonder the great prophets of Israel fought tenaciously to recall Israel to covenant faithfulness and counter-cultural distinctiveness. Don't be the same as everyone else: dare to be as different as God is different.

With all this in mind, it's clearly no accident, that the vocational charter of Israel contains the crucial, almost parenthetic, statement 'although the whole earth is mine' (Ex. 19:5b). Like Abraham, Israel exists to mediate the blessings of God to the wider world. Here is the most selective covenant arrangement imaginable, one that excludes the most powerful civilisations of the ancient world, like China and indeed Egypt. But right at the very heart of the process of choosing one nation, is inserted the significant reminder that God's eyes are still on the whole earth. Israel is meant never to forget that her special privileges and exclusive status are to serve God's plans for every nation and all his creation. The danger of turning inwards in self-serving and nationalistic ways is all too apparent. Israel is, undoubtedly, the 'jewel in God's crown', but the crown God wears is not that of a tribal or even national god; he is the one creator and ruler of the world. The challenge Israel faced (as the church still does) was to avoid reducing the one creator God to an ethnic, national or racial God. Worse still would be either to domesticate God into a mere household god who blesses the family or to privatise him as a purely 'spiritual' god of the individual soul. God gave Israel the Law, so these dangers could be avoided. The Torah was the charter of covenant loyalty, framed as general principles and spelt out in detail to cover every aspect of life.

At this point it is crucial to state again that the basis of Israel's relationship with God is redemption and grace. In fact, the reminder that God brought Israel out of slavery in Egypt prefaces the Ten Commandments or ten words.

The Maker's Instructions

God did not give the Law so that by keeping it Israel might be saved and qualify to be accepted as his people. The Law was given to a people *already saved* – Israel was already the recipient of God's grace and mercy and saving love. So, why did God give Israel the Law? The Law is essentially a description of how a covenant people are expected to live. God says in the Law, 'This is what it looks like to be my covenant people, a holy nation. Live like this in obedience to my commands and you will display covenant loyalty. As you obey, you preserve and maintain your identity as my covenant people. This law-abiding love, this heartfelt obedience, this true worship, this social justice – these define who you are'.

It is often more helpful to use 'Torah' because the word 'Law' sounds so narrowly legalistic to English-speaking readers of the Old Testament. In its broader canonical meaning Torah embraces the first five books of the Bible – which comprise far more than 'laws' in the strict sense and include the foundational redemptive narratives we have been discussing. It constitutes Israel's directions for living. Torah, rooted as it is in the wider creation story (Gen. 1–11), is like the booklet manufacturers enclose with a new electrical product; in other words it contains the *Maker's Instructions*.

The books of Proverbs, Ecclesiastes and Job would later spell out in aphorism and saga how to find this wisdom of the Creator's wisdom in both the mundane routines and tragic crises of living. In Willem Van-Gemeren's words, God's covenant with Israel (the Mosaic covenant) 'is a sovereign administration of grace and promise by which the Lord consecrates a people to himself under the sanctions of Torah'.[7]

As we noted earlier, the Torah is loosely modelled on the ancient near eastern covenant treaties made between kings and their subject peoples. This is clearer in Deuteronomy than in Exodus, but the staple formula is evident in the latter – the preamble, outlining the previous history of the relationship and re-asserting the priority of the sovereign lord; general stipulations on how the relationship can be maintained, ruling out explicitly any independent foreign policy (or, in our case, other gods); specific and detailed case laws showing how the covenant treaty applies to varied areas of living; the provision of witnesses to the agreement; the statement of sanctions against covenant breaking; and the means by which the covenant treaty can be perpetuated in the future.

Ten(der) Commandments

The ten words (or commandments) are directly spoken by God and broadly reflect the treaty form. They embrace the vertical and horizontal dimensions of relationship. They spell out that just as the relationship with Yahweh as king is the beginning of covenant, so this covenant relationship is the key to a just and free society. The first prohibition, 'have no other gods beside me', is foundational for the whole covenant. The tenth, 'you shall not covet', seeks to close the door to every violation of covenant. This is perhaps why Paul, in typical Jewish fashion, singles out the tenth commandment as epitomising sinfulness and links coveting so closely to idolatry (Rom. 7:7; Col. 3:5).

Ron Mehl astutely calls them truly 'ten(der) commandments'.[8] They reflect God's redeeming love and desire to preserve the liberty of his sons and daughters. These 'words' are given to guarantee Israel's freedom under God and to create a pro-life society where worship regulates work; a society where people are free to make long-term commitments to marriage and property because these are protected from the lust and envy of others; one which is not haunted by violence or driven by acquisitiveness, but healed by neighbourly love and cleansed by truthful speech.

Of course, our modern world has made the mistake of equating freedom with rebellious independence from God. As has been rightly said, ours is not so much a *permissive society* as a *transgressive* one. Yet, the 'ten words' are not intended as legalistic 'sound bites' for moralistic people keen to make compliant citizens in a conventional society. Rather, they are the radical means by which the creator God's ordering of chaos at creation is replicated at the social level, so that heaven's will is done on earth. Rather than being relics of an outmoded social order, therefore, the 'ten words' are liberating signposts pointing to the renewal of human community in Christ. They come as the 'maker's instructions' for a better world, they are an act of re-creation.

The case laws that follow enshrine basic human rights and social responsibilities. They constitute a charter of freedom. What is envisaged for Israel is, in a sense, an extension of and an institutionalising of the exodus. Through Torah, God intends to create the just, free, caring society that was denied Israel in Pharaoh's oppressive, slave-driven Egypt.

This covenant – as an extension of the one with Abraham – is similarly sealed with the shedding of blood (Ex. 24). 'This is the blood of the covenant' declares Moses as he sprinkles both the makeshift altar and the people gathered to hear the book of the covenant read. The burnt offerings and fellowship offerings mentioned, together with the sin and guilt offerings emphasised so strongly in

Leviticus, institutionalised the sacrificial principle at the core of Israel's worship. They no doubt resonated at a deep psychological and spiritual level with the earlier sacrificial blood shedding of the Passover lamb and continued to be effective as the means of grace, which dealt with the people's sins and so expressed or repaired the covenant relationship.

Creation's Goal

In the same way that previous covenantal stages have been characterised by a special sign, so God's covenant with Israel is marked with a sign: in this case *the observance of the Sabbath* (Ex. 31:12–18). If it is true that human beings are the *crown* of God's creation, it is equally true that the Sabbath is the *goal* of creation. Everything God has made aspires to that end. The Sabbath sanctifies time. It invites us to look back to the God who rested from his creation task and model our lives on the rhythm of God's labour and rest. It encourages us to imitate God's creative labour as worshippers, not restless workaholics.

The practical benefits of Sabbath were obvious, with animals and fields included in the regular respite from being worked. The Sabbath was, above all, a treasured gift for ex-slaves; it reminded them of the grace that had saved them from the unremitting, round-the-clock, production lines of Egypt's slave economy. Sabbath also inspires hope and urged them to look forward, not merely to the Promised Land, but beyond to the intended goal of creation, when all things would be renewed in the coming kingdom of God. To share in God's ultimate rest, when God 'rests' from his redemptive work in the new creation, will be our final inheritance of salvation. Keeping Sabbath, then, was to be yet another way in which Israel acted as custodian of God's story. Israel exists, in Heschel's words, 'in order to dream the dream of God'.[9] Israel exists as the people who mark God's time.

Praise and Presence

All that has been said so far about Israel's privileges and role leads to the conclusion that she *exists for the praise and worship of God*. The aim of redemption is worship. Nothing emphasises this more than the seemingly disproportionate amount of text devoted to the planning and construction of the Tabernacle under Moses' supervision (Ex. 25–30; 35–40). Under ancient covenant treaty conditions, the first priority is a palace for the king. Since Israel's king is God, his palace is a shrine; its key piece of sacred furniture, the ark, serves as the footstool of his throne. God is owed worship and not merely homage. Furthermore, this tent-like sanctuary is designed to be his 'dwelling-place' in Israel (Ex. 25:8).

Yahweh is a God who from the beginning of the story exhibits a strong desire to be with his people. The one God, whose Spirit roams everywhere, concentrates his holy presence among the people in the sanctuary in the holy of holies. The pillars of cloud by day and fire by night are the visible tokens of that presence. Erecting and dismantling this portable Tabernacle every time Israel camped and decamped – in each case to a precise formula – may occasionally have seemed, more of a blessed nuisance than a blessed privilege! But Israel could never forget how tenaciously this annoyingly persistent God stuck to his dream of travelling the wilderness with them. The later building of the Temple on one fixed spot may have obscured this but the Tabernacle as a movable shrine perfectly expressed this commitment of his presence.

Following the loss of the Temple, it was the prophet Ezekiel who received and shared the stunning revelation that God had even come into exile in order to be with his people. When Israel fell from grace in worshipping the golden calf, what most appalled Moses was the threatened withdrawal of God's presence and its replacement by an angel (Ex. 33:2–3). If your presence does not go with us then we are not going anywhere! When the Tabernacle was eventually constructed on its God-given lines, God filled it with the glorious cloud of his presence (Ex. 40:34). So the gracious disclosures and promises connect up to form what one scholar terms the 'Emmanuel principle', which lies at the heart of this covenant: 'I will be what I will be for you, I will be your God and you will be my people, I will be with you'.[10] God dwelt among his people in Tabernacle and Temple and Israel beheld his glory. This fell a long way short of incarnation but it was on the same road.

Microcosm of Creation

Although the Tabernacle has often been misconstrued as a coded picture of salvation, it is more helpful to see it as *a microcosm of creation*. It represents a creation-in-miniature, marked by all the features found in the first chapter of Genesis. The parallels are intriguing: the seven occasions on which the LORD spoke to Moses, ending with the Sabbath; the bringing of the rich resources of God's world into order and beauty; the action of the creative Spirit of God inspiring the craftsmanship for the work; the way Moses inspects the work, pronounces himself satisfied and blesses it; and the commencement date on the first day of the first month. *All* of these features echo the Genesis account. In other words, as the

Sabbath sanctifies *time,* so the Tabernacle sanctifies *space.* In the midst of a fallen, disordered, rebellious world, there is one place where the original beauty, design and purpose of creation as a vehicle for God's glorious presence is made visible. On a small-scale, where God dwells with Israel and is worshipped, everything is 'just as it was at the beginning'.

We turn finally to Deuteronomy, which closes the Torah. Deuteronomy is presented as a series of speeches given by Moses to the children of Israel on the verge of the Promised Land. Forty years have elapsed since the exodus and Sinai. Israel has painfully learnt the cost of her continual grumbling and complaining in the wilderness. Disobedience has turned an eleven-day journey into a forty-year detour! Obedience, it appears, is by far the best short cut when dealing with God. Now Moses gives a 'second reading' (*deutero*) of the Law (*nomos*) – not another Law but the covenant charter of Sinai renewed, expanded and re-applied to the new generation poised to enter the Land.

Remarkably, towards its close, even *before Israel occupies the Land*, Moses warns that she may lose the Land! Moses is recorded as re-iterating the blessings that attend covenant obedience and the judgmental curses that follow disobedience (Deut. 27–28). Moses then summons Israel to renew the covenant with God (Deut. 29). In doing so he anticipates that Israel's future covenantal unfaithfulness will incur the judgments of God, which culminate in the ultimate curse of *exile from the Land* (Deut. 28:63).

Once more, though this time tragically and negatively, Israel's story re-enacts the human story. Israel's exile from Canaan – a place so often described by the Old Testament in Eden type language – sadly mirrors the expulsion of Adam and Eve from the Garden of Eden.

Moses issues this warning before the people have even set foot in the Land! What Moses foresaw became grim reality 800 years later in the Babylonian exile. By the time the Torah takes final canonical shape, during that very exile from the Land, his warning has become past tense: 'In furious anger and in great wrath the LORD uprooted them from their land and thrust them into another land' (Deut. 29:28) – to which the exilic editors have wryly added 'as it is now'!

Even more remarkably, Moses does not point Israel to the sacrificial system as the means of dealing with this depth of her sinfulness. Rather, in terms that foreshadow Jeremiah and Ezekiel, Moses looks for hope beyond exile to a new initiative of God that will create radically new covenant conditions. One way of seeing how radical a change will take place is to compare Deuteronomy 10:16, where God commands the people to circumcise their hearts, with Deuteronomy 30:6 where, we are told, the LORD will circumcise your hearts! Command becomes promise. Human obligation becomes divine gift. Already, before the ink is dry on the old covenant, the new covenant is hinted at!

History from the Underside

This is the pain and promise of Israel's vocation. For his part, Paul – in the light of Christ – reads the world's story through the story of Israel. For him, Israel embodies the larger human story. Positively she embraces the human vocation. The Law was added to Israel so that sin might increase. It is as if it was also Israel's vocation to be the place and people under God's law where the world's sin would be gathered, heaped up and finally dealt with (Rom. 5:20–21). Paul is clearly reading the Christ story

through the lens of Deuteronomy 27–30 from which
he quotes in this part of his letter and which underlies
his whole argument here (cf. Rom. 10:5–22).'Did they
stumble so as to fall beyond recovery? Not at all; rather
because of their transgressions salvation has come to the
gentiles' (Rom. 11:11). Paradoxically, dare we suggest it,
Israel's failure is written into the plan from the beginning!
Israel remains the channel of God's blessing, even in her
failure; such is the amazing paradox of salvation and the
mysterious ways of God.

So, exodus and exile bracket Israel's Old Testament
story! The irony is deep – from slavery in Egypt to captivity in Babylon, from where Abraham had come a millennium earlier! *What a story!* This history is unusual if
not unique. The 'winners' usually write history. History
is usually the top-down story of conquerors, leaders,
victors, a history told by the powerful, successful and
influential. Such stories are told in the victory annals of
the Egyptian Pharaohs, Assyrian potentates and Babylonian Emperors. But the story of Israel is history from the
'underside' – the story of the powerless and the poor –
with passionate prophetic protest and innocent suffering
held out as the way to redemption and glory.

God so loved the world that he chose Israel. God so
loved Israel – and through Israel the world, that he finally
sent his only son to act out the story of Israel and her God
by embodying the one and incarnating the other.[11]

Notes

[1] Christopher J.H. Wright, *Deuteronomy*, 57.

[2] Peter Enns, *Exodus*, 197.

[3] Ibid. Enns' whole discussion, utilising Terence Fretheim's commentary on Exodus, is helpful in seeing the creational dimension of
God's controversy with Pharaoh.

[4] Herbert Butterfield, *Writings on Christianity and History*, 79.

[5] Terence Fretheim, *Exodus*, 209.

[6] John Durham, *Exodus*, 263.

[7] Willem VanGemeren, *Interpreting the Prophetic Word: An Introduction to the Prophetic Literature of the Old Testament*, 237.

[8] Ron Mehl, *The Ten(der) Commandments*.

[9] Abraham Heschel, *Moral Grandeur and Spiritual Audacity: Essays*, 10.

[10] Palmer Robertson, *Christ of the Covenants*, 46ff.

[11] See Wright, *Knowing Jesus*.

God is Committed to
Crowning His Son King

David's destiny
2 Samuel 7; Psalm 2; Psalm 89

It Was 'The Morning After the Night Before'

Our attention is drawn to a man slumped in a chair in a
state of shock. We realise that he is a king but the close-
up of his face reveals deep turmoil. He is evidently strug-
gling with profound and mixed emotions. His mixture
of pain and incredulity directly results from what has
happened the night before. As a typical ancient king,
he had spent the previous evening with his advisors
sharing with them his consuming ambition to build a
'house' for his god. In his day, the scale and grandeur of
the sanctuary-cum-palace showed how much the king
valued the god whose endorsement buttressed his rule.

His leading advisor, a court-prophet, no doubt keen to
avoid the king's displeasure, readily 'rubber-stamps' the
proposal. 'Great idea, my lord, go ahead; plans will be
drawn up immediately'. But during the night events take
a different turn altogether. One problem with being a

prophet of God is that God resolves to get his word in edgeways; he wakes his messengers up in the middle of the night – if need be – to get a hearing! His sleep interrupted, the prophet is ordered to tell the king that he is forbidden to build a house for God. Instead, God will build a 'house' for him, and will also give him a throne and kingdom that will last forever, along with the assurance that God will be his father and he will be God's son.

The time was 3000 years ago; the place Jerusalem, a recently captured Jebusite stronghold; the prophet was Nathan; the king was David. Can you imagine the trepidation with which Nathan entered David's private quarters the next morning? 'Thus says the LORD: Do you want the bad news or the good news first O king? The "bad news" is – "No, you cannot build a house for me!" says the Lord. "No, your plans are vetoed by higher authority!" "No, your dream must die, your ambition is disappointed!" But "the good news" is, although you can't build a house for God, *God will build a house for you!* In fact, God promises you four things – *a house* (in the sense of a dynasty), *a throne, a kingdom that will last forever* and *a special Father-son relationship.*'

So the 'morning after the night before' finds David emotionally reeling from the blow of having his hopes dashed and from being made such astonishing promises. God's plans and dreams, it seems, are always more than we can ask or imagine. So David is pictured sitting bewildered and humbled before the LORD, probably in the tent-tabernacle he has erected for worship in Jerusalem. He reflects ruefully and wonderingly on what has been told him. 'Who am I, O Sovereign LORD, and what is my family, that you have brought us this far? And as if this were not enough in your sight, O Sovereign LORD, you have also spoken about the future of the house of your servant' (2 Sam. 7:18–19).

Charter of Humanity

Our understanding of what David says next (2 Sam. 7:19) depends on whether we give lesser or greater weight to the phrase that literally means 'and this is the law of man'. The New International Version opts for the minimalist translation, 'Is this your usual way of dealing with man, O Sovereign LORD?' However, certain Old Testament scholars note that in some ancient languages, notably Acadian, the phrase 'the law of man' refers to human fate and destiny. This leads Walter Kaiser to translate it as 'this is the charter for humanity', which is surely a preferable translation.[1] Bill Dumbrell agrees with this, commenting that 'in the oracle delivered to him, David rightly sees the future and destiny of the human race as involved'.[2] No wonder David is apparently overwhelmed, praying only that God would see fit to keep his word.

2 Samuel 7 has, not surprisingly, been called an 'ideological summit' in the Old Testament. With the fourfold promise of a lasting house, throne and kingdom within a special father-son relationship, it is 'a mountain peak of redemptive history'[3] when God *makes a firm covenant with David and the Davidic kingship.*

Although the word 'covenant' does not occur in 2 Samuel 7, this commitment of God is rightly celebrated as covenantal in Psalm 89.

> I will sing of the LORD's great love forever; with my mouth I will make your faithfulness known through all generations. I will declare that your love [*hesed*, 'covenant love'] stands firm forever. You said, "I have made a covenant with my chosen one, I have sworn to David my servant, 'I will establish your line forever and make your throne firm through all generations.' " (Ps. 89:1–4).

The psalmist celebrates the special anointing and relationship, and the worldwide role, which God has promised to the Davidic dynasty:

> I have found David my servant; with my sacred oil I have anointed him ... He will call out to me, 'You are my Father, my God, the rock, my Savior.' I will also appoint him my firstborn, the most exalted of the kings of the earth. I will maintain my love to him forever, and my covenant with him will never fail (Ps. 89:20, 26–28).

This psalm neatly links the Davidic covenant with God's earlier covenant commitments. In speaking of the Davidic descendant as destined to be king of kings over the whole earth, it connects him directly with Noah's 'covenanted earth' and Abraham's 'all nations'. As Dumbrell says:

> Second Samuel 7 with its notion of the Davidic covenant as 'humanity's charter' provided for the future of the race under the leadership of the Davidic house and thus foreshadowed the fulfilment of the Abrahamic promises.[4]

God's King, God's Son

Psalm 89 also clearly joins the Davidic promises to God's covenant with Israel. Calling God his father and being addressed as God's 'firstborn' son, ties the king closely to God and God's people. As God's 'son' the king of Israel represented God's kingship, but the Father-son entitlement was only an intensified and focused form of the basic covenant pledge God had made to Israel because 'sonship' language had first been applied to Israel as a whole (Ex. 4:22f.). Being called God's 'son' meant that the king represented both God and the people of God. The national hopes and destiny of Israel were embodied in the king. This explains why the biblical narrative ceases to tell the story of the children of Israel and concentrates on telling the story of the kings, or, better perhaps, tells Israel's story through that of her kings. When the kings of Israel and Judah walk covenantally (which was rarely) the people prosper: when they fail in covenant faithfulness or fail to lead the people in covenant obedience, the people share the fate of their kings. In this sense G.B. Caird was not exaggerating when he said, 'The king did not merely represent Israel: he *was* Israel'.[5]

In the light of this, it is hard to overstate the importance of God's covenantal commitment to kingship in Israel, even though the monarchy got off to a very bad start. By the end of the period of the Judges, the divine experiment of Israel as a 'holy nation' in the Promised Land had degenerated into moral and social anarchy. The book of Judges sounds a society's epitaph like the dull tolling of a funeral bell: 'In those days Israel had no king; everyone did as he saw fit' (Jdg. 21:25). According to 1 Samuel 8, this stirs up a popular clamour for a king and a deputation comes to Samuel to demand one so that they can be like every other nation (1 Sam. 8:5). Sadly, this is the wrong reason because it directly repudiated Israel's destiny, which was to be *unlike* any other nation. As Samuel points out, this is tantamount to rejecting God himself as king because the people of Israel are meant to live 'theocratically', that is directly under *God's* rule.

Furthermore, the Israelites chose the 'wrong man', opting for Saul with his obvious 'head and shoulders' suitability and so threatened to thwart God's choice of David, the man 'after his own heart'. Samuel conceded to their demand and God endorsed their choice, no doubt as an act of judgment. Samuel, however, remained aware that kingship was God's intention for Israel – Abraham and Sarah having been promised kings in their descendants. Nonetheless, Samuel warned the people of the disastrous consequences of humanly engineered monarchy, anticipating just how oppressive and self-serving the kings would become.

New King, New Kingdom

God, nevertheless, remained capable of exploiting the royal category for his own purpose and glory even though bad and power-hungry kings – and with few exceptions they were bad – misused their position for their own ends. In God's hands, the office of kingship was redeemable and might become redemptive. So, as the ancient historian saw, God's covenant commitment to David remained as a 'lamp that would never go out' even in the darkest days of the most evil kings (2 Kgs. 8:19). Even though Solomon and not his father, David, built the Temple (God's house) and evil kings would come and go; God's covenant love for the Davidic king was unconditional: 'When he does wrong, I will punish him … But my love will never be taken away from him' (2 Sam. 7:14–15). 'If his sons forsake my law … if they violate my decrees … I will punish their sin … but I will not take my love from him … I will not violate my covenant' (Ps. 89:30–34).

The failure of the kings was apparent by the time of the exile. Prophetic hopes thus began to centre on a new 'David' who would rule righteously and bring in God's just and peaceable kingdom (Jer. 23:5f.; 33:15f.; Ezek. 34:23–24; 37:24).

The Old Testament histories tell us very little about how kings were crowned in Israel, but something of the covenantal significance, it seems, was conveyed to a new king at his coronation. In 2 Kings 11 we read of the coronation of Joash, the boy king in Israel:

> Jehoiada brought out the king's son and put the crown on him; he presented him with a copy of the covenant and proclaimed him king. They anointed him and the people clapped their hands and shouted, 'Long live the king!' ... Jehoiada then made a covenant between the LORD and the king and people that they would be the LORD's people. He also made a covenant between the king and the people (2 Kgs. 11:12, 17).

We may surmise that each subsequent king in the Davidic line in Jerusalem heard afresh at his coronation the privileged affirmation applied to him: 'You are my son, today I have begotten you'. Psalm 2 is likely evidence of this.

God Laughs, God Decrees

Psalm 2 was probably first sung at the coronation of a king in Israel. The prophetic singer first sings out what he sees – the nations in uproar, their heads of government engaged in furious debate at a world summit conference. For all their disagreements, he sees them as constituting one vast conspiracy 'against the LORD and his anointed' (Ps. 2:2). The bottom line of all their arrogant manifestos, humanistic agendas and well-spun policy statements is 'let us break their chains ... and throw off their fetters' (Ps. 2:3). The prophetic singer reveals that the power-struggles in our world are attempts to carve up God's world into spheres of influence, from which God has been excluded. Evidently the men of power intend to run God's world without him.

What the psalmist hears and sees next lifts us to an altogether loftier vantage point where we see a bigger picture. Our visionary singer sees the throne in heaven, but it's what he hears that rivets our attention – the sounds of derisive laughter: 'The One enthroned in heaven *laughs*' (Ps. 2:4). This divine derision cuts the rulers of this world down to size and puts all human pretension into true perspective.

Now God speaks directly. As the babble of arrogant competing voices fades, one voice rises decisively above them, announcing his decision: 'I have installed my king on my holy hill Zion' (Ps. 2:6). Glimpsing into God's Oval office, or Cabinet Room, we realize that the casting vote is *already* in; we realise that it has already been decided who is destined to rule the whole world. God's anointed king in Israel is *destined to be Lord of the world!* The rulers of empires and vast nation states can never get their heads round this because it seems too far-fetched. Is Zion – one of the hills on which Jerusalem is built, and often a synonym for the city itself – the seat of world-rule? At best, it is a puny hill and Jerusalem an insignificant place in an unheard of minor kingdom. As for the king of Israel who reigns there, what authority has he got? So the Pharaohs and Nebuchadnezzars are confounded by God's ways; and for the same reason Caesar Augustus and Pontius Pilate end up as mere footnotes to the royal story of God's Messiah.

The psalmist then lets Israel's anointed king speak as he claims for himself the divine promises of the Davidic covenant: 'I will proclaim the decree of the Lord. He said to me, "You are my son; today I have become your father. Ask of me, and I will make the nations your inheritance and the ends of the earth your possession' (Ps. 2:7–8).

A Man Born to be King

Fast-forward to two men standing, dripping wet, on a riverbank. The heavens open, the Holy Spirit dove-like alights on one of them and that voice from heaven speaks again saying, 'You are my son' (Mk. 1:11). As we hear the ancient declaration again through the pens of the Gospel writers, we realise that whatever else we know about Jesus of Nazareth, we can be sure of one thing: he is a *king*; Israel's king; God's anointed king. Almost immediately – it seems obvious now – Jesus announces the good news of a change of government, proclaiming, 'The time has come … The kingdom of God is near. Repent and believe the good news!' (Mk. 1:15).

One person, at least, should not have been surprised. Thirty years earlier, as a young Jewish up-country girl in Nazareth, she had received an astounding visit from the highest angelic messenger in God's court:

> Do not be afraid Mary, you have found favour with God. You will be with child and give birth to a son and you are to give him the name Jesus. He will be great and will be called Son of the Most High. The Lord God will give him the throne of his father David, and he will reign over the house of Jacob for ever; his kingdom will never end (Lk. 1:30–33).

Thirty years later, Jesus, as God's son-king, confronts the personified evil of Satan in the Judean wilderness, just as David had confronted Goliath. Jesus is shown and offered all the kingdoms of the world if he will bow down and worship the Evil One, but this Son of God, knowing that he only has to ask the Father for the nations to become his inheritance and the ends of the earth his possession, crucially refuses to sell his crown cheap to any old devil!

When, three years later, Jesus approaches the city where Israel's kings always came to be enthroned, he is hailed in popular enthusiasm as the long-awaited messianic deliverer. But he arrives, incongruously, as a gentle king on a donkey, not as a militaristic warlord on a horse. He comes not to build the Temple, like Solomon, but to replace it, like David, with larger dreams. He comes to be crowned not in a palace on Mount Zion, but on a cross-shaped throne on Golgotha hill – he reigns from the tree.

In the aftermath of Easter, the apostles turn again to Psalm 2 for help in explaining the deeper issues at stake in the seemingly arbitrary crucifixion of Jesus (Acts 4:21–30). It shows them that just as God's long salvation comes to its climax in the events of Easter, so too does the long battle with evil. Like a boil that is allowed to swell before it is lanced, so evil is allowed to burgeon until it comes to its head and is dealt with at the Cross. By referring to the psalmist's prophetic song, therefore, the apostles are not merely finding emotional solace in an apt Scripture but are rising to the meaningful conviction that they are caught up in God's bigger story. Herod and Pilate are unlikely bedfellows, confirming the psalmist's view that sin dupes us all into being – even unwittingly – accomplices in a conspiracy against God and against his anointed. Rulers like Herod and Pilate, are really mere stooges, the front men for darker forces. But to pit puny pragmatism against God's mighty eternal plans is to be outwitted and outdone at every turn. His enemies, their job done, might roll down their sleeves, congratulating themselves on having washed their hands of this troublesome young prophet. But Jesus won't go away that easily. Their lasting frustration will be to discover just how much they have contributed to their own defeat and the triumphant outworking of God's strategic plan. The devil's last chagrin will be to realise his contribution to Christ's victory.[6]

Conversely, Jesus' irrepressible disciples rebound from setbacks, pray irresistible prayers and proclaim an unstoppable gospel. Theirs is the story of a superior and unshakable kingdom. Their destiny is not told in the small print of a Roman Governor's report to headquarters of 'a little local difficulty' he has managed to deal with. Their destiny is written large in the sovereign plans of a sovereign God. To know this is to find oneself not in the grip of an inexorable fate, but in the embrace of an unfailing love.

Living Lord

Above all, it is Jesus' resurrection from the dead that confirms he is Son of God and messianic king. After all, a king who lives forever reigns forever. As Paul proclaims to the synagogue worshippers in Antioch, in words which blend 2 Samuel 7:14 and Psalm 2:7, 'What God promised our fathers he has fulfilled for us, their children, by raising up Jesus. As it is written in the second Psalm "You are my Son, today I have become your Father" ' (Acts 13:33). The day of Jesus' resurrection was also his coronation as king when his sonship was confirmed. Paul and Peter view David as a prophet (Acts 2:30; 13:34) whose hope for a descendant on the throne who would 'not see decay' (Ps. 16:9–11; Acts 2:25–28; 13:35–37) is answered by the resurrection of Jesus – the gift of 'the holy and sure blessings promised to David' (Is. 55:3; Acts 13:34), which means Jesus is David's Lord', as well as son (Ps. 110:1; Acts 2:34–35).

As far as Paul is concerned, only the resurrection of Jesus – whom Paul had encountered on the Damascus Road as 'alive and well and reigning' – would ever have convinced him that Jesus was the true Messiah and not a dead and discredited messianic pretender. As G.B. Caird has argued:

> the mere fact that a dead man had risen from the grave could not have won for him the right to the title of messiah. It was because Jesus had died and risen as *Israel's representative* that he was now thought to reign over God's people at the right hand of God.[7]

In this one man – her representative king – Israel's hoped for resurrection-vindication as God's covenant people had taken place, solo. No wonder Paul could write to the Christians living in Imperial Caesar's Rome, where the good news of the Emperor as 'son of god' was currently being promulgated, that

> the gospel [God] promised beforehand through his prophets in the Holy Scriptures regarding his Son, who as to his human nature was a descendant of David, and who through the Spirit of holiness was declared with power to be the Son of God by his resurrection from the dead: Jesus Christ our Lord (Rom.1:2–4).

By virtue of his resurrection, Jesus eclipses everything David was and fulfils everything David stood for. Jesus' resurrection has launched him into a new realm of reality, a sphere of human existence characterised by the unlimited powers and possibilities of the creative Spirit of God. The resurrection happened in history but came from beyond history as the spearhead of God's invading kingdom. The Jesus who is proclaimed in the gospel is Israel's true Messiah and the world's true Lord. Jesus commissions heralds like Paul to announce, throughout the Roman Empire and beyond, Jesus' accession to the world's throne and to claim the allegiance of all.

The Lion King

The writer of Hebrews also takes up this theme, skilfully exploiting the Davidic Covenant in his presentation of Jesus as God's full and final word. In the overture to their exhortation, they refer directly to the promises made to David, seeing them fulfilled in Jesus, the son-king (1:5ff.; 2 Sam. 7:14f.). They develop this in later chapters by connecting God's promise to the king of a 'father-son' relationship (2 Sam. 7:14) with Psalm 110:4 where the king as 'a priest forever according to the order of Melchizedek'. Its use enables the writer of Hebrews to link 'son', 'king' and 'priest' in a breathtakingly creative way (Heb. 5:4–6).

According to the Torah part of the covenant story, kings and priests were kept apart as distinct offices – interestingly enough the only king to have ever got away with performing a priestly function was David. The writer of Hebrews works back from Psalm 110 to the original and only other reference to Melchizedek in the Old Testament (Gen. 14) to join son, king and priest effectively together. He notes that the strange priest-king of the primeval Jerusalem who met Abraham on the road was the one to whom Abraham paid tithes. Employing a curiously rabbinic-style argument, the writer asserts that since the seed of Abram's priestly descendants, the Levites, was in his body at the time, they too, as it were, submit to Melchizedek and their priesthood is subsumed under his. Melchizedek represents, therefore, a *superior* priesthood. Furthermore, the writer of Hebrews construes the silence of Genesis about Melchizedek's predecessors or successors as typical of an *eternal* – as well as a superior – priesthood. It is this office of priesthood that Jesus now holds by virtue both of his eternal sonship and especially of his resurrection to an indestructible life (Heb. 7:16). This king is God's son in the ultimate sense of sharing the eternal divine nature; he is not simply an adopted or honorary heir. He is son-king, priest forever.

Jesus lives and reigns to make intercession. As son, priest and king who represents his people and his world, he embodies all that Israel as God's firstborn Son and priestly kingdom was ever meant to be. This Son does not merely represent God; he incarnates God. All this makes Jesus the 'guarantee of a better covenant' and the mediator to the world of all the covenantal blessings promised to Abraham (Heb. 6:13–20; 7:22; 9:15).

It is left for the apostle John, by Spirit-inspired revelation, to envision the 'lion-king' silhouetted on the skyline of history. Jesus is the lion of the tribe of Judah, the root and descendant of David, and the custodian of the scroll of God's covenant purposes for all humankind; he is the only one worthy to implement God's plans. Jesus is the Lord of the world and the king of kings, head over an international multitude that it is impossible to number, just as Abraham could not count the stars in the night sky. All this began with the dashing of David's dreams by a God who can 'do far more than you could ever imagine or guess or request in your wildest dreams' (Eph. 3:20, *The Message*).

The evidence for this is Jesus, the high king of heaven, heaven's bright sun and the keeper of the keys of David that open the door to God's eternal kingdom. Beyond this door there are no tears or broken dreams, no disappointments or regrets. Beyond this door there is no night: it's always bright and sun-drenched morning.

Notes

[1] Walter C. Kaiser, *Toward an Old Testament Theology*, 155.

[2] Kaiser, *Toward an Old Testament Theology*, 155. cf. Dumbrell, *Covenant and Creation*, 152.

[3] Robert Gordon, *1 and 2 Samuel*, 235. McComiskey, *Covenants of Promise*, 25.

[4] Dumbrell, *Covenant and Creation*, 163.

[5] G.B. Caird, *New Testament Theology*, 166.

[6] The idea and language come from P.T. Forsyth's, *The Justification of God: Lectures for Wartime on a Christian Theodicy*, 205.

[7] Caird, *New Testament Theology*, 309.

God is Committed to
Changing His People from the Inside Out

The prophetic hope
Jeremiah 31:31–34; Ezekiel 36–37;
2 Corinthians 3

> By the rivers of Babylon we sat and wept when we remembered Zion. There on the poplars we hung our harps, for there our captors asked us for songs, our tormentors demanded songs of joy: they said, 'Sing us one of the songs of Zion!' How can we sing the songs of the Lord while in a foreign land?

Nothing expresses more acutely the pain of the Babylonian exile than Psalm 137 with its evocative images of 'the day the music died' by the rivers of Babylon when harps were hung, discarded on the willow trees and the plaintive question hung in the air: 'How can we sing the songs of the Lord while in a foreign land?' Desolation has deepened into futility. The taunts of their tormentors pick at their emotional wounds. Unwilling to forget Jerusalem, but haunted by the malice of those who clamoured for

Jerusalem's destruction, the exiles savour the bittersweet memories of an illustrious past. At the end of the psalm, the dark violence of the victimised spirit erupts in an outburst of raging resentment from which we recoil (Ps. 137:8–9). The best that can be said of such an expression of brutal rage is that it is better directed to God in angry prayer than hurled at people in vengeance.

The emotional intensity of Psalm 137 is matched only by the book of Lamentations, which has been called the most 'tear-stained book' in the Old Testament. As its name suggests, it is a great outpouring of grief over the destruction of the Temple and Jerusalem at the hands of the ruthless pagan invaders. From the first of several deportations in 606BC down to the demise of Jerusalem in around 586BC, the protracted Babylonian conquest of Judah brought the long slow death of a nation. Lamentations captures poignantly the sense of national bereavement. For the exiles, and no doubt for those left behind, the pain felt terminal. Many of the exiles must have felt the loss of kingship, Temple and the Land as the virtual end of everything – the end of Israel's unique identity and destiny, even perhaps the death of God.

Graveyard of a Nation

In a prophetic vision, Ezekiel, who was one of the first to be taken to Babylon, saw the state of Israel as a valley full of bleached and dry bones – one vast cemetery with the dead humiliatingly left unburied, allowing the vultures to strip the carcasses and the elements to dismember the skeletons. Challenged as to how these bones can live again, Ezekiel sees hope and, shrewdly enough, puts the onus back on God: 'O Sovereign LORD, only you know' (Ezek. 37:3).

Ezekiel obeys the command to prophesy to the bones and they come together and flesh re-forms. He also prophesies to the *ruach* ('breath' or 'wind') and the breath or Spirit of God enters the bodies and they stand on their feet – this living army of God is raised from the dead. As Old Testament scholar, Donald Gowan has put it, 'The prophets interpreted the exile as the death of the old Israel and then promised that God would start over with resurrection in the form of a new, forgiven people'.[1] The paradoxical hope offered by the prophets is that salvation and restoration lie on the other side of 'death and resurrection'.

Isaiah's visions of hope are cast in equally extravagant language. 'The wilderness will rejoice and blossom; like the crocus it will burst into bloom' (Is. 35:1). God will provide 'water in the desert, streams in the wasteland' (Is. 43:20). 'Mountains and hills will burst into song and all the trees of the field will clap their hands' (Is. 55:12). The new world will be thornless. Isaiah, who consistently joins creation and redemption, is convinced that the God who created is the one who redeems. 'No half God could redeem a world it took a whole God to create. To redeem creation is a more creative act than it was to create'.[2] In short, there would be no half-measures; final salvation will be a new act of creation.

Leopard Changing Spots?

The trauma of exile concentrated the prophetic mind and evoked powerful images of judgment and hope. In a memorable picture, Jeremiah laments the persistent disobedience of kings and people who seem unable to change their sinful patterns of behaviour: 'Can the Ethiopian change his skin or the leopard change its spots?

Neither can you do good who are accustomed to doing evil' (Jer. 13:23). The prophets, whose word was consistently rejected, might well have agreed with a modern commentator that 'people are not changed by moral exhortation but by transformed imagination'.[3] These prophets of exile knew only too well that a transformed world implied changed people. Later, Jeremiah's scepticism about the people's ability to change was answered by God's promise of a new covenant. God will deal directly with the deep-seated disobedience of his covenant partner in this new covenant arrangement. God promises to create a new covenant people who would be changed and empowered to keep covenant with him.

Jeremiah 31:31–34 is the key passage. The covenant promised now will not be like the covenant that bound Israel to God at Sinai (Jer. 31:32) – not that there was anything intrinsically wrong with the 'old covenant'. The breakdown in covenant faithfulness occurred on the human side of the relationship, not the divine – it was Israel's deep-seated failure to keep covenant (cf. Jer. 31:32) that broke the covenant.

Four elements of the new covenant promise are spelt out:

1. A heartfelt grasp of the defining story by which God's people live, creating a new disposition to obey God.
God promises to 'put my law in their hearts' – this represents not so much a change of law as a change in the way the covenant is administered. The Law, which was previously external to the people, written on tablets of stone, is now to be internalised and imprinted on the hearts of God's covenant partners. God's people will have a new 'mindset', a new inner dynamic, disposing them to do God's will from the 'inside out'. This promises to produce

what Jeremiah later calls a 'singleness of heart and action' (Jer. 32:39).

Such a promise mirrors the challenge posed by Moses to an Israel poised to enter the Land (Deut. 30). Moses prophetically warns of the curses that will come upon a covenantally unfaithful people in the Land, culminating in the ultimate curse, exile. Even before Israel has entered to possess the Land, Moses is looking to the tragic end of the story when Israel, by her persistent disobedience, forfeits the Land. But in an extraordinary move, Moses offers the people hope. God, he says, will even then bring his people back from exile to the Land. In words that strikingly match the new covenant promises of Jeremiah, God pledges to turn his demand 'circumcise your hearts' into a promise: 'The LORD you God will circumcise your hearts so that you may love him with all your heart and with all your soul, and live' (Deut. 30:6; cf. 10:16). All this is made clear in Jeremiah. God, it seems, is intent on having a covenant partnership that works, come what may!

It is helpful to recall that 'Law' or 'Torah' constitutes more than commandments or legal obligations. Torah enshrines the founding stories of how the one creator God called Abraham, Isaac, Jacob and Joseph to join his plan of salvation for the world. Torah tells how God invested his love in a particular people, Israel, redeeming them and making them his covenant partner with a special vocation to bring blessing to the nations. The laws he gave were intended to define what it meant to be a people with this story, challenged to live out the story of this holy God and no other. This was their story; this was their song. Israel, however, failed to live by the story God had scripted for her and hankered after the self-made stories of the surrounding pagan nations. How will God get this people to live by God's story?

The new covenant promises that God will write this defining story inside them. By this 'story implant', God's people are newly disposed to obey him. They will begin to show their real identity and become the covenant community God desires, as they think and behave distinctively. New covenant ethics is not primarily about correct behaviour and right decisions but about the formation of character and becoming a faithful, obedient covenant partner.

2. A strengthened sense of security in belonging to God and God's people.
God re-affirms the heart of the covenant: 'I will be their God and they will be my people.' These words crystallise as a formula, the bond of mutual commitment that – from the beginning – was meant to characterise God's special relationship with Israel (Ex. 6:7; Lev. 26:12; Jer. 30:22; 33:1; Ezek. 36:28; 37:23). Despite failure and defeat the bond is now to be intensified and renewed. God's people are to be re-established as his own possession. The repercussions of this promise would prove to be truly amazing. Some two centuries earlier, Hosea had already held out the hope that God would one day say 'to those called: "Not my people", "You are my people" and they will say; "You are my God" ' (Hos. 2:23). But even such far-seeing prophets as Hosea and Jeremiah could scarcely have envisaged the day when those far removed from God's original vow – the Gentiles throughout the wider world – would lay hold of this promise for their own inclusion in God's covenant family (Rom. 9:25; 10:19; 2 Cor. 6:16). Peter would, one day, be able to encourage the new covenant communities in time-honoured terms, as God's 'chosen race, a royal priesthood, a people belonging to God, that you may declare the praises of him who called you out of darkness into his wonderful light', reminding

them – especially, no doubt, the Gentile believers among them – that 'Once you were not a people, now you are the people of God' (1 Pet. 2.10).

3. *An unprecedented assurance of knowing God personally.*
In the oracle's words, 'No longer will a man teach his neighbour, or a man his brother, saying, "Know the LORD, because they will all know me, from the least of them to the greatest", declares the LORD' (Jer. 31:34). The emphasis on the word 'all' implies the 'democratisation of the knowledge of God'. Knowledge of God is accessible to everyone and is no longer confined just to priests or prophets. But 'knowing God' in Old Testament terms is not a matter of having some private or mystical religious experience. In fact, the words 'from the least to the greatest' alert us to the profound social implications of the new covenant. 'Knowing God' – especially in Jeremiah – always involves knowing what kind of God he is, namely that he is a God of justice. 'Let not the wise man boast of his wisdom or the strong man boast of his strength or the rich man boasts of his riches, but let him who boasts boast about this: that he understands and knows me, that I am the LORD, who exercises kindness, justice and righteousness on earth, for in these I delight' declares the Lord' (Jer. 9:23–24). As Jeremiah challenged king Jehoahaz, son of the godly Josiah: ' "Did not your father have food and drink? He did what was right and just, and so all went well. He defended the cause of the poor and needy, and so all went well. Is that not what it means to know me?" declares the LORD' (Jer. 22:15–17).

Knowing God in this deep and pervasive way is not an escape into spiritual dreamland. It is a life-changing encounter that promotes social justice – loving your neighbour through loving God and loving God through loving your neighbour. If you do not 'know' your neighbour in this way, you do not know God. The apostle John has much to say about this in his epistles (cf. 1 Jn. 2:4ff.).

4. A radical forgiveness of sins.

Undergirding all the other provisions of the new covenant is God's solution to the deep-seated problem of human sin and covenant unfaithfulness: 'For I will forgive their wickedness and remember their sins no more' (Jer. 31:34). In one sense, this is nothing new. Forgiveness was always available under the old covenant. With proper use of the sacrificial system, joined to sincere repentance, Old Testament believers, like the psalmist, could celebrate the joy of forgiveness: 'Blessed is the man whose transgressions are forgiven, whose sins are covered' (Ps. 32:1). Clearly, Old Testament sacrifices were effective, but they were only temporary and needed to be constantly repeated – a point the writer to the Hebrews later exploits in expounding the blessings of being in the new covenant (Heb. 8:6–10:22). As mentioned earlier, neither here nor in Deuteronomy 30, which anticipates restoration beyond exile, is there any mention of the sacrificial system as being adequate to deal with the deep-seated sinfulness that has led to the judgment and 'death' of exile. God will do a 'new thing' that will bring lasting forgiveness and a permanent state of 'non-condemnation' where sins are remembered no more. Jeremiah is not told how God will do this. At this stage in the story, God is simply pledging to exercise his amazing grace, working on both sides of the relationship to make covenant work.

Heart Transplant

Ezekiel helps us to understand how this new covenant will work by supplementing the picture Jeremiah paints. As befits a man who was trained as a priest, Ezekiel uses cultic or sacrificial language to do this. He describes how God will effect a complete change of heart in his covenant people:

> I will sprinkle clean water on you and you will be clean. I will cleanse you from all your impurities and from all your idols. I will give you a new heart and put a new spirit within you; I will remove from you your heart of stone and give you a heart of flesh' (Ezek. 36:25–26).

Soft, responsive hearts will replace the hard, obdurate and unresponsive hearts of God's disobedient people.

Furthermore, the Spirit of God will reinforce the weak and fragile human spirit. God's life-breath will be poured into the renewed heart – an action that mirrors the original in-breathing of Adam which made him a living being (Gen. 2:7): 'I will put my Spirit in you and move you to follow my decrees and be careful to keep my laws. You will live in the land I gave your forefathers; you will be my people and I will be your God' (Ezek. 36:27–28). Ezekiel promises that God's Spirit, will be poured into the hearts of God's covenant people to motivate and empower them to faithful covenant behaviour and practice. This will happen in the midst of Israel, in the Land where unfaithfulness had led to exile – God's name will be hallowed where once it had been disgraced. The hallowing of his name is God's first concern. (According to Jesus, it should be our first priority in prayer.) God will redeem his reputation by creating a new covenant people who are filled with his Spirit. As we have seen, this will amount to a 'resurrection' of God's people from the dead, achieved by the prophetic word and powerful Spirit of God (Ezek. 37). The gift of God's Spirit saturates the new covenant community with refreshing and life-giving water, which is poured out on parched ground (Is. 44:3).

New Kingship

Of course, it is not only the people who have failed and need renewal; the kings also have consistently failed. After the emergence of kingship in Israel the role of the prophets took on a new dimension (cf. 1 Sam. 9:9). One function of the prophet was to remind the kings that they held their kingship in trust as stewards of God's sovereign rule. The prophets acted as the 'guardians of the theocracy'.[4] The prophets often proved a thorn in the side of those kings who failed to lead the people in covenant faithfulness, and who, by abusing their powers, finally forfeited their claim to the privileges and perpetuity of the Davidic covenant.

Once the failure of the kings had become apparent at the time of the exile, the prophets began to project hopes of a new kingship. A new David, 'a righteous branch' who 'will do what is just and right in the land' (Jer. 33:15–16) will be raised up by God. Jeremiah, for example, envisages the renewal of the Davidic and Levitical office, backed by God's fresh covenant commitment (Jer. 33:17–21). Significantly, Jeremiah links the prospect of future kings and priests with God's foundational promise to Abraham: 'I will make the descendants of David my servant and the Levites who minister before me as countless as the stars and as measureless as the sand on the seashore' (Jer. 33:22). In the thread of God's great strategic plan of redemption, the stories of Jacob and David are guaranteed to come to a satisfactory conclusion but only by the unbreakable covenant fidelity of God (Jer. 33:26). Ezekiel envisages the coming of God as the Shepherd-Ruler of his people and the sending of a Davidic prince to put things to right (Ezek. 34). Isaiah prophesies the return of God: 'Here is your God!' (Is. 40:9). God will lead the homecoming exiles on the road across the desert, returning as king in Jerusalem to be at the centre of his people's life again. This will be the best story imaginable – the good news of God's kingdom of justice, peace and salvation (Is. 52:7f.).

New Exodus

Standing back to gain a wider perspective we can see that exodus and exile are the two poles around which the Old Testament story of Israel revolves. There is terrible irony in this, as we have noted before. According to the Old Testament, Israel's story began when she was enslaved in Egypt; her story effectively ends in slavery in Babylon – which is even more ironic when you consider that this is where Abraham had come from to begin the faith journey over one thousand years earlier! But the hopes of the exilic prophets are even more remarkable

• Exodus gave birth to a nation for God out of slavery through deliverance and redemption.
• Exile yields promise of a new people of God redeemed this time out of the deeper slavery of sin through 'death and resurrection'.

What is envisioned is a new covenant community, newly motivated to obey God, deeply secure in belonging to God and being his people, with an all-pervading God consciousness; what is foreseen is a grateful community, breathing the fresh air of forgiveness, and empowered by the creative Spirit of God, under the Lordship of God, through his appointed Messiah. This depiction of new covenant realities begins to sound like a description of vibrant Christian experience (cf. Acts 2) and it is. However, before this dream can ever materialise, there is a price to pay. It is Isaiah, in particular, who strikes this deeper note.

Situation Vacant

Uniquely, Isaiah shows that the transformation heralded in the promise of new covenant and new kingship will only take effect through the shameful suffering and ignominious death of a mysterious servant of God. This servant will be endowed with the Spirit, but he will not raise his voice in the streets in a self-promoting way. He will both *be* Israel and will have a ministry *to* Israel; he will thus fulfil 'old' Israel's vocation of being a saving light to the Gentiles. He will speak words that sustain the weary, and an easy yoke to replace a burdensome law – only to be beaten and spat upon for his pains (Is. 42; 49). Runners with 'beautiful feet' will convey the good news of the advent of God's kingdom but there will be few takers (Is. 52:7–53:1). The servant will be despised, rejected and crushed, cut-off from the land of the living and cast forth into the land of exile, alienation and forsakenness. Mysteriously, he will bear the sins of the people and atone for them. His solo work will achieve the vindication of the justified many. As a result, he will be raised, lifted up and highly exalted (Is. 52:13–53:12). The end of all the servant's labours will be the renewal of all God's works – the re-creation of new heavens and a new earth (Is. 65:17; 66:22).

Who is this servant? Did Isaiah know? 'Probably not' is the answer to the second question. As G.B. Caird said of the prophet, 'It was as though he was publishing an advertisement: "Wanted: Servant of the Lord: all applications welcome" accompanied by a job description'.[5] As we now know there was only one applicant for the job who fitted the description!

To ask another pertinent question: how long did exile last? Exile as an historical event lasted barely seventy years, as Jeremiah promised, but 'exile' as a state or condition of being under judgment and awaiting the fulfilment of promises of restoration and new covenant, was an entirely different matter. There is evidence in Israel's penitential tradition that 'exile' would last longer than seventy years. Ezekiel in an enacted parable upped the figure to 430 years (Ezek. 4:4–6) and Daniel to 490 years (Dan. 9:24–27). Daniel and Ezra, in words written after the physical return to the Land, both pray as if Israel were 'still slaves' in exile (Dan. 9:3–19; Ezra 9:8–9; Neh. 9:36).[6]

For the next four centuries – except for the brief period of the Maccabees – Israel remained under pagan domination, first Persian, then Greek, and then Roman. Some perceptive thinkers, documented in Jewish theology, thought Israel was undergoing the judgment of God for her sins and was, therefore, still 'in exile'. In the four centuries between the return from Babylon to the coming of Jesus, no Jew that we know of seriously imagined that the new covenant promises had been fulfilled. The only exception was the small Qumran monastic sect that emerged 150 years before Jesus. They called themselves the 'Covenanters'. After the fall of Jerusalem in AD 70, when threatened by the Roman armies, they buried their precious Scrolls in the caves beside the Dead Sea.

In short, the true fulfilment of the prophetic vision awaited the arrival of God's servant. It awaited the appearance of the one who, in Isaiah's words, was to be 'a covenant for the people' (Is. 42:6; 49:8). It seems the hope of the prophets was held in trust for someone who could embody all God's covenantal investments.

Better Covenant

It is clear that the new covenant did not come into effect until, on the eve of his atoning death, the suffering servant of God broke bread, poured wine and said: 'This is the new covenant in my blood' (Lk. 22:20). Jesus confidently asserts that the Passover will be fulfilled in the kingdom of God on the other side of a new exodus brought about by his death. Mysteriously and marvellously, God's strategic plan comes to fruition in his servant-king who, by the blood of his sacrificial self-offering, inaugurates the new covenant agreement, initiates a new exodus, and guarantees the advent of God's kingdom.

The New Testament writer to the Hebrews celebrates the dawn of this new covenant era by citing Jeremiah's new covenant oracle in full – the longest Old Testament quotation in the New Testament (Heb. 8:7–13). Jesus, he declares, is God's unique Son, the king sharing God's throne, the High Priest of the heavenly sanctuary. By virtue of his death, resurrection and ascension, Jesus became the mediator of a better covenant (Heb. 7:22). He eclipses Moses and the Levitical priesthood of the old order, because 'the ministry Jesus has received is as superior to theirs as the covenant of which he is mediator is superior to the old one, and it is founded on better promises' (Heb. 8:6).

Jesus, by his sacrifice, achieves what the sacrifice of animals could not. He is the 'mediator of a new covenant, that those who are called may receive the promised eternal inheritance' – an 'inheritance' which the writer of Hebrews linked to the promises made to Abraham (Heb. 9:15; 6:12–13). As a consequence, they argue, the old covenant is obsolete. There was nothing intrinsically wrong with it; it's simply past its 'sell-by' date. It remains as a revelation of God's will for his people: but it no longer regulates our lives, it is not the administration under which we are now serving.

The Letter or the Spirit

The connections between the prophetic vision of God's new covenant people and the realities of life in Christ are never more clearly spelt out than when Paul writes to the Corinthians (2 Cor. 3). Pressed to produce letters of recommendation endorsing his ministry, Paul points to the Corinthians as evidence for the work God has done through him. In words that echo the Old Testament, Paul says that the letters Christ has written through his ministry are inscribed not on tablets of stone (as with the Law; see Ex. 31:18) but on the hearts of the Corinthian believers (this combines the new covenant terms; see Ezek. 11:19–20; 36:26; Jer. 31:31). It is the gospel that has brought about such a change, preached by those who, like Paul, are 'ministers of the new covenant'. The difference between the old and new covenants could not be greater: it is the difference between life and death – 'the letter kills, the Spirit gives life'.

This statement is often misunderstood to the detriment of the actual text of Scripture, but it has nothing to do with a supposed distinction between a literal and a spiritual reading of the text. Rather, the distinction Paul is making is between the fact that the Law sentences sinners to death but was powerless to do anything about it, while the gospel of the new covenant brings atonement, forgiveness and produces authentic covenantal life. The Spirit who achieves this is the mark of the new age in which the new covenant operates. Where the old covenant condemned, the new covenant brings righteousness, vindicating and securing covenant membership for repentant sinners. Where the old covenant had glory, fading though it was, how much more glorious is the new covenant whose splendour is permanent?

New Covenant, New Kingship, New Creation

The exilic prophets projected hope: the promise of a new covenant under a new kingship leading to a new creation. In 2 Corinthians Paul clearly shadows this prophetic outline of events. 'Anointed (or 'Christed') by the Spirit and sealed as belonging to the Messiah's people (2 Cor. 1:21–22), we are ministers of the new covenant (2 Cor. 3:6), servants of the new servant-king, Jesus Christ the Lord (4:6) and already share, 'in Christ', in God's new creation' (2 Cor. 5:17). 'If anyone is in Christ – new creation' (as the text literally reads) has a scope which ought not to be restricted to the personal, individual sphere of 'being born again' of 'becoming a new person'. Much more is involved. 'If anyone is in Christ, a new creation' means that when we come to faith in Christ we enter the 'new realm of reality' ushered in by God's raising of Jesus from the dead.

To be saved from sin is to be saved from self-centredness and from triviality as much as from tragedy.[7] Like Noah, we are set down by grace in a brave and bigger new world. Anyone who is 'in Christ' becomes a harbinger of God's future, a prototype of what all God's created works are set to become. To be reconciled to God is certainly to have the barrier caused by sin broken down and fellowship with God restored. But this means being reconciled to things as they may become in God's new order and not to things as they are. Salvation is not a technique for surviving in, escaping from or even being adjusted to a worryingly dysfunctional world. To lower our sights to this level would be to reduce the ministry of reconciliation to a ministry of coping and 'to substitute an accommodation for the consummation we are to seek'.[8] Instead, our reconciliation involves a radical re-alignment with what God has already begun to do (and still intends to do) to renew his creation. Peace with God, therefore, does not make us passive spectators of a world passing away but exposes us to the glory that transforms. To be in the new covenant in Christ is not merely to keep up with the times, it is to be ahead of the times.

Nowhere does Paul wax more lyrical about this than when writing his letter to the Christians in Rome. The old covenant and its Torah could not deal with the deep problem of sin and create genuine covenant living, but God has achieved it through the sacrificial sin offering of his Son and the gift of his empowering Spirit.

> There is therefore now no condemnation for those who are in Christ Jesus, For the law of the Spirit of Life in Christ Jesus has set me free from the law of sin and death. For God has done what the law, weakened by the flesh, could not do: by sending his Son in the likeness of sinful flesh and as a sin offering, he condemned sin in the flesh so that the just requirement of the law might be fulfilled in us who walk, not according to the flesh but according to the Spirit' (Rom. 8:1–4, NRSV).

Thus the new covenant community is born – the company of the forgiven-forgivers, the uncondemned sons of God, who live by the Spirit. The language of the exodus permeates this passage but it is in the service of a greater exodus and far-reaching redemption. With slavery to sin behind them and marked out by the Spirit as God's covenant family, the true sons and daughters of God call on him as 'Abba-Father'. Led not by a pillar of fire and cloud, but by the immediate light of God's Spirit, God's covenant family marches towards its God-given inheritance; except that, in this scenario, its promised land is no partial Canaan, but nothing less than a redeemed earth. God's new exodus people pioneer the way to a renovated and transformed creation, freed from its bondage to decay and made resplendent in the glorious freedom we are growing up to enjoy. None of this is without cost. The assurance of being saved into God's big story is not a self-serving, self-protective insurance scheme. The Spirit witnesses within us as to who we really are. In turn, we demonstrate that true identity by our willingness to suffer for the world in fellowship with the Messiah. Yet this company lives with hope and longing, surrounded by frustration and decay, in a world growing old. It offers itself as a sample of that newness which all creation longs for. The new covenant people stay prophetically alert to the world's sensitivity, crying out in the darkness. Every sigh of regret, shrug of resignation, tear of grief, shout of protest, outraged cry at injustice, 'every signal of transcendence' and gasp of sudden joy is registered sympathetically on the church's heart as the birth pangs of a better world. The deep 'groan' of the old creation is matched and echoed by the deep groaning of the church's intercession, by our heartfelt cries of 'Abba-Father', by the sharp pang of pity, exuberant joy, a hope against the odds, by the peace that passes understanding, and an audacious faith that baffles the experts.

In all these ways – by tiny steps and fleeting gestures – as members of the new covenant community we serve as tokens of the new creation, and live out the promise of a thornless, tearless, world. Knowing far, far less than this, Noah got out of the ark as the first step to a new world. Knowing what we know now, ought, at least to make our getting out of bed each morning just a little more worthwhile!

Notes

1 Donald Gowan, *Theology in Exodus: Biblical Theology in the Form of a Commentary*, 221.

2 P.T. Forsyth, *The Person and Place of Jesus Christ*, 86; and *Justification of God*, 123.

3 Walter Brueggemann, *Hopeful Imagination: Prophetic Voices in Exile*, 25.

4 Geerhardus Vos, *Biblical Theology, Old and New Testament*, 186.

5 Caird, *New Testament Theology*, 316.

6 Anyone wishing to follow up this fascinating but still much-debated issue of the continuing 'exile' of Israel as the backdrop to Jesus and the Gospels would need to consult N.T. Wright's, *Jesus and the Victory of God* which emphasises this scenario. Detailed support for it is offered by James M. Scott: 'For as many as under the works of the Law are under a Curse', in Craig A. Evans & James A. Sanders (eds.), *Paul and the Scriptures of Israel*, 187–221; this is summarised in Scott's article 'The Restoration of Israel' in Gerald F. Hawthorne, Ralph P. Martin & Daniel G. Reid (eds.), *Dictionary of Paul and his Letters*. Craig A. Evans endorses this view in his essay 'Jesus & the Continuing Exile of Israel' in Carey Newman (ed.), *Jesus and the Restoration of Israel: A Critical Assessment of N.T. Wright's 'Jesus and the Victory of God'*, 76–100.

7 Peter L. Berger: 'A rediscovery of the supernatural ... will not only be ... an overcoming of tragedy. Perhaps, more importantly, it will be an overcoming of triviality. In openness to the signals of

transcendence the true proportions of our experience are rediscovered.' See, *A Rumour of Angels: Modern Society and the Rediscovery of the Supernatural*, 119.

[8] Richard J. Neuhaus, *Freedom for Ministry*, 73.

God is Committed to *Fulfilling all His Promises in His Son, Jesus*

Matthew's 'Messiah report'

Jesus Has Been Called 'The Man Who Fits No Formula'

To me, he now seems a more enigmatic, more elusive, more scary, less cosy figure than he did when, as a small boy, I embraced him as Lord and Saviour. Jesus was never a religious professional or Zealot revolutionary. Still less was he – as the boffins of the 'Jesus Seminar' have suggested – a wandering Cynic philosopher or gnostic guru. At a more everyday level he confronts us as radically and culturally different. Jesus was not middle class, or from the western world. He was not even a Christian! He was a first-century Jew.

The story of Jesus is, in fact, the climax of the longer, earlier story of Israel told in the Old Testament Scriptures. The note that has recurred throughout this book is that without understanding something of the earlier stage of the story we can never hope to understand Jesus.

Conversely, without him, the Old Testament makes no final sense. Matthew makes this clear at the outset of his Gospel in his somewhat stylised version of the genealogy of Jesus. This genealogy, which is in effect a condensed history of Israel, arranged as three main epochs, roots Jesus in the larger story. Matthew first links Jesus directly with Abraham through whom 'all the nations of the earth will be blessed'. He then connects him to the Davidic line of kings in whom the people's fate rests. Lastly, he views the Jesus story as the true sequel to the exile in Babylon – that 'death' of Israel from which, according to Isaiah, only God could save and, according to Ezekiel, only by 'resurrection'.

We again note the crucial significance of the exile as the immediate seedbed for the evangelists' presentation of Jesus. As we shall see, each of them ties Jesus closely to John the Baptist, the 'voice in the wilderness', seen by Isaiah as heralding the return of God as king to Zion and thus declaring that the exile in sin and under judgment was over at last. The one who bears the name 'Yeshua' would 'save his people' (Israel) from her sins, and lead her (albeit through death) into the new promised land of salvation (Mt. 1:21). Abrahamic promises, Davidic dreams, prophetic hopes at exile are all coming to fruition at last in Jesus.

Filled-full

Matthew reinforces this point by his characteristic use of the language of 'fulfilment' (Mt. 1:22–23; 2:15, 17, 23; 4:14; 12:17–21; 13:14, 35; 21:4; 27:9; etc.). By saying that Jesus 'fulfils 'the Scriptures, Matthew does not mean that isolated predictive proof-texts launched from the Old Testament land on target in Jesus. Something much bigger than this is going on. Rather, Matthew seeks to show that the whole pattern of Israel's story is being gathered up and reproduced in Jesus. That entire story is being 'filled-full' by Jesus. He embodies the vocation and destiny of his people. The 'man who fits no formula' conforms his life to this scriptural shape.[1]

In writing his gospel, of course, Matthew is telling us an even larger story: the God who has always been with Israel is now with them in person to do for them, and the world, what only he could do.

> The embodied Word is about the new turn taken in the Great Story. The plot has moved from the triune God's call to the world to life together, to the world's rebel cry of 'No!', to God's covenantal promises – universal in Noah, particular in Israel, always long-suffering under our continuing hostility. Only God, first-hand, enfleshed, can turn the tide. So comes Emmanuel, God with us.[2]

Matthew, using his 'fulfilment' terminology, quotes from Isaiah: 'The virgin will be with child and will give birth to a son and they will call him Immanuel – which means, "God with us" ' (Mt. 1:22–23, which cites Is. 7:14). In its original context, this was not a messianic prophecy but a word to Ahaz about the imminent defeat of his enemies, which would be a sure sign of 'God-being-with-him'. Reflecting on the true identity of Jesus, Matthew sees in Jesus the ultimate sign of God-being-with-his-people; how much more 'with-his-people' can God get than to become one of them? But this is to anticipate Matthew's final conclusion (Mt. 28:18–20).

Exodus and Exile

From the beginning, Matthew's aim is to demonstrate how Jesus recapitulates the whole story of Israel. He wants to show how Jesus re-enacts the pattern of events in Israel's history so as to bring to completion and fulfilment the purpose for which God chose Israel. The two traumatic events that bracket the Old Testament story of Israel are alluded to in Matthew 2:13–21 – the exodus, the dramatic beginning; and the exile, the effective end of her life as an independent nation under God.

Matthew describes how Joseph, Mary and the child flee from the wrath of Herod, taking refuge in Egypt. This, incidentally, is prompted by Joseph's dream – just as his famous namesake's dream had first led to the children of Israel being in Egypt. More significantly, Matthew sees their re-emergence as fulfilling words of the prophet Hosea: 'Out of Egypt I called my son' (Mt. 2:15b; Hos. 11:1). Hosea is referring to the early description of Israel as 'God's son' (Ex. 4:22). But, again, it is not the fulfilment of a predictive prophecy. In fact, Hosea's words have no future reference at all but are an historical reflection on Israel's exodus from Egypt. Once again, Matthew is making the larger point that Jesus recapitulates Israel's story by beginning where she began – in Egypt. He comes up 'out of Egypt' as God's 'son', the true Israel of God and Matthew immediately alerts us to the fact that a new and greater 'exodus' is under way.

Then Matthew brings the exile into focus with a quotation from the prophet Jeremiah (Mt. 2:17–18; Jer. 31:15). The words come, significantly enough, from Jeremiah 31 where the prophet describes the 'new covenant', and refers to Israel as 'God's son' (Jer. 31:20, 31ff.). Responding to the pain of the Babylonian exile, Jeremiah pictures Rachel, the original mother of Israel, weeping for her descendants who were taken into captivity. Matthew perceives that her grief is being felt again in the agony of the mothers around Bethlehem whose children have been murdered in Herod's savage purge. This exilic reference is consistent with the viewpoint – held, as we saw earlier, by some Jews since the return to the Promised Land, including, it would appear, Daniel and Nehemiah – that Israel's real 'exile' of unforgiven sin and divine judgment was not yet over.

By drawing exodus and exile together, Matthew is already indicating the scale of what this child will achieve. It is already clear that Jesus will gather up both ends of Israel's story, starting where she started enslaved in Egypt and again in exile – and bringing her out in a greater exodus, by a greater redemption, returning her not merely to the Land but to her God.[3]

Jesus' baptism at the hands of John gives further weight to this view of what is going on. The voice from heaven, as we have seen, endorses Jesus as the true Davidic king whose sonship is affirmed to be truly messianic by the anointing of the Holy Spirit. Furthermore, the divine words: 'You are my son, whom I love; with whom I am well pleased' (which are a conflation of Ps. 2:7 and Is. 42:1, with echoes of the offering of the only beloved son, Isaac) mark Jesus out as a servant-king who is set on an ambiguous and mysterious royal road that must pass through suffering and humiliation on its way to glory. That Jesus undergoes a 'baptism for sinners', when by all accounts he was not one, could only have been seen by Matthew as a further demonstration of the extent to which Jesus would identify with Israel. He does this both positively, in embracing Israel's role, and negatively, by being 'numbered with transgressors'. Jesus intended to 'fulfil all righteousness' through baptism by pursuing his own destiny and demonstrating the covenant faithfulness of God acting to save, vindicate and restore Israel (Mt. 3:15).

New David, New Israel

This is immediately underlined by the narrative describing Jesus' temptations (Mt. 4:1–11). Just as David once strode out to confront Goliath, so Jesus, the newly anointed king-in-waiting, now strides out to meet the evil challenger to God's rule. Jesus' forty-day test re-enacts, as it were, the temptations that Israel faced and failed to resist during forty years in the wilderness and thereafter in the Promised Land. The three references from Deuteronomy serve to confirm this. The contrast, however, is stark because, as Ben Meyer puts it, 'whereas ancient Israel had collapsed under the test in the wilderness, the Israel of God of the last days, Jesus himself, emerged victorious from it'.[4] Jesus is being tested as 'the son of God', which is perhaps a faint echo of the privileged calling of Adam himself. Luke implies as much by inserting the genealogy of Jesus between the baptism and temptations and tracing Jesus' roots back to 'Adam, the son of God' (Lk. 3:38). It is more likely that Matthew is concerned to link Jesus with the covenantal sonship of Israel's king (2 Sam. 7:14; Ps. 2:7), and Israel, whom the king represented (Ex. 4:22–23; Hos. 11:1). Deuteronomy describes the wilderness period as a 'test' for Israel because, as Moses said, 'as a man disciplines his son, so the Lord your God disciplines you' (Deut. 8:1–5).

Jesus' first challenge is to pre-empt God's provision by turning stones into bread to meet his own needs. Like Israel before him, Jesus is tempted to the sin of unbelief, which is to live other than by God's word. Re-affirming Israel's covenant charter, Jesus replies with a quotation

from Deuteronomy to the effect that 'Man does not live
on bread alone but on every word that comes from the
mouth of God' (Deut. 8:3; Mt. 4:4). Urged, secondly, to
throw himself from the pinnacle of the Temple, while
'naming and claiming' Psalm 91 as his protection, Jesus
resists what he sees as presumption, putting God to the
test, by again citing the Deuteronomy command, 'Do not
put the Lord your God to the test' (Mt. 4:5–7; Deut. 6:16).
Thirdly, when offered the kingdoms of the world on
condition he bows down and worships Satan, Jesus –
knowing from Psalm 2 that he only has to ask the Father
for the nations as his inheritance – repudiates the idea of
idolatry, insisting, again in words from Deuteronomy,
'Worship the Lord your God, and serve him only' (Mt.
4:10; Deut. 6:13).

The thrust of the temptations is clear: 'If you are the
true Israel, God's "son", if you are her representative
king, God's "son", then go the way of Israel and her kings
before you', but – savingly – Jesus refuses. Israel continued to be bedevilled by the sins of unbelief, presumption
and idolatry throughout her life in the Promised Land,
but Jesus is saying, in effect, that where Israel had failed
to rise to the covenant challenge and abide by the
Deuteronomic ideal, he will not fail. As Chris Wright
says, 'On the shoulders of Jesus as the Son of God lay the
responsibility of being the true son, succeeding where
Israel had failed, submitting to God's will where they had
rebelled, obeying where they had disobeyed'.[5]

Christ's Faithfulness

The upshot of our reflections so far shows that we owe
everything to the covenant faithfulness of Jesus. Standing
back from Matthew for a moment, it is worthwhile to

connect what he has shown us with Paul's view of the crucial role Jesus plays in the redemptive plan of God. For example, Paul tells the Romans that God's saving righteousness 'comes through faith in Jesus Christ to all who believe'. The phrase 'faith in Jesus Christ', if transcribed literally from the Greek, reads '(the) faith of Christ'. It is traditionally translated (e.g. NIV) as a reference to our faith in Christ. But an equally possible and attractive option is to translate it as 'the faith' or 'faithfulness of Christ', thus avoiding the tautology of the usual version. Significantly, the phrase occurs – and elsewhere in the Pauline epistles (e.g. Gal. 2:16; 2:20; 3:22–23; Phil. 3:9) – in a strongly covenantal context. It is better, therefore, to opt for the translation the 'faith of Christ' or probably more accurately 'faithfulness of Christ'. Paul's argument to the Romans, at this point, requires the emergence of a faithful Israelite. In Tom Wright's words, 'This, declares Paul, is what we have in Jesus: as Messiah, he brings Israel's intended covenant obedience, covenant faithfulness, to birth at last, not just being an example of a faithful Jew, but the climactic and decisive faithful Jew'.[6] On this basis, Romans 3:22 might be translated, 'God's righteousness is revealed, through the faithfulness of the Messiah, for the benefit of all who believe'.[7]

In other words, Christ's own faithfulness answers the problem of Israel's unfaithfulness while, at the same time, embodying the faithfulness of God in salvation (cf. Rom. 3:3). In Bruce Longenecker's words, 'Jesus' faithfulness serves as the embodiment of covenant fidelity, through which God's covenant fidelity flows to the whole world'.[8] In the same way, Paul's heart-felt witness to the Galatians, reads: 'I live by the faithfulness of the Son of God who loved me and gave himself for me' or 'I live by the faith of the Son of God' (Gal. 2:20, NRSV margin; see also Gal. 3:22–23).[9]

The faithfulness shown by Jesus to the covenant plan of God – even unto death on the cross – is the basis for our faith in him. Our faith passes through his faith. We trust in his trust. We count on his faithfulness. This aligns well with Paul's similar emphasis on the 'obedience of Jesus' as crucial to our salvation (e.g. Rom. 5:19; Phil. 2:8). In other words, we are justified by faith in Christ's faithfulness.

New Moses, New Covenant

We call it the 'Sermon on the Mount', but to its original hearers it must have sounded more like the radical manifesto of a new revolutionary political party. Far from being a conventional appeal to traditional morality, Jesus is issuing a powerful challenge to Israel to live up to her true vocation. Those in Israel, chafing under Roman rule and impatient for a change of government, hear that the kingdom of God is for the 'poor in spirit'. Those looking for the 'consolation of Israel' are assured it will come, but only to those who mourn over theirs and the nation's sin. Blessed are the heirs of the Abrahamic promise who expect to inherit the earth, but only as they become meek, like Jesus (and, for that matter, Moses). It is right to seek personal and social satisfaction, but such fullness will come only through those who crave God's justice above all else. Those desperate to receive mercy are told to show mercy. Those who aspire to Israel's original status as God's 'sons' must make peace not war. Against all odds, the kingdom belongs, not to those who inflict violence in order to seize it, but to those willing to suffer violence in order to receive it joyfully as God's just rule (Mt. 5:3–12).

Jesus is addressing the people whom God chose to be a holy nation, a kingdom of priests, a light to the

Gentiles. But Israel had lost its distinctive saltiness. Meant to be light to the nations, Israel has become a people groping in the dark for her own survival. A people intended to be such a God-filled community that would bring the nations flocking to it, had lost its attractiveness (Mt. 5:13–16). Yet this vocation is written deep in the Law and the prophets; nothing has been abolished but everything is different. It is now Jesus' way of being Israel that fulfils the true intention of the Law and the prophets (Mt. 5:17–19). The Law (Deut. 30) and the prophets (Jer. 31; Ezek. 36) point to this renewal of covenant in which righteousness is established as the deepest reality of the human in a way that surpasses any Pharisaic imitation of it (Mt. 5:20).

In Scot McNight's words:

> The blessing about which Jesus speaks, especially in the beatitudes, is therefore the realisation of the fullness for which Israel has been longing; the return from exile, the coming of God to Zion, the inheritance of the whole land, the expulsion of God's enemies from the land. The creation of a new heart for obedience to God's Torah, the reversal of injustices, and the glorious fellowship of the unified family of God.[10]

The tragic consequence of Israel's failure to live up to her covenant privileges and responsibilities is that God's name has been brought into disrepute and his reputation tarnished in the eyes of a pagan world. Israel incurred God's wrath because she blasphemed God's name in this way (Ezek. 36:16–21). Israel's disgrace is God's disgrace. When God restores his people, says the prophet in a tough word of grace, it will not be for their sake but to rehabilitate his holy name among the nations (Ezek. 36:22–23).

First priority then, says Jesus, for a people praying for restoration is that God's name be hallowed once again before a watching world. God's longed-for forgiveness, which floods an exiled people with joy creates a community of forgiven-forgivers, echoing the revolutionary Jubilee vision of ancient Israel (Lev. 25) – a society built on fairness, generosity, mercy and truth, and not on debt, extortion or vindictiveness. The stakes are high: it's now a life and death issue (Mt. 7:13–14). But, beware, because false prophets are about. They will sell you another version of the story and lead you down another road. Wise men once beat a path to his door in acknowledgment of his wisdom. The wise person, like the wise nation, only builds the 'house' of personal or national security on a sure foundation (Mt. 7:24–27).

New Joshua, New Conquest

Fresh from his baptism, anointing and triumphant confrontation with evil, Jesus 'went throughout Galilee preaching the good news of the kingdom and healing every disease and sickness among the people' (Mt. 4:23f.). The concept of 'gospel' derives from Isaiah 40 – 66. It is where Matthew, Mark and Luke all begin their stories of Jesus. Mark starts with Isaiah's projected 'voice in the wilderness' who prepares the way of the Lord and heralds the 'good news' of God's return, linking Jesus to John the Baptist, who prepares the way for him (Is. 40:1–11; Mk 1:1–8). Matthew develops Isaiah's portrait of God's servant who would heal and teach in humble self-restraint to bring the good news of God's justice and peace (Is. 52:7; 53:4; 42:1–4; Mt. 4:23; 8:17; 12:18–21). Luke uniquely pictures Jesus announcing his 'manifesto of ministry' by expounding Isaiah's vision of God's Spirit-empowered deliverer as now being enacted in his preaching of 'good news' to the poor and marginalised in Israel (Is. 61; Lk. 4:16–21) in his home-town synagogue in Nazareth. The gospel of Jesus is a continuously 'breaking news' story.

God's kingdom is unlike any other, as is the conquest that Jesus wages to establish it. Joshua wielded the soldier's sword; Jesus wields the Spirit's sword. Jesus fights a battle of stories with metaphors and miracles. The 'new Joshua' comes, evicting the demonic powers from the land and shattering preconceived ideas with sharp-edged parables of the new kingdom.

> From Jordan, where this second Joshua passed through the waters en route to conquest, to Jericho, whose wall of disbelief collapsed when blind Bartimaeus, authentic disciple, gained sight by faith, to Jerusalem, where the first Joshua never marched the Prince of peace made his triumphant way. Joshua, the new Joshua, was marching on.[11]

Son of Man

We might say at this point that Jesus acts 'as' Israel 'for' Israel. It is not without significance that Son of God, servant of God and Son of Man all convey incorporative and representative functions. This accounts for Jesus' whole ministry. His favourite way of referring to himself was as 'the Son of Man'. He did so exclusively. Never during his ministry and only once after Easter did anyone else speak of Jesus in this way.[12] 'Son of Man' was not a traditional messianic title when Jesus used it. In the prophets, especially Ezekiel, it means simply ' the human one'. Jesus spoke of himself as 'the Son of Man' in three main contexts:

1. When speaking of his authority, as he did when he forgave the sins of the paralytic he had just healed (Mt. 9:6).
2. When predicting his suffering and death to his disciples (Mt. 16:21).
3. When anticipating his future glory (Mt. 16:27).

What did this customary self-reference suggest? In all likelihood, Jesus was evoking the memory of one of the prophet Daniel's dreams.

Daniel dreamt that the world's kingdoms were ravaging God's people like wild beasts until the 'one like a Son of Man', trailing clouds of glory, who saves the day by coming to the throne of the Ancient of Days, arrived. There he is vindicated and receives sovereign power over the nations (Dan. 7:13–14). The interpretation of Daniel's dream makes clear that the Son of Man is a representative figure because his reception of a kingdom is synonymous with the reception of the kingdom by 'the saints, the people of the Most High' (Dan. 7:27). The role envisaged for the Son of Man fits well 'with Jesus' identification of himself with Israel. As Son of Man he represented them. He shared their experience. His destiny was theirs and vice versa'.[13] That the Son of Man comes to God's throne wreathed in clouds of glory also suggests that he shares in some indefinable way in the essential nature of God. This would indeed become clear.

Meanwhile, Jesus had chosen a title that was mysterious and ambiguous enough to force people to 'watch this space' before making up their minds too soon about him. In G.B. Caird's helpful summary, his use of the Son of Man as a title served a number of purposes. It

enabled him, without actually claiming to be Messiah, to indicate his essential unity with mankind, and above all, with the weak and humble ... [It encapsulated] his special function as predestined representative of the new Israel and bearer of God's judgment and kingdom. Even when he used it as a title, its strongly corporate overtones made it ... an invitation to others to join him in the destiny he accepted. And when he spoke of the glory of the Son of Man, he was predicting not so much his personal victory as the triumph of the cause he served.[14]

Coming in Glory

What are we to make of the Son of Man 'coming in glory'? Jesus consistently maintains that this will occur in 'this generation', that is within the lifetime of his contemporaries. This question comes to a head when, at his trial, Jesus tells the High Priest, Caiaphas, 'In the future you will see the Son of Man sitting at the right hand of the Mighty One and coming on the clouds of heaven' (Mt. 26:64).

That the glory which attends the Son of Man's coming carries overtones of divine status may account for the High Priest's violent reaction as he charges Jesus with blasphemy. But when and how will the Son of Man 'come'? In coming to God's throne, does he descend to earth or ascend to heaven? Daniel's text can be read either way. Scholarly opinions are divided, though the majority have traditionally opted for a reference to the Second Coming. It is, however, unlikely that Jesus was offering the High Priest a box-seat at the parousia from which he might view the Son of Man's descent. Given the way in which, in the final week of his life, Jesus is bringing Israel's whole future to a point of climax and decision, it is much more likely that he has the upcoming tragedy of AD 70 in view, when the destruction of the Temple and the

city of Jerusalem would indeed vindicate him as God's
true prophet.

In any case, Caiaphas gets more than he bargained for.
Chris Wright's conclusion is worth quoting in full:

> By casting himself in the role of the Son of Man in the sense of
> Daniel 7, Jesus was claiming to represent the true people of
> God, the saints of the Most High. But he was standing in the
> presence of the High Priest, Caiaphas, who occupied that
> role. He was before the Sanhedrin, the representative court of
> Israel, in Jerusalem, near the Temple its most holy place. And
> in the midst of all these people and places, dripping with
> holiness and the very essence of Israel, Jesus calmly claims to
> be the Son of Man in its full Danielic symbolism, the one
> whom God will vindicate and entrust with supreme author-
> ity. He was claiming to inaugurate the salvation and restora-
> tion of the people of God, to be the one who would be
> presented on their behalf to the Ancient of Days.

But, adds Wright,

> in Daniel 7 the enemies of the son of man/saints of God were
> the beasts. Who then were these enemies of Jesus? His mean-
> ing and its implied threat were clear and quite intolerable.
> Chief Priest or Chief Beast? No wonder Caiaphas tore his
> robes.[15]

But how did everything come down to this? What was it
about Jesus that brought him to trial and judgment by the
Israel of his day? Why did his covenant faithfulness clash
so violently with the culture of first-century Judaism?
What effect did his way of being God's covenant partner
have on the institutions and traditions of the Israel he was
born into? What does Jesus do, in other words, with the

inherited story of Israel to upset his contemporaries so much?

Israel Redefined

One answer to the questions that have just been posed is that Jesus redefines Israel as the true people of God against the urgent backdrop of the anticipated catastrophe of AD 70. This assessment can be filled out under a number of headings.

1. *Jesus reaches out to regather the people*

'I was sent only to the lost sheep of the house of Israel' (Mt. 15:24). This is evidently his top priority. Moved with compassion, he seeks out those who have been cast out by the false shepherds of the flock of God (Mt. 9:33; Lk. 15:1; Jn. 9:35; 10). He presents himself as the final restoration shepherd of Ezekiel's vision (Ezek. 34), a Prince of David's line on whom blind men call for help, and Israel's God come to do what the appointed leaders are failing to do. His shepherding activity of healing, gathering and feeding the wounded, scattered, hungry sheep of God's flock is inevitably an indictment of Israel's current shepherd-leadership.

2. *He reassigns leadership of God's people*

'He chose twelve' (Mt. 10; Mk. 3). This was a powerful symbolic gesture, paralleling the twelve tribal heads of Israel, and signifying that in the restored Israel the traditional leaders would be replaced by artisans and fishermen. 'Jesus said to them, "I tell you the truth, at the renewal of all things, when the Son of Man sits on his

glorious throne, you who have followed me will also sit
on twelve thrones, judging the twelve tribes of Israel" '
(Mt. 19:28).

3. Jesus reintegrates Israel's Scriptures

Matthew explains Jesus' use of parables by quoting
Psalm 78, 'So was fulfilled what was spoken through the
prophet: "I will open my mouth in parables, I will utter
things hidden since the creation of the world" ' (Mt.
13:34–35). Jesus is saying that the new things are a commentary on what is happening in his messianic ministry.
They are new not in the sense of being novel but in the
sense of being previously hidden away in the Old Testament. If there is novelty, it lies in their being brought
together in a creative synthesis by Jesus. He brings 'various pieces of revelation into new perspectives',[16] gathering them up into a unified message and enacting them
before the interpreters' eyes. 'Thus Messiah is Son of
God but also suffering servant. Jesus is the royal king and
son of David foreseen in Scripture (Mt. 21:4–11) but also
the stricken shepherd equally foreseen in Scripture (Mt.
26:31)'.[17] Jesus' own self-understanding is of a 'Messiah
who unites in himself streams of revelation from the old
covenant that had not been so clearly united before'.[18] In
this sense, Jesus 'fulfils' the law and the prophets because
they 'comprehend certain patterns, types, predictions,
declarations, which cumulatively look forward to him
who "fulfils them" '.[19] This calls to mind the well-known
and somewhat cryptic remark of C.H. Dodd when discussing the skill with which the New Testament writers
interpret God's previous revelation in the light of Christ:
'To account for the beginning of this most original and
fruitful process of rethinking the Old Testament we
found need to postulate a creative mind. The Gospels

offer us one. Are we compelled to reject the offer?'[20] Each of the Gospel writers say 'no' in their own way and points to Jesus as the one who made 'fulfilment' possible and gave the first lessons in it. Matthew might well have been thinking of himself when he said: 'Every teacher of the law who has been instructed about the kingdom is like the owner of a house who brought out of his storeroom new treasure as well as old' (Mt. 13:52).

4. Jesus redraws the boundaries of covenant participation

Jesus is the 'boundary breaker'. He redefines who is acceptable and welcome in God's kingdom. Provocatively, he enacts this at his table-fellowship to which, in God's name, he invites outcasts, sinners, tax collectors and the poor. By eating meals with such people, Jesus explicitly criticised those, like the Pharisees, who were drawing tighter boundaries around the holiness of God. At the same time, he was effectively and prophetically identifying the kind of people a loving Father could create through repentance and forgiveness. So to the repentant renegade Zacchaeus, Jesus announces: 'Today salvation has come to this house, because this man, too, is a Son of Abraham' (Lk. 19:9). His healings and exorcisms were not only works of compassion and signs of power; they were also acts of social reinstatement that signified the healing and restoration of Israel.[21] Criticised for healing a crippled woman on the Sabbath, Jesus points out to his critics his recognition of her as a true 'daughter of Abraham' (Lk. 13:16). The aim and outcome of the healing ministry of Jesus was to reclaim the dignity of the sick or possessed and restore them to their rightful place as fully participating members of God's renewed family.

5. *Jesus reconstitutes Israel around himself*

The *ecclesia* of God will be built on a new foundation rock, i.e. confession of Jesus as the Christ (Mt. 16:18). As C.H. Dodd put it:

> The Messiah is not only the founder and leader of the new people of God: he is its 'inclusive representative'. In a real sense he is the true Israel, carrying through in his own experience the process through which it comes into being.[22]

Jesus immediately makes clear what that process involves:

> From that time on Jesus began to explain to his disciples that he must go to Jerusalem and suffer many things at the hands of the elders, chief priests and teachers of the law, and that he must be killed, and on the third day be raised to life' (Mt. 16:21).

This was throwing down the gauntlet to his contemporaries: 'Take up your cross and follow me'. It is as if Jesus was saying: 'Come and be Israel my way. Come down into death with me, the suffering servant Israel and rise up with me your anointed messianic king as the new covenant people of God cleansed, forgiven and empowered to be the Israel God intended.' Already pre-figured by Hosea (Hos. 6:3) and expanded later in Ezekiel's vision of the dry bones (Ezek. 37), the restoration of the people of God will take place when 'resurrection' as a metaphor becomes resurrection as an actuality. 'Thus to a unique degree, Jesus is seen as the goal, the convergence-point, of God's plan for Israel, his covenant promise'.[23]

Matthew's closing chapters bring the conflict to a head. Jesus rides into Jerusalem as messianic claimant, to face Israel and her rulers with the ultimate covenantal challenge. Neither the Temple, the present generation, the current leadership of Israel, nor Jerusalem can be affirmed as they are. They must go through a radical death and resurrection with him to survive (Mt. 21 – 25). If not there is catastrophe ahead. Jesus would go ahead of the people into the eye of the storm and take that judgment from Roman hands upon himself. The judgment he predicts will be the judgment he is willing to bear. But if they do not respond within a generation, they will see destruction and his words vindicated. Matthew skilfully echoes Israel's renewal of covenant before entering the Promised Land (Deut. 27–28) by showing that the 'blessings' of the Sermon on the Mount (Mt. 5–7) are now matched by prophetic 'woes' (Mt. 23) as Jesus forces Israel to its conclusive covenant crisis.

6. *Jesus represents a threat to the Temple and Jerusalem*

So, in the final week of his life, Jesus goes up to Jerusalem: where else would Israel's king go to be crowned? But he doesn't come with blatant hubris on a war-horse. Instead, he arrives on a donkey in baffling humility. He heads straight for the Temple: where else would David's 'greater son' go to do a greater work than Solomon? Jesus had already subverted the Temple's sacrificial ritual and usurped the role of its priests by pronouncing God's forgiveness and pardon on the streets. His 'cleansing' of the Temple – a powerful prophetic parable – spells the end of the Temple and its replacement by the new Temple of his risen body where the concentrated holiness and glory of God could be encountered.

In parable after parable told during the final week of his life Jesus presses home the challenge. God is addressing the 'terminal generation' and calling in the accounts (cf. Lk. 11:50–51). The Jerusalem authorities are his reluctant audience and prime target. The story about two sons, expanded so memorably by Luke, contrasts an officially compliant, but inwardly rebellious Israel with 'prodigal Israel', which was now coming home from exile in the far country – the Israel which had been lost but now was being found, which was dead but was coming alive before their eyes (Mt. 21:28–32; Lk. 15:1; 11–32). The 'son' is finally sent to the tenant farmers, who have consistently eliminated the owner's agents, of the vineyard. They reject and kill him and refuse to yield up the stewardship they were meant to hold in trust, but 'when the vineyard owner comes' there is only judgment left (Mt. 21:33–46).

The parables about a returning master, a landlord looking for a return on his investment, or wedding virgins in varying states of readiness (or otherwise) for the arrival of the bridegroom must be seen in context as Jesus' sharp challenges to the Israel of his day. They are not primarily about his second coming but about his first coming and the return of God as king to claim his rightful rule in Israel.

7. Jesus rewrites the Passover meal

Jesus reshapes the foundational ritual of Israel's national life, which looked back to the exodus, by looking forward to his own death, placing his body and blood, at the sacrificial centre and making it the seal of the new covenant. Did Judas trade this secret as part of his treachery to add fuel to an already inflammatory situation? We will never know. But Jesus had already caused enough trouble to provoke the question that surfaced with vehement emotion that final week: 'Who is this person and by what authority does he do and say these things?' It is a good question. Who has the right to retrieve the lost sheep of

Israel in a sovereign way? Who has the right to re-assign the leadership of Israel to men of his choice? Who has the right to redraw the boundaries of covenant participation? Who has the right to reconstitute the nation around himself? Who has the authority to present himself as the final answer to the plight of the people and to re-script the essential covenant meal of Israel's worship? Who has the right to do and say all this?

Suffering and Glory

Only the cross and resurrection would begin to answer these questions. Jesus' death was as strange as his life. He died alongside political rebels and took the place of Barabbas, a revolutionary leader, although Jesus was not one! The Romans killed him because they thought he was the Jewish Messiah and so a danger to them; the Jews condemned him because they thought he wasn't, and so a threat to them! He went to the cross 'as' Israel 'for' Israel.

> The Messiah's resurrection was Israel's redemption. God had done for Jesus the Messiah what they were expecting him to do for Israel. But in Jesus as Messiah, he had, at a deeper level, actually done it for Israel. The new age had dawned.[24]

As we recall the text that prompted our journey, we picture him alive and resurrected from the dead, opening the eyes of the Emmaus two who reflected: 'Did not the Christ have to suffer these things and then enter his glory? And beginning with Moses and all the prophets, he explained to them what was said in all the Scriptures concerning himself' (Lk. 24:26–27). G.B. Caird commented:

We look in vain for Old Testament predictions that the Messiah must reach his appointed glory through suffering, unless we realise that the Old Testament is concerned from start to finish with the call and destiny of Israel, and that the Messiah, as king of Israel, must embody in his own person the character and vocation of the people of which he is leader and representative.[25]

His life and death is shaped to the pattern of exodus suffering and deliverance, and of exilic death and resurrection. As king of Israel and Son of God, Jesus incorporates and recapitulates Israel's story. By his death he inaugurates the promised new covenant, releasing the blessings of Abraham to all humanity. By his resurrection he makes the first down payment on a brand new creation. As Tom Wright says, Matthew, Mark and Luke all

tell the story of Jesus, and especially that of his cross, not as an oddity, a one-off biography of strange doings, or a sudden irruption of divine power into history, but the end of a much longer story, the story of Israel, which in turn is the focal point of the story of the creator and the world.[26]

The Promised World

As for Matthew, he has consistently presented his work as a new Deuteronomy, with contemporary Israel facing a life or death challenge in its confrontation with Jesus. Matthew ends with Jesus, Moses-like, gathering the remnant of Israel around himself on a mountaintop. But the contrast is remarkable. What was it that Moses had urged Israel to do: 'go into the Promised Land, observe the Torah and God will be with you always'?

Now Jesus stands on a mountain to commission his small disciple-band: 'Go, not just into a Promised Land but into the promised world; teach people not what Torah says but what I have commanded you'. Even more remarkably, the pledge he gives is not: 'And God will go with' but 'I will be with you to the end of the age'. Matthew thus ends his gospel where he began it, with 'Emmanuel – God-with-us'.

So if, as his friends, we ask again the question posed by his enemies: who is this person? With Matthew and with hindsight we have to say: no one has the authority to do and say these things except Israel's God in person. Vinoth Ramachandra, a Sri-Lankan theologian, summarises brilliantly when he says of Jesus: 'He embodies the identity and mission of Israel by embodying the identity and mission of Israel's God'.[27] At his royal command a new covenant people is launched on the world with a restored Abrahamic mission to bring the blessings of God's salvation and grace to all the nations.

Notes

[1] For a useful discussion of Matthew's treatment of 'fulfilment', see Don Carson, 'Matthew' in Frank Gaebelein (ed.), *The Expositors Bible Commentary* Vol. 8, 90–5, 141–5, 320–3.

[2] Fackre, *Doctrine of Revelation*, 120–1.

[3] See the excellent comments of Don Carson, 'Matthew', 95.

[4] Ben Meyer, *The Aims of Jesus*, 240–1.

[5] Wright, *Knowing Jesus*, 124.

[6] N.T. Wright, 'New Exodus, New Inheritance: the Narrative Substructure of Romans 5 – 8', in Sven Soderlund & N.T. Wright (eds.), *Romans and the People of God: Essays in Honour of Gordon Fee on the occasion of his 65th birthday*, 32. The impetus for this way of understanding 'the faith of Christ' is usually credited to Richard Hays, *The Faith of Jesus Christ: An Investigation of the Narrative Substructure*

of Galatians 3:1 – 4:11. See also Richard Hays, 'Crucified with Christ: A synthesis of the Theology of 1 and 2 Thessalonians, Philemon, Philippians and Galatians', in Jouette Bassler (ed.) *Pauline Theology*, Vol. 1, 232; 'Adam, Israel, Christ – The Question of Covenant in the Theology of Romans: A Response to Leander E. Keck and N.T. Wright' in David Hay and Elizabeth E. Johnson (eds.), *Pauline Theology*, Vol. 3, 75. On discussing the implications for our own obedient response see Richard Hays, *The Moral Vision of the New Testament: Community, Cross, New Creation: A Contemporary Introduction to New Testament Ethics*, 27–32.

[7] Wright, 'New Exodus', 32.

[8] Bruce W. Longenecker, 'Covenant Theology', in Richard Longenecker (ed.), *The Road to Damascus: The Impact of Paul's Conversion on His Life, Thought, and Ministry*, 133. For a more extended study see Bruce W. Longenecker, *The Triumph of Abraham's God: The Transformation of Identity in Galatians*, especially chapter 5.

[9] The Reformation principle of *sola fide* ('by faith alone') can only be strengthened by this reading since it re-instates the 'middle term' in the logic of our salvation – namely the obedient, covenant faithfulness of Jesus Christ even unto death on which, uniquely, our saving faith in God relies.

[10] Scot McNight, *A New Vision of Israel: The Teachings of Jesus in National Context*, 153–4. I am especially indebted in this whole section to Wright, *Victory of God*, 287–97.

[11] James Wm. McClendon, *Systematic Theology* Vol. 2 – *Doctrine*, 235.

[12] Stephen in Acts 7:56.

[13] Wright, *Knowing Jesus*, 152. See also Ben Witherington, *The Christology of Jesus*, 240.

[14] G.B. Caird, *The Gospel of Luke*, 94–5.

[15] Wright, *Knowing Jesus*, 152–3.

[16] Carson, 'Matthew', 322.

[17] Ibid.

[18] Ibid.

[19] Ibid., 323.

[20] C.H. Dodd, *According to the Scriptures: The Sub-structure of New Testament Theology*, 110.

[21] See, for example, N.T. Wright, *The Challenge of Jesus: Rediscovering Who Jesus Was and Is*, 47.

[22] C.H. Dodd, *The Founder of Christianity*, 106.

[23] C.F.D. Moule, cited by R.T. France, *Matthew – Evangelist and Teacher*, 210. This understanding owes a good deal to France's influential

and newly re-issued work *Jesus and The Old Testament: His Application of Old Testament Passages to Himself and His Mission*. This whole section is heavily indebted to the analysis of Tom Wright: see note 26 below for details.

[24] Wright, *Knowing Jesus*, 148.

[25] G.B. Caird, Luke, 258.

[26] N.T. Wright, *The New Testament and the People of God*, 396. This is the first of a groundbreaking series of projected books that explore the biblical, cultural and Jewish context for Jesus and the church. Volume 2, *Victory of God*, (explores the Synoptic Gospels). This whole perspective on Jesus can be viewed in popular form in Wright's, *The Original Jesus: The Life and Vision of a Revolutionary*; *Who Was Jesus?*; *Challenge of Jesus*; also, 'Jesus and the Quest', in Donald Armstrong (ed.), *The Truth about Jesus*, ch. 1; and in even briefer summary in the article on 'Jesus' in Sinclair B. Ferguson and David F. Wright (eds.), *New Dictionary of Theology*, 348–51. I am, it is obvious, immeasurably indebted to the stimulating work Tom Wright is doing. This is an appropriate place to acknowledge further helpful contributions from evangelical circles, all of which I have found very instructive: Scot McNight, *A New Vision of Israel*; David E. Holwerda, *Jesus & Israel: One Covenant or Two?*; Peter W.L. Walker, *Jesus and the Holy City: New Testament Perspectives on Jerusalem*. On the even more intriguing (or controversial) question as to whether Jesus fulfilled the role of the Land as well as Temple and City see Gary M. Burge 'Territorial Religion, Johannine Christology and the Vineyard of John 15' in Joel B. Green & Max Turner (eds.), *Jesus of Nazareth: Lord and Christ*; Gary M.Burge, *John*; Philip Johnston & Peter Walker (eds.), *The Land of Promise: Biblical, Theological and Contemporary Perspectives*.

[27] Vinoth Ramachandra, *The Recovery of Mission: Beyond the Pluralist Paradigm*, 236.

9

God is Committed to
Re-uniting Everything Under Christ's Lordship

Paul's apostolic vision
Ephesians 3:1–21

Most of us love a good mystery. Many people's bedtime reading is a good crime-mystery, an Agatha Christie or more gruesomely, a Patricia Cornwell. I have, myself, been known to nod off after a chapter or two of Colin Dexter's Oxford-based sleuth, Inspector Morse, or John Grisham's legal beagles. For other people, there's nothing more soporific than a tense spy-thriller, a John Le Carre or a Tom Clancy.

Scientists also love mystery. Stephen Hawking, in that brave, 'dalek-like' voice, probes the 'mystery of the universe'. The Human Genome Project – arousing either awe or fear – unravels the very 'mystery of life' by charting the DNA code of the human person itself.

Paul obviously relishes a good mystery too: he uses the word three times in this short section of his letter to the Ephesians (Eph. 3:3, 4, 9). But when Paul uses the word 'mystery', it's in neither of these two senses.

Although, as we shall see, the unjust murder of an innocent victim is at the heart of the drama Paul is telling. He was not of course, using scientific language when he used the word 'mystery', although the scale of such research – cosmic vastness and the individual creaturely complexity – is precisely the scope of the gospel he proclaims.

Open Secret

The word 'mystery' (Greek, *mystērion*) was a technical term used for the secret initiation rites of the so-called 'mystery-religions' of the Greco-Roman world. Today, some extreme New Age groups seem to be re-brandings of these 'mysteries' – cults, for example, like the headlines examples in Waco, Texas or the 'Solar Temple' sect in Canada and Switzerland. Again, this is emphatically not what Paul is speaking of.

So what does Paul mean when he uses the Greek term *mystērion*? The English translation 'mystery' conjures up something spooky, dark, obscure, baffling, esoteric, even incomprehensible. The ancient philosophers graded *mystērion* at the upper echelon of the knowledge scale, attainable only by the persistent and ultra-clever disciple. But in Paul's use of the word we are not to think of the solution to a mysterious crime or entry to a mystery religion or elevation to an exclusive academy of higher knowledge. Rather, Paul draws on Jewish and Old Testament categories – from the Book of Daniel through to the Book of Enoch – when using this word. For him *mystērion* is a secret that lies beyond the reach of human reason; a secret that could never be uncovered or known unless God took the initiative and made it known to us. And that, Paul declares, is precisely what God has done.

In the gospel, God has made known to us his deepest and most secret intentions. Paul uses words like 'revelation' ('apocalypse') ... made known ... insight into ... revealed' (Eph. 3:1–5). The mystery is no mystery at all for Paul: it is an open secret – the shared 'sacred secret of God's plan of salvation'.[1] Paul has been 'let in' on the secret of God's strategic plan. He has been given the 'inside story', been taken behind the scenes and shown a glimpse of God's strategy for human history and he celebrates God's revelation of the 'mystery of his will' at the start of this letter (Eph. 1:9–10).

Long-range Plan

The scope of God's strategy is breathtaking. In Eugene Peterson's stirring paraphrase: God 'set it all out before us in Christ, a long-range plan in which everything would be brought together and summed up in him, everything in deepest heaven, everything on planet earth' (Eph. 1, *The Message*). In an earlier era, J.B. Phillips captured the essence of this stunning revelation:

> God has allowed us to know the secret of his plan, and it is this: he purposes in his sovereign will that all human history shall be consummated in Christ, that everything that exists in heaven or earth shall find its perfection and fulfilment in him.[2]

In his exposition of these texts, Martyn Lloyd-Jones relishes the strategy:

> The perfect harmony that will be restored will be harmony in man, and between men. Harmony on the earth and in the brute creation! Harmony in heaven, and all under this

blessed Lord Jesus Christ, who will be the head of all! Everything will be united in him ... That is the message; that is God's plan. That is the mystery which has been revealed unto us ... Do you know that these things are so marvellous that you will never hear anything greater, either in this world or the world to come?[3]

All believers – not just an elite – have been initiated into this 'mystery'. We have had a tip-off from unimpeachable sources; a leak from the highest authority has come to our notice; a file marked 'Top Secret' has fallen into our possession; 'classified information' is now in our hands – and hearts.

Paul emphasises the God-givenness of this revelation by recalling that it was God's grace that shared this secret with him (Eph. 3:2–3). He makes no claim to having deserved to receive this privileged information. In fact, in his ignorance, he was bent on thwarting God's purpose, but on the Damascus Road, God broke open Paul's worldview and blinded him with an amazing revelation of Jesus.

Why is Paul making so much of knowing the 'mystery' at this point in Ephesians? He does not address a specific problem in this letter, but he does write to the believers in Ephesus to raise their awareness of the dimensions of their salvation and the high privileges of their Christian identity. If Paul is forcefully to remind and reassure the Ephesians about their real identity in Christ, then he can give no greater example of this than himself. He is evidence of a career, a ministry and a destiny passionately absorbed by this secret strategy of God, disclosed to him by the sheer grace of God, centred intensely in Christ, with shattering cultural and cosmic repercussions. The 'mystery' – this strategic plan of God – is Paul's magnificent obsession. If we, too, are in need of

reassurance about who we are, where we've come from
or where we're going – Ephesians is a powerful shot in
the arm.

God's 'X-files'

We must make a number of moves to track down this
secret strategy of God.

1. Christ is the centre (Eph. 3:4)

Everything focuses entirely on who Jesus is, what has
been achieved through and in him, and what is projected
for and by him. This is why 'in Christ' is Paul's instinctive
way of describing the central reality of our lives as Christians. Everything of our saving involvement in this plan
occurs 'in Christ'. Everything that God destines for the
redemption and perfecting of his creation is 'in Christ'.
This 'top-secret' plan is truly the 'X-files'!

Jesus had teased his contemporaries that the 'mystery
of the kingdom' was hidden in him, the seed sown into
the ground in death to bring forth fruit (Mk. 4:11).
Elsewhere, Paul glories in the supreme paradox of the
cross. It is precisely in the crucifixion, which is the height
of folly, that God works the deepest magic of his divine
wisdom and confounds the wisdom of the powers: it is in
the extreme weakness of the crucified Christ, crushed
by the powerful violence of evil, that God's strength is
made perfect. The Corinthians are reminded: 'We speak
of God's secret wisdom, a wisdom that has been hidden
and that God destined for our glory before time began.
None of the rulers of this age understood it, for, if they
had, they would not have crucified the Lord of glory'
(1 Cor. 2:7).

2. An idea whose time has come

The next move is just as crucial. The mystery had not been revealed to previous generations as it was now to God's holy apostles and prophets, by the Spirit (Eph. 3:5); the 'as' in this verse is not meant to blunt Paul's thrust at this point. He is not conceding that there was a partial disclosure of this secret in the Old Testament that has subsequently been expanded. Rather, full weight must be given to the 'now'. Paul is in eschatological mood, contrasting the 'then' with the 'now' to highlight the decisive difference Christ has made. This is not to say, of course, that the Old Testament did not envisage the Gentiles being touched by God's plan. But the *manner* of their inclusion in God's covenant family, on an equal footing with Jewish believers and in the one body of Christ, is an entirely new feature of God's plan. This has been made possible and has become clear only through the coming and achievement of Jesus. The emphasis is confirmed by what Paul says elsewhere. For example:

> Now to him who is able to establish you by my gospel and the proclamation of Jesus Christ, according to the revelation of the mystery hidden for long ages past, but now revealed and made known through the prophetic writings by the command of the eternal God so that all nations might believe and obey him – to the only wise God be glory for ever through Jesus Christ. Amen. (Rom. 16:25–27).

With Holy Spirit inspired hindsight, the 'mystery' is seen to be the fulfilment of Old Testament prophetic promises. This history-borne hope is now disclosed as the eternal purpose of God. Paul speaks in similar vein to the Colossians when he writes of 'the mystery that has been kept hidden for ages and generations but is now disclosed to the saints' (Col. 1:26). Paul is not dealing in abstractions or vague generalities, but in historically conditioned revelation. There was a time when this secret was hidden but the situation has changed because it is now out in the open.

Through the Holy Spirit, God entrusts his secret to the apostles and prophets. The singling out of 'apostles and prophets' as God's' holy' ones may suggest something about the authority of the New Testament as Scripture. In the Old Testament, God's 'secret' was disclosed only to his prophets (Amos 3:7), to those who stood in God's privy council or secret assembly (Jer. 23:22). Just as their revelation became foundational Scripture, so, by analogy, those who receive and transmit the *mystērion* of God – namely the New Testament apostles and the prophetic figures associated with them lay the foundation for the New Testament as authoritative Scripture (Eph. 2:20). Furthermore they do so – as did the Old Testament prophets – through the Holy Spirit who sanctifies them for this special task of receiving and passing on the secret plan of God in Jesus Christ.

3. One new human race

Staying on the trail of this 'mystery' in our search through the text, we stumble on the particular aspect of the secret Paul is relishing. 'This mystery is that through the gospel the Gentiles are heirs together with Israel, members together of one body, and sharers together in the promise in Christ Jesus' (Eph. 3:6). Paul is marvelling over the formation of an unprecedented new community that embraces two groups – Jews and Gentiles – who represent the bitterest divisions that tear the human race apart. 'In Christ' who is our peace, and through his peace-making death on the cross, there has come about an astonishing, unheard of reconciliation of Jew and Gentile (cf. Eph. 2:11–22).

The inclusion of 'uncircumcised' Gentiles on an equal footing with Jewish believers in the one family of God, through faith in Christ, is especially notable because, as Paul reminds the Ephesians, they were previously 'excluded from citizenship in Israel and foreigners to the covenants of the promise' (Eph. 2:12). The plural 'covenants' and the singular 'promise' indicate again that the *several* covenants serve the *one* promise-plan of God. The Gentiles have been introduced to all these in the single strategy of God. In John Yoder's memorable phrase, this demonstrates 'the social novelty of the covenant of grace'.[4] Created by God through the grace of the cross and the genius of the Holy Spirit, this new body is the place where pride and exclusiveness are overcome, where the ethnic hatred and religious bigotry that still bedevils our world is swallowed up in Christ. The down-to-earth, incarnational, relational reality and victory of God's strategic plan – where Unionist and Republican in Northern Ireland, Serb and Croat, Arab and Jew can join hands and lives in Jesus Christ – is revealed. The product of such a miracle is justifiably described as one 'new human race' (Eph. 2:15).

Grace Not Race

Throughout his apostolic career Paul consistently fought for this aspect of the big mystery of God bringing all things under the Lordship of Christ. He warned the Galatians about the danger of Jewish Christian exclusivism and legalism. He upbraided the Roman church for Gentile Christian arrogance. Grace not race, faith not law, Spirit-motivated obedience from the heart not external signs like circumcision are the true identity markers of the new covenant people of God. In Paul's mind, Israel, in line with Noah and Abraham, had always had a larger vocation, not to be displaced but to be the nucleus of a worldwide covenant family of faith. So startling is this new unity in the church that Paul coins three new words especially for it, each with the prefix – meaning 'with' – *sungkleeronóma* ('joint heirs'), *sússooma* (' joint-body') and *summétocha* ('joint sharers').

One more step of discovery leads us to the reminder that the emergence of such a unified community fulfils the heart-felt intention of God in creating the world in the first place (Eph. 3:9c). God created us and gave us being with a view to our becoming his faithful children, in loving and obedient partnership with him (Eph. 1:4–5). God the Holy Father always intended there to be a perfect creaturely counterpart to his eternal Son; in short, a bride for Christ (Eph. 5:25ff.).

The one creator God always intended to realise his creation's potential and to bring it to perfection in alliance with his mature sons. Since our great rebellion, under the terms our sin has set, that destiny must pass through frustration, groaning, suffering and go the way of the cross before it can again enter into its appointed glory. Creation can only be brought to its intended goal through the cross and resurrection of the one faithful covenant partner. We are reminded, if reminder were needed, that this stunning unity and togetherness has always been God's intention: it has always been his aim to redeem his creation, not replace it with something else.

We need to establish for our own security that what we share in Jesus is 'Plan-A', there has never been a 'Plan-B'. The blueprint of history is not rigidly determined. Rather, it flows out of the fatherly-heart of a

God who took the responsibility for creating this world
knowing he had the power and love to redeem it. In
Christ, the Father is set to achieve that worldwide family
in a perfected creation which before the Fall – before
even creation itself – he had set his heart on. Through the
gospel, in the revelation of this 'mystery', we are in touch
with the ultimate purpose of all reality. Salvation is not
the abolition of our status as creatures in favour of some
higher spiritual existence; it is the redemption and not
the dilution of our humanness.

This does not exhaust the scope of the 'mystery'. Paul
describes the impact of this secret plan on the cosmic
forces in the heavenly realms (Eph. 3:10). Even stranger is
that it is 'through the church' that the revolution rumbles
round the heavenly realms. Did Paul really say, 'through
the church'? Apparently, he did, so that it is through a
church in which the cross has broken the ability of the
powers to divide and rule, that God's multi-coloured
wisdom is flaunted before their disbelieving eyes.
Andrew Lincoln comments:

> By her very existence as a new humanity in which the major
> division of the first-century world has been overcome, the
> church reveals God's secret in action and heralds to the hos-
> tile heavenly powers the overcoming of cosmic divisions
> with their defeat.[5]

Division saps the church's strength and weakens its
impact. Unity demonstrates to the cosmic powers and to
those human institutions that welcome them that God is
wise enough to find ways of bringing about his ultimate
purpose to unite all things in Christ (Eph. 1:10–11).

Narrative-shaped Living

Everything we do as believers – as those who are 'in Christ' – makes sense because it is connected to God's big story, illuminating who we are in Christ and what we are here for. For this reason Paul views Christian marriage as a vivid sign of the greater mystery of Christ and church (Eph. 5:31–33).

The question for the contemporary church is not so much whether we should allow divorce and remarriage as if the church's vision is defined by an agenda set by a dysfunctional society. As Christians we ought to be asking the bigger question: 'why get married at all?' Beyond the pro-life, pro-choice standoff, looms a larger issue: 'Why do we have children at all?' In each case, the New Testament's answer is because marriage and child-bearing enshrine the great mystery; both tell out the big story. To choose not to abort a foetus for reasons of convenience but to carry it to full term; to carry through the pro-life project; to bear, nurture and sustain a created life whatever it turns out to be; to commit and to vow and be faithful and to keep covenant until death or desertion breaks that covenant – to do any or all of these things is to tell the story of the one creator God who did not abort his creation experiment even at the Flood but promised never to disown his creation until his redemptive purposes were complete. It is to illustrate the narrative of a God who made covenant with Israel and remained – as Hosea did – obstinately determined to redeem his love, even if it cost him the life of his only Son on the cross.

Even in the western world it will soon be a definite Christian act of faith and testimony to get married because marriage only makes sense if it is connected to the big story of God's covenant love for his people, Christ's sacrificial passion for his bride the church.

Husbands then sacrifice for their wives because Christ did: wives submit to husbands who do that, and both live to tell the tale.

Living in and living out the bigger narrative of God is the Christian rationale for every action and relationship. We work because God works. He made the world in six days and pours out his life to maintain it. That is the kind of God he is. But God also rested. He looked forward to the weekend and could enjoy it all the more for having achieved something worth doing! We also need to embrace the rhythm of work and Sabbath rest. We forgive because as Paul reminds us 'God in Christ forgave you' (Eph. 4:32). We tell the truth not because it will always make people like you (they may get enraged), or because it will guarantee your children will like you or advance your career prospects with the company. 'Jesus does not say that if we turn our cheek we will not be hit. He just reassures us that if we live as he lived we shall be living the way God rules the world'.[6] The point is clear: if you know who you are in the big story, you know what you're here for. This narrative-shaped way of living worked in the first century and continues to be relevant today.

First-century Ephesus was a centre for the Artemis ('Diana') cult. The city attracted many visitors as a consequence. The tourist industry flourished. Its theatre was a civic pride and the entertainment industry kept the popular audience enthralled and passive most of the time. Economically, the city relied heavily on idolatrous worship because many people were employed to meet the consumer demand for replicas of the goddess. All these things defined who you were in Ephesus. Did you go with the crowd? Did economics, idolatry, entertainment or consumerism define who you were? From the beginning the Christians in Ephesus – many of them converts of Paul[7] – had learned a different story.

[You were taught in Christ] in accordance with the truth that is in Jesus. You were taught ... to put off the old self, which is being corrupted by its deceitful desires; to be made new in the attitude of your minds; and to put on the new self, created to be like God in true righteousness and holiness (Eph. 4:21–24).

New Story, New Script

What might this look like in practice?

- *Consider Rufus and Paula, two young people with normal healthy appetites who have been thinking of moving in together. They were in love, so they thought, but marriage was a bit of a joke really, though perhaps inevitable. Paula for one was resentful of the male-dominated, hierarchical ideas which ruled Ephesian approaches to sexuality.*

  But it all changed when the Gospel came to town. Rufus was now learning how to act out the Jesus and God story by laying down his life as a carpet of honour for his new wife to walk on. As for Paula, she smiled at herself at how much easier she was finding it to respect and honour her husband in turn. He didn't put her down in public nor did she make fun of him behind his back with her friends as she had seen so many other couples do.
- *Julia worked as an usherette and part-time barmaid at the 20,000-seat theatre at the top end of town. Being an usherette was generally assumed to make you available, and she had had her fair share of being abused and exploited by men. But now, since becoming a Christian disciple, she was learning a different story of unconditional love from God. She now saw herself in a new light, the light of God – in fact, she liked to think of herself as a 'daughter of the light'. Surrounded, as she still was, by impurity and debauchery, she felt strangely clean. She'd even stopped telling bawdy stories herself, and*

all the uncleanness around her didn't seem to stick to her so much as it once had. True, she wasn't so popular as before, but she had gained a whole new self-respect.

- *Aristarchus was the manager of a silversmith's workshop down by the harbour, and a colleague of his Trade Union leader, Demetrius. His firm made silver-images of the famous goddess, Diana, whose Temple was a star attraction in town and whose influence cast a heavy shadow over everything. Since those apostles had arrived his trade had taken a knock but they were his heroes now. He had heard a different story and was learning to live by it. Life was still insecure, he was still on a short-term contract but he'd branched out into making models of the other buildings and sites around town. He was a poorer but happier man.*

- *Alexander and his wife Tryphosa ran a bookshop near the Theatre. Until recently they had made a good living by selling occult books and magic paraphernalia. Then had come that unforgettable day when they had succumbed to a 'deeper magic' and a superior Name and had willingly joined so many former customers in the book burning in the town square. Alexander could still scarcely believe what had happened. This was their livelihood going up in smoke! But they had never regretted it. The deep haunting oppression he and Tryphosa had felt for years had lifted. He was no longer as dark and fearful as he had once been and Tryphosa slept better at night. She'd even been healed by the name of Jesus. Now they knew they had a greater Spirit inside them and, even the book trade was picking up a bit again with maps and travel guides selling well.*

- *Rufus, Paula, Julia, Aristarchus, Alexander and Tryphosa couldn't wait for the weekend when they could be together with the others for a few brief hours perhaps in the Tyrannus Hall where the visiting preachers still taught as Paul had done himself at the beginning. And then, every week, they went to Alexander's place where they sang till they could drop about the mercy of God, about the cross of Jesus, and where they felt him present with them by the Holy Spirit as they broke bread and drank wine together. 'Together' – that was it – being in it together made so much difference; they could tell the story to each other every week and learn together the grace and truth to live it out.*

God's Special Agents

What is Paul's role in all this? Like every Christian, he may, in Jacques Ellul's words,

> be sent out as a spy to work in secret, at the heart of the world, for his Lord; to prepare for his Lord's victory from within; to create a nucleus in this world and to discover its secrets, in order that the kingdom of God may break forth in splendour.[8]

Paul is God's special agent ('Paul 007' perhaps) and we can take our cue from him (Eph. 3:7–9; 6:19–20).

God's special agents live by grace alone. Grace gifts them with divine favour and forgiveness; it calls and commissions (Eph. 3:2); it lets them in on this amazing secret (Eph. 3:3). So God's grace flows in, over and out of Paul; it is like a mighty power and freeing energy (Eph. 3:7–8). Grace carried the day with Paul because he regarded himself as the 'least of all the saints'. He exemplifies the attitude Karl Barth urged on twentieth-century disciples of 'not wanting to be the heroes of our own conversion stories'.[9]

Paul insists that grace has been given him to preach the unsearchable riches of Christ – a description that suggests a picture of a reservoir so deep that soundings cannot reach the bottom of it. No limit can, therefore, be put on its resources. Now that is a mystery! Paul receives grace (Eph. 3:9) in order to make plain to everyone the administration of this mystery, 'to bring it to light ... to make everyone see'. Paul does not, like the cults with their murky mysteries, hide the gospel message in dark rites and obscure sanctuaries to which only an elite are initiated and can enter. God's secret is exactly the opposite. The mystery of God's strategic plan is an open secret for everyone to share.

It is significant that the inner sanctum of the Solar Temple sect was covered in mirrors, so that when the members worshipped all they saw were pathetically idol-atrous reflections of themselves. The church, however, is full of windows, not mirrors – windows which let light out and allow those outside (the world and the spiritual powers) to look in and see the open secret of God's love and grace in Jesus Christ being worked out.

This gospel breaks open the closed shop of ethnic exclusivism and heals the wounds of racial hatred. It blows the lid off the stale and murky mysteries of the cults and sects. Every nook and cranny of our tired and musty world – even the prison cells where God's special agents are held – are aired by the bracing fresh air of freedom. The God whose eternal purpose is being worked out in Christ is a God whom we 'may approach with freedom and confidence' (Eph. 3:12) so that we may boldly come to, and boldly go from, his presence.

Premature Ambassadors

Paul's 'suffering' in the course of duty alerts us to the dangers faced by a special agent inside enemy territory. We must never let down our guard or lose contact with base. We remain subversives with the gospel of peace.

Paul's situation also prompts us not to be discouraged by those of our agents who, operating behind enemy lines, suffer pain and imprisonment for their daring deeds – Paul was one of them (Eph. 3:1; 6:20). To recount the noble company of apostles and martyrs is to perpetuate the memory of those of our agents who are 'missing, presumed dead'. 'Pray also for me' Paul urges the Ephesians, 'that whenever I open my mouth, words may be given me so that I will fearlessly make known the mystery of the gospel, for which I am an ambassador in chains' (Eph. 6:19–20). This appears an incongruous state for an ambassador to be in, but in Richard J. Neuhaus's brilliant words:

> We are premature ambassadors, having arrived at court before the sovereignty of our king has been recognised. It is awkward, of course, and our authority is very much in question. We must resist the temptation to relieve the awkwardness by accepting a lesser authority from another kingdom.[10]

True-love Story

What a breathtaking mystery story this is – God's strategic plan! – but the mystery is not mere mystification! It is something that can be received, grasped and communicated. Yet it remains a mystery for all that, in that it partakes of the transcendence and infinity of God. It cannot, therefore, be contained. It can, however, be known and it surpasses knowledge (Eph. 3:19). The riches of Christ and the riches of the Father's glory cannot be searched (Eph. 3:8, 16). The ways and wisdom of this gracious God are multifaceted. They confound the evil intelligence of the cosmic powers (Eph. 3:10). The mysterious will of love in Christ is unfathomably high, wide, long and broad. Only the saints across all the ages can begin together to quantify it (Eph. 3:18–19). We experience the immeasurable fullness of God himself (Eph. 3:19b) and this lies beyond anything we can ask or imagine (Eph. 3:20). It will take eternal ages of unfolding joy to do justice to the glory that radiates in the church (Eph. 3:21).

This story, to paraphrase Chesterton, answers the yearning for romance by being a love story, and answers the needs of philosophy by being a true story. And the end of all things is the harvest of glory. The end of all hunger for righteousness, every quest for joy, all homesickness of soul, coincides with God's ultimate intention for our salvation. Our best self-interest finally converges with God's sole interests and glory. 'To him be glory in the church for ever and ever.' Every aspect of this sovereign strategy moves majestically to magnify his grace and glory (Eph. 1:6, 12, 14).

- The Father's eternal plan (Eph. 1:5–6) to gather a family in love moves into our time and space world to pick us up in his saving hand and it's all 'to the praise of his glorious grace' (Eph. 1:6).
- His historic action in Christ (Eph. 1:6–7) redeeming us at the cost of his blood, forgiving us by grace, sharing with us his stupendous secret strategy for the world, fills us with an unspeakable sense of amazement and wonder so that we exist 'for the praise of his glory' (Eph. 1:12).
- His intimate involvement with us by the Holy Spirit, (Eph. 1:11–14), invading our lives with his empowering presence, leaving the indelible stamp of his claim upon us, continues to redound 'to the praise of his glory' (Eph. 1:14).

The end of all things is be cherished from before the world's foundation, to share in the Trinity-life of the one creator God, to know with all the saints the four-dimensional love of this God in Christ and, in the Spirit, to be embraced for ever by the same love with which the Father eternally loves the Son.

So God's being glorified and our being fully satisfied in him are one and the same goal. To see this is to become, as John Piper puts it, 'a Christian hedonist'. As he rightly insists: the chief end of all things is to glorify God by enjoying him for ever.[11] This is the eco-system of the divine life, the glory of God's love and will flowing out to us and back to God again in loving praise and covenant faithfulness. God's is the true love that makes the world go round!

When I'm gripped by a good mystery, I can't put it down. But this gospel of God's strategic plan is the one mystery so gripping that it can't and won't put us down forever!

Notes

[1] Murray J. Harris, *Colossians and Philemon: Exegetical Guide to the Greek New Testament*, 75.

[2] J.B. Phillips, *The New Testament in Modern English*.

[3] D.M. Lloyd-Jones, *God's Ultimate Purpose: An Exposition of Ephesians One*, 206–7.

[4] John H. Yoder, *The Royal Priesthood*, 80.

[5] Andrew Lincoln, *Ephesians*, 187.

[6] William Willimon and Stanley Hauerwas, *Lord, Teach Us: The Lord's Prayer & the Christian Life*, 46.

[7] See Acts 19.

[8] Jacques Ellul, *The Presence of the Kingdom*, 45. For the imagery of the Christian as a spy see also Virginia Stem Owens, *And The Trees Clap Their Hands: Faith, Perception, and the New Physics*.

[9] Karl Barth said this in Basel in 1937 as reported in *A Karl Barth Reader*, 36.

[10] Neuhaus, *Freedom for Ministry*, 71.

[11] John Piper has challenged us with his many books emphasising this point and drawing on the work of Jonathan Edwards. See *Desiring God: Meditations of a Christian Hedonist*, *The Pleasures of God: Meditations on God's Delight in Being God*, *The Purifying Power of Living by Faith in Future Grace* and *God's Passion for His Glory: Living the Vision of Jonathan Edwards*.

10

God is Committed to
Renewing the Whole of His Creation

John's Revelation on Patmos
Revelation 21:1–22:5

Our curiosity about the future is insatiable. Eagerly, if somewhat sheepishly, we read our horoscopes, gaze into our crystal balls and try to sneak a look into what lies ahead. More pretentiously, big business hires expensive trend-analysts or futurologists in an attempt to predict the market. Others, more pessimistically, lapse into shrug-the-shoulder mood and prophesy doom. No longer, it seems, do we expect the men in white hats to ride over the hill to our rescue; it is more likely that men in white coats will come to carry us away and certify us. On either prognosis, it's all a bit of a lottery; and we don't even get the weather forecast right all the time! And right here John shouts his good news to us.

'I saw ...' (Rev. 21:1)

Swept up by the prophetic inspiration of God's Spirit, John is taken to a high-mountain vantage point and shown a stunning vision of the future (Rev. 21:10). They say 'on a clear day, you can see for ever' – and this was an exceptionally clear day! As if from far below, we shout up to John on his lonely pinnacle of vision 'what can you see from there, John?' John replies, 'I can see a sparkling new world, a whole new creation'. 'What does it look like?' 'It looks like a city but stretched out in all directions. It's like a new kind of Jerusalem teeming with people from every nation, as if up for an international festival, enjoying the presence of God'. 'What else can you see?' 'I can see that no one's crying, there are no cemeteries, no prisons; I can see no one in pain or suffering any disease; and I see … I think I can see … I can't believe it … I feel sure I can see … God! I can see God's face! And yet everything is radiating such a glorious light that I'm not sure what I see; when I stare at the face of God, more often than not I see a face I know so well, the human face of Jesus'.

This is John's seventh and final vision; it is the ulti-mate vision. We might shout to him to be more specific but we'll make ourselves hoarse. Once again we are reminded that 'people are not changed by moral exhorta-tion but by transformed imagination'.[1] Nowhere is this insight more necessary than when approaching John's Revelation. Crassly literal minds will be blinded to the truth. Intriguing images, dazzling visions, majestic meta-phors, stunning symbols are the currency of trade in the last book of the Bible. These images sharpen and fade, merge and separate before our very eyes as if on a giant computer screen. They dazzle and enlighten us. And the way in which they stir our imagination makes what they portray more not less real.

It is these intensely poetic words that, we are assured, are trustworthy and true (Rev. 21:5) and convey divine authority and disclosure. Revelation celebrates in graphic pictorial form that the one creator God has never relinquished his control of things and that Jesus Christ, the slain Lamb, has already won the decisive victory over a personal Satan and institutional evil through the cross and resurrection. John stands in the long tradition of the biblical prophets in seeing and showing these ultimate realities to us. In one sense, there is nothing new in John's Revelation at all: it has all been said before! Although the book lacks any direct and complete citation from the Old Testament, almost every line of it is soaked in echoes and allusions to the first part of Scripture. In other words, John superbly gathers up all the previous threads of biblical prophecy and weaves them into a majestic gospel tapestry.

So what does John see?

1. *The new creation*

'I saw a new heaven and a new earth' (Rev. 21:1).

The Bible moves in a sweeping narrative from first creation to new creation. The strategic covenant commitments and the dramatic redemptive intrusions come to this. The continuous energising of God's creative Spirit and the never-ceasing flow of God's history-making Word – it has all been leading to this. On this Hebrew prophets and Jewish Christian apostles agree. Isaiah was entrusted with the intention of God: 'Behold, I create new heavens and a new earth; the former things will not be remembered.' (Is. 65:17; cf. 66:22). Throughout Isaiah chapters 40–55, the prophet holds together creation and redemption: it is the creator who redeems and in redeeming creates again. Peter has seen the death of the old world in the cross of Jesus and the birth of the new world in the resurrection of Jesus. So in answering critics of God's slowness in keeping his promises, he re-affirms Isaiah's vision: when the cosmos is melted down to its constituent elements, it will be a day of judgment and resolution. 'But', he urges, 'in keeping with his promise we are looking forward to a new heaven and a new earth, the home of righteousness' (2 Pet. 3:11–13).

God has not written off his good creation. 'Late great planet earth?' explodes Lewis Smedes, 'Nonsense; the very notion is probably the sickest heresy to corrupt the Christian hope'.[2] What lies ahead is not some merely spiritual salvation but the ultimate reconciliation of spirit and matter, the reclaiming and restoring of God's own good creation.

John's 'no mores' say it well. 'No more sea' (Rev. 21:1) – which is not meant to disappoint sailors and swimmers or lovers of beaches and oceans. In Scripture the 'sea' represents the forces of chaos brought under control at the first creation, the untamed, restlessness of evil and disorder that now has no place in the new creation. Death is no more (Rev. 21:4) – so there will be no more mourning, crying, pain, disease, cot-deaths, cancer, Alzheimer's, widows and orphans, bereavement or funerals. The God, who stooped once in his Son to wash the dust from tired feet, will wipe every tear from every grief-stricken eye – this is truly the 'old order passing away'. Alongside the 'no more' we ought to put the 'much more', because this will not just be 'paradise regained' as if all will be returned to how it was before. Everything will be transformed and enhanced, be better than before, with every potential fulfilled and every seed-bearing fruit. The Christian hope: is for a redeemed earth for which you and I will need, and receive, brand-new resurrection bodies.

Lewis Smedes once asked a Christian audience, 'do you want to go to heaven when you die?' Many hands showed. Then he asked, 'Given the chance, would you want to go tonight?' In the embarrassed silence just a few hands went up! Finally he asked, 'would you like to see the world we live in set completely to rights, with no more colds or cancers, no prisoners or slaves, no rape or murder, no cruelty or war; where only love, justice and peace would prevail?' A frenzy of hands gave him his answer. That, Smedes assured his audience, is just the world Christians can expect.

Paul, like Isaiah and Peter, saw it too. The world groans and waits for it, he said, and so do we. Our hope, intercession and willingness to suffer might just turn out to be the birth pangs of the new world. We are not going to heaven; heaven is coming here! As Smedes said, 'If a new world tomorrow is what you really want, you want to go to heaven. For heaven is nothing more than this earth made new. What else would a good creator plan for his earthly creatures?'[3] It is not that finally we get to go to heaven; heaven is where God is and, as Adrio König says, 'heaven is on earth if God is there'.[4] We are not going to heaven: heaven is coming here.

This is reinforced by the second great image John sees in which the new creation is viewed as a city.

2. *The New Jerusalem*

'I saw the Holy City, the new Jerusalem, coming down out of heaven from God' (Rev. 21:2). Just as the angel invited John to a desert to see Babylon, the great whore, come crashing down (Rev. 17:1ff.), so now he is invited to a high mountain to view the coming down of the Holy City as God's bride. God's new city alights on a mountaintop (Rev. 21:10). Here are echoes of the ancient myth of the mountain of the gods, which had been merged with mount Zion in the vision of the Hebrew psalmist when he sang, 'Great is the Lord and most worthy of praise, in the city of our God, his holy mountain' (Ps. 48:1). According to Ezekiel the Garden of Eden was set also on a mountain

(Ezek. 28:12–16) so that what we have is a fusion of images, Jerusalem with Paradise restored.

The Jerusalem John sees is a *heaven-sent city* (Rev. 21:2, 10). Again, the emphasis is on heaven coming here. It comes 'from God' – it is a God-designed and God-made city. Abraham left Ur, the epitome of Babylonian civilisation, turning his back on the city man was building, setting out on the great faith adventure, 'looking forward to the city with foundations whose architect and builder is God' (Heb. 11:10).

This Jerusalem is a *holy city* – the dwelling-place of the holy God (Rev. 21:2, 10). The descent of this city more than matches the downfall of the unholy city pictured earlier (Rev. 17–18). This explains the symbolism of its remarkable shape: it is as wide and high as it is long (Rev. 21:16) – in short a perfect cube. The significance of this derives from the holy of holies in the Temple, which was a perfect cube (1 Kgs. 6:20). In other words, in this new world – this new Jerusalem – all is sacred, everything is holy space, everywhere is filled to the same intensity with the holy presence of God. No wonder a Temple is redundant there (Rev. 21:22).

This is a *glorious city* that is brilliant with the radiant glory of God (Rev. 21:11). It stands in stark contrast to the city of Babylon, which represents all that humankind has built without God. Babylon glorified itself and was the dwelling-place of demons (Rev. 18:2, 7). The New Jerusalem is the dwelling-place of God and shines with his glory. The Bible is a 'tale of two cities' – Babylon and Jerusalem. Salvation depends on coming out of the one culture and becoming a citizen in the other, so that your name is enrolled in the 'Lamb's book of life' (Rev. 21:27).

The New Jerusalem is a *unified city* (Rev. 21:12–14). The city is home to a new covenant community, which unites believers from before and after Christ's coming. The city's gates are inscribed with the twelve tribes of Israel and its foundation stones with the names of the twelve apostles (Rev. 21:12, 14). In tune with this, John has already heard the rehearsals for the song of Moses and the Lamb (Rev. 15:3).

It is also an inclusive and international city (Rev. 21:24–27). Within it is an international company of people fulfilling and far-exceeding what Abraham was promised and what he dreamed of (Rev. 21:24). Abraham was promised descendants as innumerable as the stars in the night sky, the grains of sand on the seashore and the specks of dust on the ground. In this way, all the nations of the earth would be blessed. Abraham believed God and it was counted to him as covenant membership. John *hears* that there are 144,000 in this company (Rev. 7:4), and so knows that God's covenant family is complete, that no one is missing, that no one is 'in' who shouldn't be there and no one is 'out' who should be 'in'. But when John looks to see this people, he *sees* a multitude from every nation, tribe, people and language group that no one could number.[5] On one reading of an earlier vision, it is suggested to John that whereas Elijah learned of only seven thousand who were *not* apostates, John learns of only seven thousand who *are* – nine-tenths of the entity being judged apparently come through to repentance and faith (Rev. 11:13). The new heaven and earth – the New Jerusalem – is the new environment prepared for this new covenant people. And it is this company, purified and redeemed, which is the bride of the Lamb; the people who are in every way the perfect complement to Jesus.

3. Wedding gifts

The nations and kings come to the city to bring tribute and honour to God. Surely, this is a magnificent symbol of the contrast with Babylon. Babylon ultimately destroys all art, music and commerce, turning them to false ends; it consumes all love and relationships by its insatiable appetite for self-aggrandisement. But all true human potential will find its fulfilment, all will be made good in the New Jerusalem; all true human history, culture and creative achievement will be gloriously redeemed, purified and returned to the praise of its creator.

Finally, the New Jerusalem is a *garden city*. With its flowering, a movement is completed full circle – from creation to new creation which restores Eden but does not go back to it (Rev. 22:1–2). There is development and expansion from a mere garden to a garden city, one with all the benefits of urban living and all the joys of country-life. There may be no more sea but the river of true life runs freely through the city-centre. 'Jerusalem from above is now the symbol and centre of the new creation. It is the meeting place of heaven and earth. All enemies are now defeated. The nations have come within its gates and the waters of paradise flow along its streets'.[6]

There is 'no more curse' (22:3), which says it all. God's judgmental curse, pronounced over the whole earth because of Adam's disobedience, is now rescinded. A thornless world appears as creation is released into the freedom and blessing enjoyed by the redeemed children of the one creator God (Rom. 8:19ff.). No darkness closes in; there is 'no more night'. There is only the full blazing glory of the light of God and of the Lamb. By the Spirit, we have already come as worshippers to this city (Heb. 12:22f.) and by faith we continue to march as pilgrims towards it.

Soberly, John allows himself a terrible glance over his shoulder into the abyss at the fate of those who have debarred themselves from being part of this (Rev. 21:8). Even the angels who have supervised the judgmental destruction of Babylon and the old order of things now want to show him something better. It is as if, said G.B. Caird, the 'demolition squad had also an interest in the reconstruction for which they have cleared the ground'.[7]

The angels want to show John that this city is a *beautiful bridal city* (Rev. 21:2, 9). The 'bride' is a long-standing Old Testament metaphor for God's people, Israel, to whom he is wed in covenant, whose exclusive love and devotion he jealously treasures, and when the prophets warn her against loving other gods. When Israel was in Canaan, she was tempted to cover her options by paying homage to Baal, the husband deity of the fertility goddess who guaranteed good crops and harvest. Hosea denounced such behaviour as spiritual adultery (Hos. 2:1–6). Israel must go into the desert wilderness in judgment, but there, amazingly, God pursues and woos his erring lover once again (Hos. 2:14–20). Even after the 'divorce' of exile, the marriage metaphor was retrieved as a suitable description of God's renewed love for his people and the effects of a new covenant relationship with him (Is. 62:3–5).

Robert Farrar Capon asks his students how the story ends:

Inevitably, I get all the correct but dull answers: the Word triumphs; creation is glorified; the peaceable kingdom comes in. And I say, yes, yes; but how does the story actually end? The class looks at me for a while as if I were out of my mind, and then offers me some more of the same: the Father's good pleasure is served; humanity is taken up into the exchanges of the Trinity. And I say again: yes, but how does the story end in fact? No answer. I try another tack: where does the story end? ... where can you read the end of the story? And eventually someone says: in the Book of Revelation – but who understands that?! I'm not asking you to understand it,

I say. I just want to know what you read there. What is the last
thing that happens? And slowly, painfully, it finally comes
out. The new Jerusalem comes down from heaven as the
bride of the Lamb. They never see it till they fall over it! It's
the oldest story on earth: boy meets girl; boy loses girl; boy
gets girl! He marries her and takes her home to Daddy! The
Word romances creation till he wins her. By his eternal flat-
tery, he makes new heavens and new earth; the once groaning and travailing world becomes Jerusalem, the bride
without spot or wrinkle.[8]

And God and his people live together ever after in the
new world.

So to the question, 'how can a city be a bride?' The final
answer is, 'because of those who live there'.

4. *The new covenant community*

'Behold the dwelling-place of God is with men and he
will live with them. They will be his people and he will be
their God' (21:3). God finally has the people he always
desired. This is the God we should have known about all
along throughout the biblical story – the God who loves
people and longs to be with them; who went for quiet
walks and conversation with Adam and Eve in the
garden in the cool of the afternoon; who camped and
decamped all those years with Israel in the wilderness
and marked his presence with a pillar of cloud by day
and fire by night; who showed up in the sanctuary built
for him with the golden mist of his Shekinah glory and
who gave himself an earthly address in the Temple in
Jerusalem.

Once more, the great summary covenant statement
resounds: 'I will be their God and they will be my people'
which runs like a recurring thread through all his

dealings in history (cf. Lev. 26:11–12). At last, the truly human ones embrace their royal vocation of reigning with him on the earth as kings and priests (Rev. 22:5).

Those who by grace share in the new order of things, share also the inheritance of David: 'I will be his God and he will be my son' which takes the amazing covenantal promise made to David and his kingly descendants of enjoying a unique father-son relationship with God and extends it to all. God's new covenant people are his royal family (Rev. 21:7).

5. 'It is done'

The last word on history belongs to the voice of him who sits on the throne: "I am making all things new" (Rev. 21:5). God declares that "it is done" (Rev. 21:6). Intriguingly, this phrase introduces the vision of the new Jerusalem which follows (cf. Rev. 21:9–22:11) just as the same phrase 'it is done' closed the trumpet judgments and introduced the downfall of the unholy city, Babylon (cf. Rev. 16:17–21).

God can truly say of salvation or judgment that 'it is done … it is finished'. The old creation is wrapped up, the old order is passing away; behold the new creation and city are ready to be unveiled. 'I am the Alpha and Omega, the beginning and the end' (Rev. 21:6). Praise and glory be to the Lord for now we know there was a beginning, there is a meaning in between, and there will be an end – and it is in his hands. He had the first word on the old creation and he has the last word on it too. And he who had the last word on the old creation has the first word on the new creation!

Living as we do – as John's readers did – in the middle of things, life sometimes seems a muddle. We wonder how we got here and whether there is any future. How can we cope with the muddle in the middle? We remember the beginning and look to the end. In that way we find meaning in the middle. For our God is with us, as the entire alphabet and not just the A and Z.

The 'overcomers' will inherit all these things (Rev. 21:7). They are not some spiritual equivalent of the Marine Corps, some SAS elite group, or the few super-powered macho Christians. They are all who fight the fight of faith and on a daily basis win some minor victory. They are those who have put all their faith in the blood of the Lamb to save them, who faithfully confess the Lordship of Jesus and who do not love their lives so much they shrink from death (Rev. 12:11). The followers of the Lamb through their own suffering and self-giving love share in the implementation of his victory over evil and death. They are those who have glimpsed the coming glory and have been captivated by John's vision. They live as heralds of the new day, harbingers of a new world, samples of the world's future. For this you get up every morning, keep fighting the fight of faith; achieve minor victories of integrity, patience and prayer. This is your inheritance.

6. *The new vision of God*

The ultimate prize, the final vision is seeing the Lamb's face (22:4). He is the one who comes into focus, who receives the bride and lays the foundations of the city. The Lamb is the temple and the light in it; he shares the throne of God. The slain Lamb who now stands to rule keeps coming into view. 'The new creation of heaven and earth is destined finally to emerge from the history of God's suffering, and to have this suffering at its centre. This new creation is to be the kingdom of the crucified Lamb'.[9]

Seeing the face of God will surely be heaven on earth – the 'beatific vision', as the mystics called it. 'There', said Saint Augustine, 'we shall rest and we shall see; we shall see and we shall love; we shall love and we shall praise. Behold what shall be in the end and shall not end'.[10] We shall rest, unlike the unrepentant wicked. We shall love for, in E.L. Mascall's words, 'in the beatific vision we shall be supremely and immeasurably happy, but we shall not be thinking about our happiness. We shall be thinking about God, and that is why we shall be supremely and immeasurably happy'. And when we see God face to face, Mascall continues:

> we shall find in him, in a far more wonderful way, anything we have had to give up for his sake, and everything good we have left behind on earth. For in the last resort, there are only two alternatives: either to have God, and in him, everything, or to have nothing but yourself. The latter alternative is what Christian theology knows as hell, the former as heaven.[11]

We will praise because, as P.T. Forsyth put it, God's love 'is homeward bound as well as outward bound. If it goes forth it also returns incessantly on Himself'.[12] With this vision dazzling his eyes and this voice ringing in his ears, John fell down to worship (Rev. 22:8): this was too true to tamper with and too good to miss. It was worth every lonely hour on Patmos. For this Noah overcame fear and stepped into the ark and with even more faith stepped out of it again. For this Abraham left comfortable retirement in search of the city of God and launched into the great unknown trusting the word of God. For this Israel was chosen and loved and covenanted with, and for this Moses confronted Pharaoh and led Israel out of Egypt. For this David left his father's flock, was anointed king and captured Jerusalem from the Jebusites. For this the prophets pleaded and were persecuted and projected the promises of God with stunning pictures and powerful words.

For this the Lamb came and lived among us. He chose twelve disciples. He entered Jerusalem and laid down his life to displace the temple. He died and rose again with a new world in his nail-pierced hands. He shares God's throne and intercedes, and is coming again.

7. Rainbow people

Just before the dawn of the new world of Narnia, as exquisite music begins to fill the air with an almost unbearable sweetness and as a thousand stars suddenly burst dazzlingly into light above his head, the old London Cabbie who has gone into Narnia with the children, comes to the realisation that all his life he might have been a better man if only he had known there were things like that![13] So would we all; so will we all.

Our entry to the big story was with Noah and God's war-bow hung in the sky as token of suspended judgment. We end with John and the bow surrounding God's throne, symbol of an overarching covenant love. We remain pilgrims, 'come wind, come weather'. But we can 'trace the rainbow' even 'through the rain'. The new covenant community is not monochrome – its members are of varied hue – nor are its experiences uniformly grey. Christ's sunlight streams through the prism of our still-being-redeemed humanity to produce a church of many-coloured graces and gifts.

As Leonard Sweet has said:

A rainbow church embraces the entire climate of the human experiences – whether the prevailing weather pattern of each soul is sunny and bright or damp and dreary. In this church,

Christians are not afraid to believe or doubt or to believe and doubt simultaneously. Members are nurtured while they experience the vast sensorium of human emotion – from stumbling in the light to dancing in the dark, from cries of 'how long?' to shouts of 'Hallelujah!'.[14]

In the bombed-out ruins of Hamburg, immediately after the Second World War, Helmut Thielicke reminded his congregation that though Christians do not know, anymore than others, exactly what will come, but they do know who will come.

This means that world history, as illustrated by the monumental stories of the Bible, is fitted and held together by the first rainbow which shone over the catastrophe of the flood and the end of the primitive world, and also by the second rainbow which John the Divine saw around the throne of God before which world history will some day end … In spite of every appearance to the contrary, our way does in fact lead from God's gracious bow at the beginning to his triumphant bow at the end. We may rest in the heart of God and find shelter in his omnipotent might.[15]

Notes

[1] Brueggemann, *Hopeful Imagination*, 25.
[2] Lewis Smedes, *How Can It Be All Right When Everything Is All Wrong?*, 151.
[3] Ibid., 152.
[4] Adrio König, *The Eclipse of Christ in Eschatology*, 235.
[5] On this point and much else see the insightful work of Richard Bauckham, *The Theology of the Book of Revelation*; and *The Climax of Prophecy*.
[6] Dumbrell, *End of the Beginning*, introduction.
[7] G.B. Caird *Commentary on the Revelation of St. John the Divine*, 269.

[8] Robert Farrar Capon, *The Romance of the Word*, 237.

[9] Jürgen Moltmann, *God in Creation: An Ecological Doctrine of Creation: The Gifford Lectures 1984 – 1985*, 90.

[10] St Augustine from the *City of God*, Book 22, chapter 30, as cited by E.L. Mascall in *Grace and Glory*, 13.

[11] Mascall, *Grace and Glory*, 54, 79.

[12] P.T. Forsyth, *This Life and the Next: The Effect on this Life of Faith in Another*, 32.

[13] C.S. Lewis, 'The Magicians Nephew' in *The Chronicles of Narnia*, 62.

[14] Leonard I. Sweet 'The Rainbow Church,' *The Christian Ministry*, March (1986), 6; cited in a development of the idea, by Donald E. Messer, *Contemporary Images of Christian Ministry*, 143.

[15] Helmut Thielicke, *The Silence of God*, 55–6.

Participating in the Story

11

Meet the God of the Biblical Story

The flexible tactics of God!

The life of Jesus, it has been said, was 'absolutely planless'.[1]

To say this is to counter any idea that God's plans form some rigid, deterministic scheme. It has been a major concern of mine all through this book to prevent just such a conclusion. So it is worth highlighting the paradoxes and ambiguities in the biblical picture of God's strategic plan.

Jesus was clearly not 'working to orders' in the sense of following the successive stages of a hard and fast 'business plan'. He did not keep a five-year diary! Jesus marched to the deep heartbeat of his Father's unwavering resolve, not that of a structured agenda. God's will was not a wall-chart that dictated Jesus' progress, but his meat and drink – Jesus ate and slept God's glory. Zeal for God's house was not an occasional surge of spiritual adrenaline but a passion that consumed him. He did not live self-consciously by ticking off today's guidance from a checklist of scriptural proof-texts about how messiahs are supposed to behave. Rather, he lived a fully

God-conscious human life immersed in the biblical pattern his life was conformed to.

In all this Jesus seems both almost 'laid back' in his relaxed approach to each day's ministry and 'driven' by the claims of the kingdom urging him on. Luke records him taking time beyond sunset to heal every one of the large numbers of sick people that were brought to him that evening. But when, next morning, the curious crowds come surging out to find him, he turns away from them with the rebuff: 'I must preach the good news of the kingdom of God to the other towns also; because that is why I was sent' (Lk. 4:43).

No one so 'planless' has ever been more 'focused' or led a more purposeful life than Jesus. Early on, he accepted an essentially prophetic vocation. He grew in awareness, not least that it would involve suffering the classic prophet's fate. Jesus did not set goals but, as Luke shows us in a vivid glimpse, bent his whole life in the direction of Jerusalem so that his 'destination was in his face' (cf. Lk. 9:51). Yet along the way he can stop to bless children, turn aside to respond to blind beggars and spend 'wasted' afternoons in the company of sinners. When at last Jesus reaches the city, he feels no self-satisfaction at merely keeping an appointment but the tearful anguish of someone forcing a decision at a moment of destiny. Jesus truly moves in mysterious ways God's wonders to perform!

Underground Stream

Paradoxically, the *hiddenness of God* has been evident throughout our story. His plan is often like a stream that runs deep underground beneath the surface events. His long-term plan is certainly not immediately obvious, even to the participants themselves. The whole is always bigger than the sum of its parts and even the individuals favoured with specific covenant commitments scarcely knew more than a fraction of the plan or gained more than a faint glimpse of it.

No one exemplifies this more than *Joseph*. Rejected by his brothers – not surprisingly in view of his arrogant dreams about his own supremacy over them – he is sold into Egypt. There, living on his wits, he rises to eminence in government so that years later, when famine strikes Judah, he receives his family again as they arrive in Egypt in search of food. In a moving disclosure scene, Joseph says to them, 'Come closer ... I am your brother Joseph, whom you sold into Egypt. Do not be distressed or angry with yourselves, because you sold me here; for God sent me before you to preserve life ... God sent me before you to preserve for you a remnant on earth' (Gen. 45:4–5, NRSV). This is remarkable. What seemed like a rather sordid family squabble involving fraternal jealousy turns out to be part of the larger story of God's purposes for the world. Later on Joseph is able to see God's hand and say, 'even though you intended to do harm, God intended it for good' (Gen. 50:20, NRSV). As Hauerwas and Willimon say of Joseph:

> The bratty little dreamer isn't the hero. The hero of the story, the One who makes it worth retelling is the author of another plan. A plan hidden but sure. Joseph tells his brothers: 'What you meant for evil; God meant for good'. God's plans will triumph. We're not told – at least here – how. The Bible can't do that. We're told that God's plans do triumph.[2]

Ruth's story – set, canonically, in the darkest days of the Judges – also shows how one widow's domestic world is lifted by redemption into vital connection with God's big saving story. Yet she did not realise how significant her story would turn out to be – a key link in the chain of God's promise plan stretching back to Abraham and forward to David (Ruth 4:18–22).

Not all Scripture so readily states the case. The Wisdom literature in particular, is often viewed as problematic for the theme taken in this book, since it hardly deals in historical, covenantal or redemptive categories. Israel's wisdom tradition is reflective and appears static and oddly at variance with the linear movement of God's strategic plan. For this reason, the Wisdom stance is often seen as an alternative, or even contradiction, to the narrative-redemptive approach we have been following of it. I prefer to see it as presupposing covenantal continuities and, paradoxically, revealing the *hiddenness* of God's plan in the mundane pre-occupations of living.

Crisis Wisdom

It is perhaps only with *Job* that we sense this concealed wisdom. We only seem to discover the God of crisis when the God of creation-order appears to fail us. We only seem to perceive the larger normative, narrative when suffering and injustice break up the regular patterns of our story. As with a deep gold-mine, everyday activity on the surface is geared to and governed by what is being worked and extracted at cost in the hidden depths far beneath at the rock face (Job 28). Only there do you find the deepest truest wisdom of the creator God that can make uncommon sense of things.

When the bottom dropped out of his normally successful world, Job goes into 'free-fall', but when he hits the rock-bottom of reality it turns out to be the everlasting arms of a tough but tender, redemptive God. As David Wells says:

> Beyond this God's people have no assurances that the dark experiences of life will be held at bay, much less that God will provide some sort of running commentary on the meaning of each day's allotment of confusion, boredom, pain or achievement.[3]

Job discovered, through crisis, a deeper order of things hidden beneath the surface of everyday events, which was not, in the end, susceptible to commonsense rationalisation, or even reducible to a cut-and-dried theological system. 'It is a new mercy of God – as his judgment always is – to let the false foundation slide from us, so that we may stand, in its debacle, on the Rock'.[4]

When God eventually speaks, he seems intent on overwhelming Job with a recital of his unrivalled power as creator. God appears to bully Job by throwing his divine weight around, as if aiming to browbeat Job into an abject submission. Is this a demonstration of divine oneupmanship, which uses a hammer to crack a nut, or is something more serious going on? Is God perhaps taking drastic measures to pierce Job's defences? Job has often confessed to a 'death wish', complaining that he hates being human (Job 7:17–21). God's rebuke, it seems, is not meant to cut Job down to size. Instead, God wants to rouse Job so that he measures up as a worthy conversation partner and co-worker (Job 38:1–3; 40:6–7).

In his miserable condition, Job has more than once sarcastically repudiated his kingly human status as celebrated in Psalm 8: 'What is man that you make so much of him, that you give him so much attention?' (Job 7:17). Job has succumbed to the lie that the more space God occupies the less room there is for us to be human. Instead of enjoying the dignity of being 'crowned with glory and honour', Job feels that God has made a mockery of his human dignity, 'stripping' him of his 'honour and his crown' (Job 19:9). But we do not magnify God by loathing ourselves. In fact, by goading Job into a stand-up, eyeball-to-eyeball encounter, God subverts Job's self-pity. God summons Job to stand on his feet 'like a man' and to look God 'in the eye' in the daring realisation of what it means to be human: 'Brace yourself like a man and I will question you and you shall answer me' (Job 38:3; 40:7). God is not impressed with Job's display of self-abasement (Job 40:4). But, far from denigrating Job, God in the end seems bent on dignifying Job's humanness.

On one possible reading of the text of Job 42:6, Job is said to repent *of* not *in* dust and ashes. Apart from its obvious penitential meaning, 'to repent' can be used in the sense of 'changing one's mind' (Jer. 18:8) or even of 'being comforted' (Ezek. 14:22). The ambiguity of the text leaves open the real possibility that Job is here 'repenting of' his low sense of self-worth; he is turning from his own self-hatred to re-engage with the One in whose image he is made. In other words, Job finds 'consolation', not humiliation, in being 'dust and ashes' humanity. Job discovers that 'dust and ashes' humanness, 'with all the suffering to which it is vulnerable, is not incompatible with royal status but now may be accepted as the very condition under which royalty manifests itself'.[5] Receiving renewed divine approval, the royal vocation to become truly human may be embraced with all its vulnerability to innocent suffering. Intimations of mortality may be the hidden clues to incarnational and cruciform glory.

God Moves in Outrageous Ways His Wonders to Perform

God's mysterious pursuit of his plan is no more evident than at the time of the exile. Jeremiah writes to reassure the exiles that God has a plan for them. ' "For I know the plans I have for you," declares the LORD, "plans to prosper you and not to harm you, plans to give you hope and a future" ' (Jer. 29:11). This is all well and good. But this hope imposes an odd immediate response: knuckle down for the long haul and, even more strangely, 'Seek the peace and prosperity of the city to which I have carried you into exile. Pray to the LORD for it, because if it prospers, you too will prosper' (Jer. 29:7). Bless your enemies and pray for your persecutors in furtherance of God's plans.

Isaiah, too, brings God's reassurance to the exiled community: 'My purpose shall stand and I do all that I please' (Is. 46:10). But then he adds, 'From the east I summon a bird of prey; from a far-off land, a man to fulfil my purpose' (Is. 46:11). The return from exile involves the calling of a pagan emperor who's never heard of Yahweh to be God's anointed and appointed agent of deliverance for his people.

It is this depth of paradoxical wisdom that Paul celebrates as he tries to make sense of the breathtaking strategy of God in history (Rom. 11:33–34). Part of the revealed secret strategy of God is that 'all Israel will be saved' (Rom. 11:26). Whether this means all ethnic Israel then or in the future, the sum total of all Jews (or all Jews and Gentiles) who respond to the preaching of the gospel, or Israel on a national scale in the future by a sovereign act of God, it will happen only in response to the new covenant promises of the prophets now made good in Jesus (Rom. 11:26–27; Is. 59:20–21; Jer. 31:33).

What about the Jews? They oppose the gospel as Paul preaches it and prove themselves to be *enemies*. Are they still special to God? Yes, undoubtedly, but they are specially loved because of their past – 'they are loved on account of the patriarchs' (Rom. 11:28). This cannot mean that they have a separate-track future. But has God not repudiated their past? No, 'for God's gifts and his call are irrevocable' (Rom. 11:29). How does God work all this out in pursuance of his long-range plan? Paul's vision is stretched almost to breaking point: 'God has [imprisoned all in] disobedience so that he may have mercy on them all' (Rom. 11:32). What a strange and severe mercy it is, and how extraordinarily paradoxical a plan! 'Oh the depth of the riches of the wisdom and knowledge of God! How unsearchable his judgments and [how inscrutable his ways]' (Rom. 11:33). In the words of Deuteronomy 29:29 – set in a context in Paul's mind as he writes Romans (e.g. Rom. 10:6, 19): 'The secret things belong to the LORD our God; but the things revealed belong to us and to our children forever.' Like Job, we may feel that we have merely touched the outskirts of God's ways but some things are sure and steadfast and revealed to us. And we are not undone by what we do not know of God. He does not have a 'dark side' that threatens to destroy our trust in what he has revealed to us.

God's Tactics

It is for reasons like this that we might speak of the *tactical flexibility of God*. 'God's strategic plan' is the sub-title of our journey. The language of 'strategy' and 'tactics' is interesting. Science, politics, business and the military all employ 'strategies'. By definition 'strategy' stands for the plans of the *powerful* imposed from above in an all-embracing way. Once again we are reminded of the post-modern rejection of 'master-stories' for being inherently oppressive.

'Tactics', on the other hand, are said to be the 'art of the weak'. The powerless are opportunists who seek to find and fill whatever gaps and spaces they can.[6] This distinction is helpful. It serves to remind us that it is God, not the church, who has the strategy. The story we have followed reveals a God who, in his *strategic* interests, is adept at accommodating himself *tactically* to the needs and opportunities of the moment. And furthermore, in pursuance of his long-range goal, God continually steps over to the side of the weak. Time and again this God gets emotionally involved with the marginalised in the patient long-term tactical battles that are part of the greater strategic war going on.

This helps to throw an eerie but wonderful light on the God whose story this is. He emerges as a God keen on entering into dialogue rather than authoritarian decree; a God who does not hastily opt for closure but keeps debate alive and his options open. This God appears curiously persuadable. He wants people to share the emotional turmoil of decision-making as if inviting persuasion, prayer and appeal.

With Noah, for example, God shares the terrible secret of his intention to judge and destroy. By singling out Noah as his confidant, God invites Noah into the heartbreaking decisions he has to make. It is almost as if God wants Noah to be the pretext for wresting some good from the situation. God's emotional vulnerability invites us to see into his deepest feelings. It sets up the reader for the amazing disclosure that even after the flood, while the sinful nature of humankind remains unchanged, God resolves to change and 'never again' flood the earth (Gen. 9:15).

God is equally flexible and open to argument with Abraham. He allows Abraham to haggle with him over the fate of those in Sodom and Gomorrah. God proposes to do something to these cities, which he 'can't hide from Abraham' (Gen. 18:17). Why not, unless God is encouraging his covenant partner to barter with him in some way? Here again we are given an insider's view of God's openness and strange vulnerability to entreaty. Pressing his case with God, Abraham argues, 'Far be it from you! Will not the judge of all the earth do right?' (Gen. 18:25). It may be going too far to say, as Walter Brueggemann does, that Abraham is being invited to help God decide what kind of God he wants to be in this situation.[7] God is after all never going to be less than the steadfast God of covenant faithfulness. But this dialogue again sharply faces us with just how versatile and vulnerable God is able to be.

Versatile and vulnerable

The dialogue between God and Moses illustrates both these points after Israel's 'fall' into idolatry with the golden calf (Ex. 32–34). God effectively repudiates his people to Moses: 'Go down, because *your* people' – note it is no longer *my* people – 'whom you brought up out of Egypt have become corrupt' (Ex. 32:7). An exasperated God has had enough of his people: 'Now leave me alone so that my anger may burn against them and that I may destroy them. Then I will make you into a great nation!' (Ex. 32:10). God wants to be left alone in his anger, but because Moses will not leave him alone, he pledges again not to leave Israel alone! With the words 'then I will make of you a great nation' God makes the same promise to Moses that he had made to Abraham as if he is offering to start all over again with him! To his credit Moses refuses. Audaciously he banks everything on God being gracious:

'Moses sought the favour of the LORD his God' (Ex. 32:11). He boldly appeals to God's self-interest: having expended so much divine energy on Israel's behalf in the past, why give up now? (Ex. 32:11). He pleads God's reputation as if to ask 'what will the neighbours think?' (Ex. 32:12), and recalls God's previous covenantal commitments, as if to query whether God has lost the plot (Ex. 32:13).

Evidently God's grace can stand the strain of this brash and argumentative praying. So, 'the Lord relented and did not bring on his people the disaster he had threatened' (Ex. 32:14). God is vulnerable and versatile, tactical and strategic, flexible and faithful. He opens himself to the intercessory negotiations of Abraham and Moses. By so doing he remains faithful to his covenant promises and long-term plan.[8]

Perhaps we can discern three levels of God's will operating here:

1. His over-arching strategic promise-plan of salvation.
2. His decisive redemptive and covenantal commitments, which he pledges never to go back on.
3. His dynamic responses to circumstances and needs, which display his tactical flexibility and emotional vulnerability.

God seems ready to respond to lament and protest, prayer and intercession, interacting with his covenant partners and disclosing more of himself in the process – and all in the interests of his long-term covenant purpose.

The language of God 'relenting' or even 'repenting' serves to highlight this paradox. It is precisely in those contexts, such as Jeremiah's vision of the potter and the clay (Jer. 18–19), which most seem to emphasise God's absolute sovereignty, that he is said to be responsive to our repentance and willing to relent (Jer. 18). Where God is said 'not to repent' (e.g. Num. 23:19; 1 Sam. 15:29), it is precisely where the text seeks to guard him against accusations of human-like fickleness or instability. As Chris Wright says of Moses' exchange with God, 'The paradox is that in appealing to God to change, he was actually appealing to God to be consistent – which may be a significant clue to the dynamic of all genuine intercessory prayer'.[9] Wright goes on to suggest that:

> Moses was not so much arguing *against* God ... as participating in an argument within God ... Such prayer not only participates in the pain of God in history but is actually invited to do so for God's sake as well as ours. This is a measure of the infinite value to God of commitment to persons in covenant relationship. God chooses in sovereign freedom to link that divine sovereign freedom to human prayer. Intercessory prayer, then, as a divine-human engagement, is not merely a human duty to be fulfilled as part of the mission of the people of God, but ultimately flows from and into God's own mission in the created world (cf. Rom. 8:18–27).[10]

God's responsive 'repentance' – dare we conclude – is tactical: his non-negotiable *un*repentance is strategic. God's profound emotional investment in this story is undeniable. In one of the high points of Old Testament revelation, God says through Hosea, 'How can I give you up, Ephraim? How can I hand you over, Israel? How can I treat you like Admah? How can I make you like Zeboiim?' (Hos. 11:8). The prophet makes us a party to God's own self-questioning and emotional turmoil. God evokes the memory of the cities of the plain destroyed with Sodom and Gomorrah. It is as if God is remembering what was done there in face of Abraham's pleading and wonders whether he can go through it again with his own people. 'My heart is changed within me; all my compassion is aroused. I will not carry out my fierce anger nor will I turn and devastate Ephraim' (Hos. 11:9). Evidently God is moved to make a new decision. 'For I am God and not man – the Holy One among you. I will not come in wrath' (Hos. 11:9). The pain of Israel is taken into his own heart for since Israel is a nation like no other nation so he will be a God unlike any other god by feeling Israel's pain in this way.

The Wisdom of the Cross

This divine hiddenness, versatility and vulnerability find their ultimate fulfilment and focus at the cross. Why do the nations rage? It is futile. 'Herod and Pontius Pilate met together with the Gentiles and the people of Israel in this city to conspire against your holy servant Jesus, whom you anointed. They did what your power and will had decided beforehand should happen' (Acts 4:27–28). Nothing, it seems, lies outside the tactical genius of this sovereign, free and flexible God; nothing, it seems, can in the end deter this God from his covenant faithfulness and love that will not let us go.

The deep hidden wisdom of God surfaces at the cross; it is 'the hiding place of God's power', where that strength, paradoxically, is made perfect in weakness:

> Jews demand miraculous signs and Greeks look for wisdom, but we preach Christ crucified: a stumbling-block to Jews and foolishness to Gentiles, but to those whom God has called, both Jews and Greeks, Christ the power of God and the wisdom of God. For the foolishness of God is wiser than man's wisdom, and the weakness of God is stronger than man's strength (1 Cor. 1:22–25).

As a result, Paul asserts:

> We do, however, speak a message of God's wisdom among
> the mature, but not the wisdom of this age or of the rulers of
> this age, who are coming to nothing. No, we speak of God's
> secret wisdom, a wisdom that has been hidden and that God
> destined for our glory before time began. None of the rulers
> of this age understood this, for if they had, they would not
> have crucified the Lord of glory (1 Cor. 2:6–8).

There is no deeper wisdom in God, no more profound
strategy, than the cross. But the Spirit has, through the
gospel, revealed this secret strategy of God to us. God's
unimagined future, 'prepared for those who love him …
has [been] revealed … to us by his Spirit' (1 Cor. 2:9–10).
As P.T. Forsyth said so memorably: 'We need not demand
happy endings if only we are made to feel the atmosphere
of moral triumph, the presentiment of a grand consummation, and the dawn of an eternal reconciliation'.[11]

The cross and resurrection of Jesus are God's solution
to the world's grave crisis. Here everything is resolved if
not answered. In the cross of my son, God says, we bore
the full weight of the load that crushes you.

> It bowed him into the ground. On the third day he rose with a
> new creation in his hand, and a regenerate world, and all
> things working together for good to love and the holy pur-
> pose of love … God's wisdom, none can trace and his ways
> are past finding out; but his work finds us: and his grace, his
> victory, and his goal become sure … [God] moves in long
> orbits, out of sight and sound but he always arrives.[12]

Here, then, is the story of an odd, angular God; a fierce,
untameable, strangely vulnerable God; a tough loving
and tender-talking, compassionate, unquenchable God

whose redemptive love alone is adequate to the great tragedies of the world. But the God who emerges from his own story, like Jesus, does not emerge unscathed. Can we speak as some do of the 'suffering God' or even – as Luther and Wesley and Moltmann have done – of the 'crucified God'? 'Like Jesus' is perhaps all that can be said. Suffice to say that, as we review God's participation in the story, God is like Jesus and in him is no 'un-Christlikeness' at all. And that is the best that can be said of God.

Notes

[1] The observation was made a century ago by the well-known Free Church preacher and devotional writer, F.B. Meyer.

[2] Willimon & Hauerwas, *Lord, Teach Us*, 63.

[3] David F. Wells, *God in the Wasteland: The Reality of Truth in a World of Fading Dreams*, especially chapter 7 for an interesting discussion of progress, providence and Peretti!

[4] P.T. Forsyth, *Justification of God*, 152.

[5] J. Gerald Jantzen, *Job*, 256–8. See also the discussion in William P. Brown, *Character in Crisis: A Fresh Approach to the Wisdom Literature of the Old Testament*, 10–1; and *Ethos of the Cosmos*, 376. See also Leo G. Perdue, *Wisdom in Creation: The Theology of Wisdom Literature*, 174–5.

[6] This discussion centring around the work of Michel de Certeau as used by Stanley Hauerwas is helpfully summarised by Samuel Wells in *Transforming Fate into Destiny: The Theological Ethics of Stanley Hauerwas*, 114–5.

[7] Walter Brueggemann: 'It is as though Abraham has posed for Yahweh a new question about what kind of god to be ...' See, 'A Shape for Old Testament Theology, 11: Embrace of Pain' in Patrick Miller (ed.), *Old Testament Theology*, 38.

[8] Walter Brueggemann has done some of his most provocative work in this area. See the chapter 'A Shape for Old Testament Theology' noted above and chapters 9–12 of his *Theology of the Old Testament: Testimony, Dispute, Advocacy*. A stimulating collection of essays considering this aspect is Tod Linafelt and Timothy K. Beal (eds.), *God*

in the Fray: A Tribute to Walter Brueggemann. The articles by Terence Fretheim, R.W.L. Moberley, Patrick Miller, and Samuel Balentine are especially helpful.

[9] Wright, *Deuteronomy*, 139.

[10] Ibid., 140.

[11] Forsyth, *Justification of God*, 211.

[12] Ibid., 154, 207.

Make the Story Your Own

'This is your life!'
Acts 13:14–52

The big red leather book is offered to the special guest in front of millions of television viewers with the solemn pronouncement, 'This is your life!' Of course, what we see is a mere glimpse – sometimes moving, sometimes embarrassing – of a person's family and friends, career and good works, successes and achievements. There is rarely a hint of a shadow over the proceedings. It's a highly selective, compressed view of one person's life. Even so, as an exercise, it brings what that individual's life has added up to sharply into focus.

At an evangelistic businessmen's dinner in Oxford, a friend, concluding his gospel message, put me on the spot by inviting me to say a few words. All I could ask the assembled high-flyers and professionals was, 'what is your story? University perhaps, trainee manager or junior doctor, marriage, children, perhaps divorce, promotion, partnership, or private practice, a little golf, a seat on the board perhaps, retirement, more golf ... then what?' Re-working famous words of J.B. Phillips, it could be that 'Your story is too small'.[1] 'Let me invite you to be

part of a bigger story – the redemptive story of God.'
Being part of this story, by faith, is to be saved. Paul is
offering his audience at Psidian Antioch something along
these lines! 'Seeing the world through God's eyes' is to
see the world as the stage for the greatest story ever told;
it is to see history as the unfolding of a great drama in
which 'God is the chief actor'.

For over two hundred years we have been sold a different story in the modern-western world. The script has
been written by philosophers, scientists, and evolutionary thinkers – it is the gospel of scientific materialism. We
have been told that the chief actor in this drama is *human
reason*: nothing can be treated as true that cannot be
proved by reason. Descartes gave this momentum over
two centuries ago with his dictum 'I think, therefore I
am'. We have inherited the critical method legacy, which
has left us doubting everything until nothing seems
certain. We have been taught that science and technology
will fix all our problems and eventually overcome all
obstacles to human development and happiness. But we
who enjoy the fruits of modern science and wonder at
human creativity are not so sure because we have also
lived to see Auschwitz, Chernobyl and AIDS. We were
confidently assured that evolutionary progress would
make the world a better place – there would be a steady
upward march to Utopia – but now we are not so sure.
Marxists preached this as a doctrine of progressive revolution, which has consumed itself and its walls have
tumbled. Capitalists urge us to cast ourselves on the
mercy of all-embracing free market economics, but too
many are finding it unforgiving as the rich get richer at
the expense of the poor.

The experts now tell us we are living in the *postmodern
world*, which sees the collapse of the 'grand narratives',
such as reason and progress, of the Enlightenment.

It is the promise of salvation on humanistic terms that is now being recognised as completely fallacious, and in the ensuing despair the post-modernists are now attacking *all* 'meta-narratives', all beliefs in an overarching meaning, all beliefs rooted in a transcendent order, all values'.[2]

The World's Lost Story

In explaining 'how the world lost its story', Robert Jenson argues that the entire Enlightenment project was self-defeating:

> The experiment has failed. It is, after the fact, obvious that it had to: if there is no universal storyteller, then the universe can have no story line. Neither you nor I, nor all of us together can so shape this world that it can make narrative sense; if God does not invent the world's story, then it has none, then the world has no narrative that is its own. If there is no God, or indeed if there is some other god than the God of the Bible, there is no narratable world'.[3]

Is there no story, no overall plot line that makes sense of anything? Is life merely 'a string of pearls whose thread is broken'? If so, then we are cast back on ourselves, each of us scrambling to write our own little story as best we can. This is the '*me*-generation', the '*now*-generation'.

We perhaps conclude that the only valid story is the story of my family and me; we, therefore, cling to the myth that family life or our children will suffice. However, marriage breakdown and dysfunctional family life raises doubts. In Britain, some eighteen million people reach out for a surrogate family three or more times a week by absorbing themselves in soap operas. Here are characters we can identify with in our struggles, an extended story we can feel part of so that, momentarily at least, we are drawn out of our domestic story into a bigger one. But our favourite characters leave the series (as eventually we all have to do). 'Soaps' go nowhere; they don't develop but merely reflect back to us the muddled and mixed story we have already settled for as our lot in life.

The situation is being made worse by the changing shape of global capitalism, which means that for many work no longer provides meaning to their lives. Richard Sennett, a distinguished sociologist at New York University and the London School of Economics, views such changes as contributing to what he describes as a dangerous 'corrosion of character'. Although successful and affluent, many modern workers lack narrative meaning to their lives because they are subject to the tension and uncertainty of 'short-termism', which may include short-term contracts, flexible working arrangements, project based companies, teamwork and consultancy. For them there is simply nothing 'long-term' anymore. The idea of a career withered on the vine long ago. There is no fabric that can build trust since no one has long-term commitments or loyalties to anything.

No Linear Narrative

To illustrate the point, Sennett recalls an interview he conducted twenty-five years ago with Enrico, an Italian immigrant to New York, who worked as a cleaner in an office block for over twenty years. It was mundane and dreary work but on the basis of its expected continuity, Enrico saved to buy his house, planned for his pension and his old age; he became a settled member of the local Italian community and put his sons through college. Sennett comments that what struck him about Enrico and his generation was how 'linear' time was in their lives: over the years 'he carved out a clear story for himself in which his experience accumulated materially and psychically; his life thus made sense as a *linear narrative*'.[4]

Rico, the elder son, benefited from the college education his father worked to provide him with. Twenty-five years on, when Sennett met him on a plane, Rico had become one of the top five per cent wage earners. However, in fourteen years he had moved his family four times, twice because his wife wanted career moves and once because his own company had been downsized. Although prosperous, he and his wife fear that they were on the edge of losing control of their lives.

Sennett sensed Rico's emotional turmoil. With no real friends, at work or in the neighbourhood through having moved so often, Rico had a special fear for his children's lack of ethical discipline. The message being sent to his family by his work history was: 'don't commit yourself, don't sacrifice, don't trust ...'. Rico wonders how he can instil such virtues in his children when they don't remotely see it modelled in his own life. Sennett comments, 'What is missing between the polar opposites of drifting experience and static assertion is a narrative which could organise his conduct'.[5] His father had one; Rico does not.

Identity Crisis

The loss of narrative meaning can have a profound effect on a person's moral character and personal identity. As Sennett explains, 'Narratives are more than simply chronicles of events; they give shape to the forward movement of time, suggesting reasons why things happen, showing their consequences.'[6]

Alister McGrath tells of hearing a lecture given by a Kiowa Apache Indian on the theme of discovering one's identity through the history of his people. As a small boy, his father took him one day to the home of an elderly Kiowa squaw. All day, she told the boy stories of the Kiowa people. She recounted their origins by the Yellowstone River and how they had migrated south. She spoke of the many hardships they faced – wars with other native Americans, great blizzards on the winter plains. She told of the glories of the Kiowa people – of great buffalo hunts, the taming of wild horses, the skill of the braves as riders. Then he learned of their humiliation at the hands of the white man, how they were forced to move south to Kansas, where they faced starvation and poverty, and finally confinement within a reservation in Oklahoma. The lecturer said that his father collected him before dark: 'When I left that house I was a Kiowa' – now he knew the story of his people, now he knew who he was, a Kiowa not just in name but also in reality.[7]

When the red book, which says, 'This is your life!', is handed to you, what will it add up to? What story will it tell? This, I believe, is where the approach we have taken to the Bible is so relevant. John Goldingay sums it up well:

It is not by chance that the bulk of scripture is narrative. This characteristic corresponds to the nature of the Christian faith. The fundamental Christian message is not an ethic, such as the challenge to humanity to live by the law of love, a challenge Christianity shares with some other religions. Nor is it a theology, a collection of abstract statements such as 'God is love' – statements that it also shares with some other religions. It is a gospel, an account of something God has done, a concrete narrative statement: 'God so loved that he gave ...'.[8]

Story-making Bias

One reason why a narrative account of what God has done is such good news for us is that we have a built-in bias towards story making, to constructing a story of our lives. But left to our own devices, we shrink the dimensions of the stage we play on and domesticate the drama. The psalmist confessed his awe at being 'fearfully and wonderfully made' but admitted that self-knowledge was 'too wonderful for me, too lofty to attain' (Ps. 139:6, 14). We are too much of a mystery to ourselves to be confident about scripting our own lives. We don't know our own characters well enough to compose a meaningful life-story that isn't fantasy on the one hand or cynicism on the other.

Through sin we have 'lost the plot'. We no longer know where we fit in, why we have entered, how we leave or, indeed, what the whole shooting match is about! How can we make it up? We have stepped on stage in the middle of the human story, so we settle for lesser stories to star in and become absorbed in sport, business, career, sex, rock music or family. Our lives are caught up in what has been called a 'tournament of narratives'. We adopt all kinds of roles and personas in the stories offered us because our hearts long for that larger story that lifts us above ourselves and fulfils us, which dwarf us without diminishing us and eclipses yet includes us. Of course, even this has its dangers and might lead us into the wrong story, selling our soul to the Führer or dying on stage in Jamestown or Waco.

Albert Speer was a man who 'sold his soul to the Führer'. Flattered originally by Hitler's lavish praise of his architectural prowess, Speer was, from 1942, in charge of all war-production and the second most powerful man in Nazi Germany. He claimed to have tried to remain aloof from the horror going on around him and did not know about the fate of the Jews. Gitta Sereny's brilliant life of Speer, over two decades in research and based on countless interviews with the man, reads like a tense, psychological thriller as she relentlessly pursues the post-war question of how much Speer knew and whether he was guilty.[9] Sentenced to twenty-years imprisonment at the Nuremburg War Crimes Trials, Speer was incarcerated in Spandau Prison. There he attended the first service led by George Casalis, the new, young Protestant Chaplain to the prison. After the service, Speer said to Casalis: 'What I want to ask you is, would you help me become a different man?'[10] Stanley Hauerwas, commenting on Speer's career as a test case in self-deception, argues, 'His self-deception began when he assumed that "being above all an architect" was a story sufficient to constitute his self'. Speer's story was evidently too small to sustain the crisis of his times. Hauerwas observes that Speer 'had to experience the solitude of prison to realise that becoming a human being requires stories and images a good deal richer than professional ones, if we are to be equipped to deal with the powers of the world'.[11]

For most of us, in less dramatic contexts, it is often only when tragedy strikes or when we fall in love, that we sense a bigger scale to our lives. We often rise to nobler proportions and achieve temporary transcendence in these circumstances. Christians sadly offer cheap grace at this point. All too frequently, truth is packaged as a static body of beliefs that we are meant to accept, possess or, worse, defend. Yet truth is a call and promise that incites risk, daring obedience and faithfulness as we embark on a journey of further discovery with God. So many of the 'principles', 'keys', or 'steps' of our Christian training programmes seem designed to enable us to fix the status-quo, to manage life rather than live it, to hunker for survival rather than leave and let go for a great adventure. So, forgetting Abraham, we cling to our household gods and freeze on the threshold of a larger world reluctant to relinquish them.

So the big question hangs in the air: Is there a bigger, better story that will show us who we are and make us different people? Paul says 'Yes, there is' and proceeds to tell it at Antioch (Acts 13:14–52). From Luke's account of Paul's preaching, we learn again that this 'bigger, better, story' is told in the Bible and it is God's story.

In this story, *the chief actor is God himself!* Paul puts heavy emphasis on God's activity – *God* chose our fathers; *he* made the people prosper in Egypt: *he* led them out; *he* endured for forty years; *he* overthrew seven nations; *he* conquered Canaan; *he* gave them judges; *he* installed and removed Saul; *he* raised up king David, ' a man after his own heart'; *he* brought to Israel from this man's descendants a Saviour (Acts 13:16–23).

The Climax of this Story is the Story of Jesus (Acts 13:26–37)

This is not the end of the story for it is still going on but it is the climax of the earlier stage of the story of God's covenant relationship and saving activity with his people Israel (Acts 13:23). As Goldingay puts it:

> To understand the Christ event we must see it as the climax to a story that reaches back into pre-Christian times, the story of the relationship between the God and Father of our Lord Jesus Christ and the Israelite people, whom that God chose as a means of fulfilling a purpose for the world as a whole.[12]

Paul employs the idea of 'fulfilment' three times (Acts 13:27, 29, 33). As we have seen elsewhere, 'to fulfil' is 'to bring something to its intended goal' (i.e. to complete, or to fill-*full* with meaning). The gospel Paul proclaims is the fulfilment of *a plan, in a person, of the promise of God*.[13]

1. The gospel is the fulfilment of a plan (Acts 13:26–27)

Of all people, the 'sons of Abraham' should have known about this since it can be traced back to him, their patriarch. God's ground plan – the plot of the big story – is, as we have seen, to bring blessing to the whole world through one family, one nation and its king. The deep irony is that the religious leaders in Jerusalem unwittingly fulfilled this previously stated plan of God by condemning Jesus. Mysteriously, there is a hint that even the failure of Israel seems to have been accommodated in God's plan from the beginning'. Clearly this is not *plan-B* because it has always been *plan-A*!

2. This plan was fulfilled in a person (Acts 13:29)

Fulfilling 'all that was written about him' is how Paul argues for it; this echoes the way in which Luke tells us that Jesus had explained the Scriptures to the Emmaus two (Lk. 24). Jesus is the pivotal character in this saving narrative. The whole story turns on the dramatic events of his death on the cross and his resurrection from the dead – viewed by Paul as a mighty creative act of God (Acts 13:30).

3. The fulfilment of a promise (Acts 13:32)

Paul sums up the gospel as the 'good news of the promise' made to our fathers, Abraham, Isaac and Jacob and especially to David. He recalls God's promise to David (2 Sam. 7:14) of a throne, a dynasty, a kingdom that will last forever and, above all, of a special father-son relationship with God. This is spelt out further in Psalms 2 and 16, and Isaiah 55. It was not David who fulfilled God's dreams – he's dead and buried – it was Jesus who died but is now alive and ruling.

Paul then presses home his case, issuing a challenge and an invitation. It is, he urges, through this person that you can be written into the story of salvation. *The challenge is the offer of being part of a bigger, better, story*! We are challenged to join God's big story, to be drawn into what he has been doing, is doing and will do in human history and on this earth! Why stay in amateur dramatics in the school hall when we are called to come to Broadway or the West End! We are being offered freedom from the failures and delusions of our own self-made stories. As Hauerwas says:

> A true story could only be one powerful enough to check the endemic tendency toward self-deception – a tendency which inadequate stories cannot help but foster. Correlatively, if the true God were to provide us with a saving story, it would have to be one that we found continually discomforting. For it would be a saving story only as it empowered us to combat the inertial drift into self-deception.[14]

This is just what the gospel story achieves in its call to ruthless repentance and radical faith. 'Forgiveness of sins' is now offered through Jesus Christ who bore them on his cross. God's forgiveness invites you to trade in the old, dog-eared, much corrected, self-approved script of your own life for the brand new, true story whose personal chapters he'll help you write! As the whole story confirms, but contrary to false rumours, 'God is not interested so much in controlling people as in giving them freedom.'[15] Scripture, especially as encapsulated in the gospel, has given us, in William Willimon's words, 'a new story, a new narrative account of the way the world was put together, a new direction for history, new purposes for being on earth'. In the early church, Willimon adds, 'to be a Christian was to be someone who had been initiated by baptism into this alternative story of the world'.[16]

Joining the Cast

The invitation is to join the cast of those who live out this story (Acts 13:39–52). Come and join the casts of thousands who are repentantly, enthusiastically, sometimes blunderingly, but always hopefully, learning their parts in this greatest story ever told! In this gospel 'everyone who believes' joins the community of faith (Acts 13:39). Whatever your family heritage, or national history, faith makes this story your story! And you join the worldwide family of faith. This, says Paul, is what it means to be *justified*. He is test-driving what will become his characteristic term. Justification is linked linguistically and theologically to the concept of righteousness especially, as it appears in the Old Testament. God is righteous because he fulfils his obligations of covenant. In the Old Testament a righteous person is someone within the covenant family of God. God justifies when he acts to restore people to membership of the covenant – to 're-righteous' them! Justification by faith means that by faith in Jesus we are declared to be in full, bona fide membership of the family of God.

Paul makes it clear that this is never a 'bed of roses', because 'scoffers' will mock, thinking it is too good to be true (Acts 13:41). Some will feel so strongly about this they will make life difficult for us by stirring up 'persecution' and talking 'abusively' (Acts 13:45, 50). But there will be others who, hearing this story, find they are enthralled and can't wait to hear more (Acts 13:42). The newly recruited actors who believe in the story enjoy the undeserved 'grace' of God (Acts 13:43c), buzz with the vitality of life which has an 'eternal' quality to it (Acts 13:48), and share exuberantly in the wild divine energy that has been let loose in the world as they are 'filled with joy and with the Holy Spirit'. These disciples relish the fact that the story is an ongoing story and that the cast list grows by the day (Acts 13:48). The challenge and the invitation is to discover your place in God's strategic plan and redemptive story.

1. What is your place in Noah's story?

As part of the new creation 'in Christ', you are called to keep your feet firmly on this old ground, respecting the earth but travelling through it as a pilgrim, walking keenly towards the future new heavens and new earth 'all landscaped with righteousness' (2 Pet. 3:13, *The Message*).

2. Where are you in Abraham's adventure?

Following in the footsteps of faith, you are challenged to live counter-culturally, not wedded to the society man is building but to the city God is building, living daringly by faith not sight, confident in trusting Jesus 'the seed of Abraham' and serving his mission to bring blessing to an accursed world.

3. Where are you in Israel's vocation?

By grace grafted on to the stock of the Old Testament
people of God, revering your Jewish roots but living free
from the burden of Torah, you are enabled to keep covenant with God through the death of Christ and the
indwelling power of the Holy Spirit as members of a
'chosen race, and royal priesthood' called to praise before
the world the God who has brought you out of darkness
into his marvellous light.

4. Where are you in David's destiny?

By redemptive transfer from the kingdom of darkness
you now find yourself in the Messiah's kingdom and
community, confessing Jesus as Lord of the world, learning with others how to be 'kings and priests' unto God for
the sake of the world.

5. Where are you in the prophetic hope?

Enjoying the blessing of the new covenant in Christ's
blood, you relish being forgiven, your heart responsive to
God, his will your growing delight, his Spirit within you
as God's empowering presence, among the new people
who serve one another as the true temple of the living
God.

6. Where are you, above all, in the Jesus story?

This for all of us is the first and crucial question. Will I
repent and embrace him as the master-story of my life?
Will I be his disciple? Am I a follower of Jesus Christ? No
one is ever too old to start on a fresh stage of the journey.
David and Jeremiah were mere striplings when God

claimed them. But Abraham and Moses were long past their supposed 'sell-by' date when they made their debuts in God's story. When John Stott's much used primer on becoming a Christian, *Basic Christianity*, was re-issued in a revised edition in 1971, he received a letter from Leslie Weatherhead, a retired doyen of Methodist preachers of a previous generation.

> Dear John,
> Thank you for writing *Basic Christianity*. It led me to make a new commitment of my life to Christ. I am old now – nearly 78 – but not too old to make a new beginning. I rejoice in all the grand work you are doing.
> Yours sincerely,
> Leslie Weatherhead.[17]

No two men came from more opposite theological poles than the refined but robustly evangelical Stott and the romantically liberal Weatherhead. But, evidently, even opposites are attracted to Jesus. 'Jesus doesn't just tell stories,' says Buechner, 'He himself is a story. Only Jesus himself is the truth, the whole story of Him'.[18] And as one of the Wise Men reflects, after visiting Bethlehem, in another of Buechner's pieces:

> What we saw on the face of the new-born child was his death. And we saw, as sure as the earth beneath our feet, that to stay with him would be to share that death.
> Is the truth beyond all truth, beyond the stars, just this: to live without him is the real death, to die with him is the only life?[19]

When the red book that says 'This is your life!' is handed over, what will it add up to? What story – or better – *whose* story, will it tell? As Stanley Hauerwas has so often reminded us, 'To be redeemed is nothing less than to learn to place ourselves in God's history'.[20] He was pre-empted along the way by St. Columba: 'Since all the world is but a story, it were well for thee to buy the more enduring story, rather than the story that is less enduring'.

Notes

1. J.B. Phillips, *Your God is too Small*.
2. Wells, *God in the Wasteland*, 47.
3. Robert Jenson, 'How the world lost its story', *First Things* 36 (1993), 3.
4. Richard Sennett, *The Corrosion of Character: The Personal Consequences of Work in the New Capitalism*, 16.
5. Ibid., 30.
6. Ibid.
7. Alister E. McGrath, *Evangelicalism and the Future of Christianity*, 10.
8. John Goldingay, *Models for Scripture*, 23.
9. Gitta Sereny, *Albert Speer: His Battle with Truth*.
10. Ibid., 23.
11. Hauerwas, *Truthfulness and Tragedy*, 93.
12. J. Goldingay, *Models for Scripture*, 48.
13. For a helpful analysis of the Plan of God theme in Luke-Acts see John T. Squires 'The Plan of God' and Darrell Bock, 'Scripture and the Realisation of God's Promises' in Howard Marshall and David Peterson (eds.), *Witness to the Gospel: The Theology of Acts*.
14. Hauerwas, *Truthfulness and Tragedy*, 95.
15. Goldingay, *Models for Scripture*, 93.
16. William H. Willimon, *Shaped by the Bible*, 21.
17. Timothy Dudley-Smith, *John Stott: The Making of a Leader*, 457.
18. Frederick Buechner, *The Clown in the Belfry: Writings on Faith and Fiction*, 135–6.
19. Frederick Buechner, *The Magnificent Defeat*, 70–1.
20. Hauerwas, *Peaceable Kingdom*, 33.

13

Made Famous by the Story

What makes life worth living?
Hebrews 11

At a critical point in Tolkien's saga, *The Lord of the Rings*, the two hobbits, Frodo and Sam wonder what sort of tale they've gotten into, and whether they will ever be celebrated in song as famous people.

Well it's a point worth pondering. What sort of tale do all of *us* find ourselves in? Do the big important plans include us or pass us by? Will *we* ever feature in songs or saga or be famous for anything? Is there an ongoing story to be part of which makes life worth living, beyond happiness, grief, work, rest and sleep?

As we face the uncertainties and challenges of a new millennium we need someone to offer us a good, big reason for living. In the future, said the American artist, Andy Warhol, from his 1960s vantage point, everyone will be 'famous for fifteen minutes'. Warhol became famous for having said it! Nowadays, given the camera's capacity for instant celebrities, we might have to add, 'famous … as long as it's on TV'. This dignifies few people, but it is better, it seems, to have loved and lost dignity on a voyeuristic chat show than never to have been on TV at all! Michael Caine, himself a famous British export to Hollywood, explained to talk show host, Michael Parkinson, the difference between a great movie *star* and a great movie *actor*. The movie star says: 'how can I change the script of the story to fit my personality?' The great movie actor says: 'how can I change myself to fit the script and the story line?'

Hebrews 11 is often called the 'heroes of faith' chapter. This gallery of biblical celebrities are striking because they were, for the most part, obscure, sometimes nameless people, who lived in out-of-the-way places, far from the madding media crowd of the modern era. They were immortalised by the drama they were part of. They were *made famous by the story*. So bold and memorable was their faith that we can, in fact, find Hebrews 11 very intimidating. But it's worth noting that the writer starts with his readers themselves as he adduces evidence of vigorous faith and not with the Old Testament heroes: 'Remember those earlier days after you had received the light, when you stood your ground in a great contest in the face of suffering' (Heb. 10:32).

The Jewish Christians, to whom Hebrews is addressed, were living through disturbing times. A long way from the action in Israel, increasingly aware of the impending disaster about to strike Jerusalem and suffering harassment and social pressure for their faith in Jesus the Messiah, they had much to be disturbed about. Their old securities were being swept away as the pagan Romans threatened much of their Jewish heritage with extinction. That was their long-range anxiety. Nearer to home was more uncertainty. Situated at the centre of the Roman Empire, they were threatened with persecution for their newfound faith. Every foundation outside of Christ was being shaken. Not a moment too soon, this great pastoral writer offers them his word of exhortation and encouragement (Heb. 13:22) by reminding them (and us) of what gave deep and lasting significance to their lives, which is being an active participant in the ongoing story of faith.

It is a note we need struck for us – even if we are at a lower level of crisis than the original readers. No one wants to put any present state of uncertainty on a par with the painful pressure of those first-century Jewish Christian believers in Rome. They lost their homes and property by violent expulsion and expropriation; they weren't worrying about the mortgage interest rate going up! Gracefully accepting a modest rise in interest rates comes just a tiny bit lower on the scale of emotional challenge than 'joyfully accepting the confiscation of your property' at the hands of the ruthless pagan powers.

After all, as has been said, it is the call of God to join him on a journey of faith as partners in the outworking of his amazing salvation purposes in the earth that gives our lives eternal significance and not our roots in plant, property or possessions. This is the note the writer strikes: don't automatically assume that you are not in the same league as the heroes; you *are* in the same story; you are in the same arena (Heb. 12:1). Their witness is meant to inspire and not intimidate you.

Future Grace

Hebrews is a special re-reading of the Old Testament story of Israel. The writer could have highlighted the long catalogue of unbelief – as he did in Hebrews 4 – but in Hebrews 11 he focuses on the gripping examples of radical obedience, passionate trust, daring risk-taking and tough endurance that is also true of the same story.

So what, briefly, are we being reminded of? The writer is pressing his readers to exercise what John Piper has called 'faith in future grace' that is 'essentially a future-orientated assurance of things hoped-for' (Heb. 11:1).[1] Faith is not simply fuelled by gratitude for past mercies. Gratitude is good and natural but even the godless can be grateful. The faith talked about here, reaches forward for the power of God because we trust him to keep his word and promises.

You can believe in future grace

Without knowing where you're going (Heb. 11:8)
We walk as children of the light but sometimes in the dark; we walk by faith not sight. It was in the deep and dreadful darkness of a God-induced trance-like sleep that Abraham received a prophetic vision of the troubled centuries ahead. He lived in the Promised Land as if he was a stranger in it, feeling rootless and unsettled and incomplete.

He erected his tents every night – often, no doubt, blowing hard and sighing: 'here we go again; is nothing permanent?' His faith was stretched – as ours is – by living in 'transition'.

Without knowing how (Heb. 11:11–12)
Abraham and Sarah confronted the reality of their own bodies and faced the impossible but from what was considered 'as good as dead' new life sprung! The seed grows, said Jesus, secretly, and even the experienced farmer cannot tell you how it happens! (Mk. 4:27 – 'though he does not know how'). That's what this kingdom is like.

'Without not knowing how' merges into 'without knowing why?' (Heb. 11:17–19)

Why sacrifice Isaac the child of promise on whom the whole promise-plan hinged? It doesn't make sense! Did Abraham wonder how on earth he would return with Isaac after sacrificing him, because believe this he certainly did! The writer to the Hebrews perceptively construes it as Abraham's faith in a God who can raise the dead. This God defies the odds, surmounts the arguments and does wonders to faith.

You can enjoy 'faith in future grace'

Without knowing 'when' (Heb. 11:13)

Abraham's faith was stretched to breaking point while waiting for Isaac to come. Even though Isaac materialised, the city never did! These all died in faith (Heb. 11:13). What an epitaph! They did not die disillusioned, embittered or nostalgic for past glories. Faith is not motivated by short-term goals or fixed on short-term gains. Faith looks beyond the visible, immediate and known. It creates waves beyond its own life span and influences the future (Heb. 11:20). As Max Warren said of the great missionary heroes of faith, 'they were buried beside the road'. When the British climbers, George Mallory and Andrew Irvine died in 1924 during their assault on Everest, the cryptic message was passed on to the world from base camp, 'Last seen, still climbing'. Oswald Chambers observed: 'Faith is faith in God when he is inscrutable and apparently contradictory in his purposes'. The temptation is always to elevate principles or dogma or techniques above a relationship with the living God and so to lay down rigidly what can, and, cannot happen. If Abraham had been a slave to his own logical consistency he might have refused to hear the angel's veto on the killing of Isaac – perhaps rejecting it as wishful thinking – in which case Isaac would have died right there and then. But fanaticism is never faith – Abraham knew God better than that. It was George Muller who said, 'Save me from tradition; save me from inherited ideas and prejudices; above all save me from pride in my own consistency'.

Of course, none of this works unless faith experiences, first-hand, the trustworthiness of God. Genuine faith believes in God as the active responder to the appetite for him, which he has already put in our hearts (Heb. 11:6) and not as a vague backdrop to life. God is a rewarder, not a refuser, not a God who has 'off days' or gets moody and capricious. This is no lottery. God makes and keeps covenants. Sarah famously proved God 'faithful' (Heb. 11:11b). True faith-people are God-orientated, God-obsessed, passionate pleasers of him – for whom even the fulfilment of our legitimate needs is good only because it pleases him to do so. This leaves the current self-absorption of much popular Christianity stone cold dead! As Heschel said: 'Abraham was not going to sacrifice his only son in order to satisfy his personal need.'[2]

Big Reasons

In Bill Hull's words, 'people need big reasons'.[3] You certainly need a big reason to do what is celebrated here. You need a 'big reason' to build an ark in a drought, to leave your own homeland at retirement age for a perilous adventure, to facedown a ruthless totalitarian dictator, to accept torture and martyrdom. That 'big reason' is nothing less than the one creator God, and his glorious plan to reclaim planet earth. This is the 'big reason' that makes these people throb with energy, hope, resilience and sacrificial love. Our story of faith is the same as theirs: astonishingly, without us they are not part of a complete story (Heb. 11:40).

P.T. Forsyth once observed that, in the end, we are required to answer not for our failures and mistakes so much as for our whole life's commitment. The final question, he said, would *not* be:

> How many are your sins and how many your sacrifices? But on which side have you stood and striven, under which king have you served or died – what is your home to which your heart returns either in repentance or in joy? Where is your heart? What is the bent of your will on the whole, the direction and service of your total life?[4]

Despising the Shame

So what is the true tale you and I have fallen into? Every disciple of Jesus has 'fallen into a story' in which 'disgrace' and 'shame' are fodder for the fire of his cross. David deSilva has helpfully researched the social stigmas of ancient middle-eastern honour-shame cultures. He writes:

> Shame is more than the experience of being dishonoured: it signifies the sensitivity toward public opinion that moves people to do certain things that will be approved by the majority and to shrink from doing the things that will be censured by the majority.[5]

Abraham bore the reproach of being an immigrant stranger for the prospect of a better country. Moses suffered disgrace in solidarity with an enslaved people with his eye on a greater reward than Egypt had to offer.

Supremely, Jesus despised the shame of being crucified as a discredited messianic pretender for the joy set before him of accomplishing his Father's plan.

In deSilva's insightful words,

> Jesus, Abraham and Moses made correct choices because they weighed honor and advantage through the eyes of faith – in the eyes of unbelievers, all three during their lifetimes would have been considered to have made foolish choices, incurring the loss of honor. Disregarding the opinions of outsiders (the world) is thus presented as a necessary step to achieving honor where it counts eternally.[6]

Faith that is this radically *counter-cultural* goes against every grain. We want to be able to control our own destiny, to manage our own lives; we do not feel at all comfortable 'not knowing where we're going'. We want to reduce everything to rational explanation and understand all mysteries with intellectual power; our pride is hurt by the realisation that we don't know 'how'. We plan our schedules and dictate our diaries, and we don't know when it's all going to come good. We feel insecure when it is suggested that Jesus did not have a plan for his life. We find it discomfiting to learn that he worshipped so little at the altar of public opinion and took no heed of special interest groups. Keeping up with the Joneses comes more naturally than keeping pace with Jesus. It is ironic that in an age of vaunted individual independence, our common inclination, even as believers, is still to be liked, to conform to social expectations, to succumb to peer pressure, to be culturally 'in-step'. Os Guinness keeps the Church alert to these issues better than anyone. In his splendid book *The Call*, Guinness commends 'holy folly' as a counter-cultural stance:

On every side we see Christians pursuing the rage for relevance, whether seeking the respect of the 'cultured despisers' of the gospel, reaching out to the contemporary 'unchurched' with a 'user-friendly gospel', or just enjoying the comforts of the age. Against all such attempts, the holy fools stand as a weeping roadblock.[7]

Hair shirts are optional but such wisdom is not.

1. No wonder Noah condemned the world by faith!

Noah's foolish obedience was a standing contradiction to a culture taken up with eating, drinking and family-making; his contemporaries not in the least bit concerned with saving anything up for what turned out to be an exceptionally rainy day!

2. Scandalous Abraham

It is not surprising that *Abraham's actions were a scandal*. He left a 'hole of bafflement' in Babylonian high society, jettisoning an honoured status for the wandering humiliation of a foreigner and 'resident alien' in a strange land.

3. Moses' choices too are socially provocative

Moses prefers partnership in suffering with God's people to the usual hedonistic life-style of pleasure and entertainment, opting for disgrace in the will of God which he regards as a better bet than all the accumulated wealth and wisdom, kudos and perks of a high-flying career in the Egyptian diplomatic service. This brand of faith reaches beyond the kitsch glitter of contemporary culture to a more abiding city (Heb. 11:10), an alternative homeland (Heb. 11:14), a better country (Heb. 11:16), a more

lasting reward, more solid joys, more lasting treasure
(Heb. 11:26), and, ultimately, to a better resurrection
(Heb. 11:35) in an unshakable kingdom. No wonder the
writer says: *'the world was not worthy of such believers'*
(Heb. 11:38). The world doesn't deserve them! How could
it? They inhabited the margins of official recognition and
made their 'way as best they could on the cruel edges of
the world' (Heb. 11:38, *The Message*). The world has no
standard of measurement than can assess such people's
true worth; they go right off the top of the scale.

This is because what matters, above all, is God's
assessment that he 'is not ashamed to be called their God'
(Heb. 11:16b). We may not know where, how or even why
or when, but we know 'who'. He dazzles us, we seek; he
leads, we follow; he challenges, we obey; he dares, we
risk; he invests all in us, we stake all on him, he calls we
answer. It is enough to keep us moving. Our review of the
story of how God deals with his followers confirms the
view of Calvin Miller:

> We keep on serving the call, even when we wonder if our
> partnership with God has been canceled. As we go on being
> faithful, we find that the call sooner or later wakes our sleep-
> ing adoration once again. We are soon back at home in the
> depths of our union with Christ. Tough times don't last for
> long, but tough saints go on forever. The calling gets us
> through the tough times. We serve because we feel called,
> and then we serve because we don't. It is not as though we
> fake it till we make it. We *take* it till we make it.[8]

Incomplete Perfection

To live this faith enables us to live with incompleteness.
'Lives relevant to God' – as Oswald Chambers used to say

– 'are open-ended and incomplete'. It is what he calls an 'incompleteness perfection'. The life of faith is as open-roofed as heaven and as open-ended as eternity, but there is nothing more certain and assured as faith's foundation. We didn't start this story and we aren't expected to finish it. Only one person has ever been able to say with total sincerity, 'I have accomplished all that you gave me to do'. Only one person could say in dying, 'It is totally finished'. But then, of course, he is the author and finisher of your faith and mine.

Jesus eschewed fame for his Father's favour. His moods were not dictated by his standing in the opinions of the experts, or by his popularity with the crowds. Nor were his movements determined by the spurious glories that cultural conformity might have offered him. He absorbed the mockery of those who disparaged him for associating with the poor and being 'a friend of sinners'. He endured opposition in ministry, despising the shame of being misunderstood and refused to allow the false expectations of his friends or the false allegations of his enemies to define who he was. He endured a shameful and degrading death on a cross and perfected his own faithfulness. By his faithful persistence, he brought to a climax the long beginning and will bring to consummation the sure end of God's strategic plan in which we are privileged to participate. To discover your place in this plan is what constitutes salvation.

No one is guaranteed celebrity status or flickering TV fame by taking part. There is only the lasting memorial of being made famous by the story that is eternal life. Time would fail me to tell of the countless and nameless believers who chose not to bend the story line to suit their own egos, but allowed themselves to be shaped by the script. Every one of them is a true 'hero of faith' – except they don't know it. They think, and with one voice, acclaim that God is the chief actor and the Messiah Jesus, the real star of the story. A passion for God's story is a passion for God's glory.

Notes

[1] John Piper, *Future Grace*, 13.
[2] Abraham Heschel, *Man Is Not Alone: A Philosophy of Religion*, 233.
[3] Bill Hull, *Building High Commitment in a Low Commitment World*, chapter 7.
[4] P.T. Forsyth, 'Christian Perfection' in *God the Holy Father*, 110.
[5] David A. DeSilva, *Perseverance and Gratitude: A Socio-Rhetorical Commentary on the Epistle to the Hebrews*, 433.
[6] David A. DeSilva, *Honor, Patronage, Kinship & Purity*, 65. See also *The Hope of Glory: Honor Discourse and New Testament Interpretation*, chapter 6, where DeSilva treats the letter to the Hebrews.
[7] Os Guinness, *The Call: Finding and Fulfilling the Central Purpose of Your Life*, 221.
[8] Calvin Miller, *Into the Depths of God*, 140.

14

Model the Future of the Story

Living in the end of the beginning
Mark 9:1–32

At first glance, Mark's account of the transfiguration of Jesus looks like a commercial for a new brand of glory-religion! From a sweeping aerial view of the landscape, the camera zooms in on a mountain and the dazzling white light that irradiates the central figure who has gone there with three friends. Cut into the film, suddenly, are two spiritual giants from a previous generation. Fame by association is the key to advertising. Associate the product being promoted with illustrious and popular people – that makes sense. Then a cloud envelops them like dry-ice at a rock concert! The voice-over – whom we discover is God – endorses the central figure in the scene as his 'son' and urges us strongly to give him our exclusive attention. Fade the cloud and, in the penultimate shot, this 'son' is left in splendid and unnerving isolation in a close up which fills the screen!

Since visiting Olympia, London's premier exhibition centre, to see the latest in television equipment and communications wizardry, I can understand a little better how technically this might be achieved. The word 'digital' was everywhere. Sharp minds were agonising eagerly over the feeding of the five thousand channels we will soon have access to. The multi-national companies with their omnipresent brand names displayed their wares and let me play with their fancy new gadgets! With one touch I could delicately manoeuvre a camera at the end of a thirty-foot boom. Adjust a small lever and I could turn the famous red of a Ferrari into green half way through a Formula One motor race by superimposing one image on another to dazzling effect. No self-respecting, computer-wise, ten-year-old would have raised an eyebrow at all this, but at my age I felt a little as George Bernard Shaw did when he visited Soviet Russia in the 1930s and said, 'I have seen the future and it works'.

So does the transfiguration scene amount to a commercial for some hyped-up, triumphalist, self-promoting 'glory-religion'? It would do, if the narrative had stopped there, but our editor, John Mark, has too much integrity for that and lets the 'film' run on. Before we know where we are – as the camera pans down the mountain – we are back in an all-too-familiar world. We recognise the world as we know it. Here we meet confused crowds, argumentative religious types, hand-wringing do-gooders, puzzled sceptics, muddled half-believers, out-of-control children and desperate parents. In short, as if in a mirror, we confront a society deranged by a demonic virus, a frightened and wounded world. What sense can be made of this sequence of scenes?

We can begin to make sense of this jarring conjunction of images by seeking to unravel the stories the editor has superimposed on one another. Of course, at one level this is the *story of Jesus.* The transfiguration narrative typically encapsulates his unique career. From the heights of unimaginable glory, dwelling in unapproachable light, he descends into the deep valleys of our world's harshest realities. He comes 'down to earth' to meet us head-on. He steps down to distract us from our futile debates, to overcome evil in heart-to-heart combat, to carry our sins up another hill, down into death, and out the other side of death into resurrection glory, so raising our hopes to life.

Eclipsed and Upstaged

Jesus' story, as we have repeatedly seen, is inextricably joined to the *story of Israel*. Why else would Moses and Elijah feature so prominently at the transfiguration of Jesus? Both are key characters in the story told in the Old Testament of Israel as God's people, chosen to bring the light of salvation to a world darkened by sin and despair. We don't know what facts Mark had at his disposal. If he knew more than he tells, then his editorial decisions are perhaps unkind to the two Old Testament figures at this point. He edits their sparkling conversation with Jesus – Luke tells us only that they talked about his 'exodus' – and leaves in Peter's understandable but fatuous sound-bite about wanting to stay and build a sanctuary on the spot.

More noteworthy is the recollection of Israel's covenantal story as having been forged in fire and smoke on the mountaintop of Sinai. This burning and holy glory of God later irradiated the face of Moses when he met God in the Tent of Meeting and finally flooded the completed Tabernacle as a glorious mist. The story that was launched in this way was widely expected to end in a similar way, with the re-appearance of Elijah and the return of the self-same glory cloud. But intertwined now with the Jesus story, this is the story of Israel with a difference, a story radically transfigured.

If we ask what explains the presence of Moses and Elijah, the answer might be that they represent the law and the prophets, respectively, paying homage to Jesus. True though that is, I suspect, in fact, that more is going on here than meets the eye. Both Moses and Elijah had direct encounters with God and experienced theophanies (Ex. 24:15; 34:29; 1 Kgs. 19:11–13); both were charismatic figures. But, above all, Moses and Elijah represent the *beginning* and the *end* of Israel's projected story. Moses was the founder of the nation, the God-appointed mediator of the torah. Elijah, as we have said, was popularly expected to come on to the scene again just before the 'end'. Jesus alludes to this commonly held belief when he provocatively suggests that 'Elijah' has already come to prepare for the 'end' in the person of John the Baptist (Mk. 9:11–13). Moses saw and reflected God's glory so that his face shone, but even Moses in all his glory was not arrayed like this! If Moses is *eclipsed*, Elijah, who inaugurated an era of miracles by defeating the prophets of Baal, is demonstrably *upstaged*.

So Israel's past and future converge on Jesus. Moses never set foot in Canaan during his lifetime. Moses now *steps out of the past* history of Israel and into the Promised Land for the first time. He lives 'inside' the fulfilment of the promise because he stands within the radiance of the Messiah. Elijah departed this life by being taken up into God's heaven without seeing death. Now, Elijah *steps out of the future* of Israel, to talk of Jesus' death on which all hopes are pinned. Moses and Elijah are both eager to discover how Jesus' suffering and death might be a new 'exodus' and a 'new departure', not just for themselves but also for the world (Lk. 9:31).

All ears are now tuned to Jesus to hear the voice of authority: all eyes are turned to Jesus to see the vision of his majesty (Mk. 9:7–8). Israel's story does not derive from Moses or climax in Elijah. Jesus is the real reason for Israel's existence and the true climax of her story. The two-thousand-year saga of Abraham's descendants finds its focus in Jesus. 'Listen to him' as the Father directs and as Moses does; look only to him as Elijah and the disciples find themselves doing. The story of Jesus, which is superimposed on the story of Israel, transforms promise into fulfilment, prophecy into realisation, hopes into reality and word into flesh. What God has already done in Jesus Christ is enough to make us confident of the final outcome.

The Valley of the Shadow of Life

The further good news of the transfiguration of Jesus is the fresh light it throws on the *story of hurting humanity*. Our human story also had a glorious beginning. However, in our sinfulness, we have fallen short of the glory of God and reneged on the glorious destiny of being God's image bearers. So, as Mark's account shows, people are confused, beset by a babble of competing claims, divided by untried opinions, riddled with doubt and scepticism, and, in the end, driven by overwhelming tragedy to their wit's end. But superimpose the story of Jesus onto this story and a strange transfiguration takes place. One sight of the majesty of Jesus and everything looks different. Disciples see him and are 'frightened' (Mk. 9:6); crowds see him and are 'overwhelmed with wonder' (Mk. 9:15); spirits see him and are panicked into 'convulsion' (Mk. 9:20). One word from Jesus winds up all debate, stills the storm of argument and lays bare the attitude of every heart (Mk. 9:14–15).

Just as Moses came down from the glory of Sinai to confront a faithless and perverse people (Ex. 32:15ff.;

Deut. 32:20), so Jesus comes down from his mountain-top glory to expose the deep cultural scepticism of an 'unbelieving generation' (Mk. 9:19). But one word from him opens up the situation to new possibilities with an assurance that 'all things can be done for the one who believes' (Mk. 9:23 NRSV). With one word from this Jesus, demons 'fear and fly', as they are rebuked with crushing authority, and lifeless children are raised to life again (Mk. 9:26–27). Lay *Jesus'* story on the world's sad story and the colours, images and perspective of everything are altered in salvation, but only through pain.

That the Messiah must suffer in order to enter into his glory (Lk.24:26) was the conviction with which this book began as it explored the encounter with Jesus on the Emmaus Road: it is foreshadowed here. The evangelist brackets the glorious manifestation of who Jesus is with his equally emphatic passion predictions (see Mk. 8:31; 9:31). Mark tells us that the disciples 'did not understand' this strange combination of suffering and glory (Mk. 9:32). But one day they would and it would transfigure their lives.

I once heard Jürgen Moltmann, a great theologian of our time, give his testimony to this when he recalled his first visit to Britain as a seventeen-year-old youth. Drafted into Hitler's armies in the last frantic days of the Reich, the teenage Moltmann was captured by the Allies in Belgium and ended up in a Scottish prisoner-of-war camp. Desperate, lonely, and afraid, his state of mind was hardly improved by the guards who showed him newly taken photographs of the recently discovered extermination camps at Auschwitz and Belsen. Moltmann recalled feeling terrifyingly alone, ashamed to be German, repulsed by the thought of going home and wanting only to die. The padre added to the disappointment by offering copies of the New Testament, not cigarettes.

Moltmann, however, took one and began to read. Coming, he said, from a non-church-going family, he read for the first time the story of Jesus' suffering and dying on the cross. Moltmann was gripped especially by Jesus' words of abandonment 'my God, my God why have you forsaken me?' There, at that point, Moltmann confessed, I found that Jesus was my friend.

Moltmann later wrote:

> The gospels do not merely draw the portrait of the miracle-man ... who is in possession of extraordinary powers: they paint the picture of God's messianic plenipotentiary who de-demonises the world, and through the 'powers of the age to come' (Heb. 6:5) makes the world whole and sane and reasonable.[1]

Unscathed World

Mark's narrative tells *our story* too as disciples of Jesus. Disciples are those entrusted with the story, engaged to tell and live it out. Disciples are those privileged with glimpses of glory who are all too often found powerless and usually puzzled. No amount of subtle editing can disguise the church's failures. It often seems paralysed by its own sense of helplessness, lack of understanding and prayerlessness. But if the story of Jesus is superimposed on to that of the disciples then there is hope even for them. In a world out of control, where natural elements like fire and water are sometimes allies of supernatural evil, the deliverance of one deranged boy is a token of that cross where all evil and sin is met and mastered, and the world 'de-demonised'. And the raising to life of one, corpse-like child heralds his resurrection and holds promise of the raising up of a whole new creation in the restoration of all things. In Moltmann's words, 'In the context of the new creation, these "miracles" are not really miracles at all: They are the merely the foretokens of the all-comprehensive salvation, the unscathed world and the glory of God'.[2] The church is called to model the story of that future. 'The church is not the kingdom but the foretaste of the kingdom. For it is in the church that the narrative of God is lived in a way that makes the kingdom visible.'[3]

As was noted at the outset of this book, it is only when the story is over that we really know who God is. When all is said and done, not all is said until all is done. In Gabriel Fackre's words, 'Only when the story is over and the book put down do we know what the writer wants us to know about its characters. Their identity is depicted in their doing, [and is] fully disclosed when the narrative has run its course.'[4] This is not to detract from the assurance that the Bible reliably and normatively reveals who God is, but simply to concede that all our knowledge, especially of God and his ways, is partial. 'Now we see but a poor reflection; then we shall see face to face. Now I know in part; then I shall know fully, even as I am fully known' (1 Cor. 13:12).

However, ' "No eye has seen, no ear has heard, no mind has conceived what God has prepared for those who love him" but God has revealed it to us by his Spirit' (1 Cor. 2:9). Inevitably, we can rarely find words adequate to describe what we have seen and are seldom allowed to do so. They are things so rarefied that we are not permitted to speak of them; some joys so full of unbearable glory as to be unutterable. But then the gift of Jesus is unspeakable even if we had a thousand tongues. Yet, what we have seen and heard in the story of Jesus is enough for us to trust our way to that ultimate unveiling. God's covenant with Noah was his commitment to preserve the old creation – upholding it even in its ambiguity and brokenness – until his redemptive work is fully done. 'Preservation is the work of the triune Providence sustaining the world in its journey to its purposed end'.[5]

Winston Churchill encouraged his nation in 1942 after the Allied Armies had won their first major victory of World War Two by defeating Rommel at El Alamein: 'This is not the end, this is not even the beginning of the end. But this is the end of the beginning'. Now in terms of the big story, we are obviously not at the end. Nor can we know, despite the lurid certainties of brash pop-prophecy pundits, whether we are at the beginning of the end, in the sense of nearing the countdown to the close of the space-time universe. With Jesus we can be content not to know. But we can be sure that we are living in the end of the beginning. If indeed we can say with Irenaeus that 'the glory of God is a human being fully alive' then we have seen God's glory in the face of Jesus Christ.[6] We have 'beheld his glory' blazing out luminously on the mountain, paradoxically from the cross, and triumphantly bursting forth upon our gloomy world in risen and Pentecostal radiance.

When George Bernard Shaw said that he had seen the communist future and it worked, he couldn't have been more wrong. As I marvelled at the technological and digital future on display I assumed it would work, though to what purpose except to show endless re-runs of old movies. But I have 'seen the glory of God in the face of Jesus Christ' and caught there a glimpse of an 'unscathed world' put right by his dying, rising and arrival in glory. I can say with confidence: 'I have seen God's future and it works'. And that's no commercial, that's the news!

Entrusted with this gospel, the church can model God's future in company with the risen Christ. Recalling how Jesus was baptised and transfigured, the apostle Peter assures his readers:

> We did not follow cleverly invented stories when we told you about the power and coming of our Lord Jesus Christ, but we were eye-witnesses of his majesty. For he received honour and glory from God the Father when the voice came to him from the Majestic Glory, saying: 'This is my Son, whom I love; with him I am well pleased.' We ourselves heard this voice that came from heaven when we were with him on the sacred mountain. And we have the word of the prophets made more certain, and you will do well to pay attention to it, as to a light shining in a dark place, until the day dawns and the morning star rises in your hearts (2 Pet. 1:16–19).

And as Stanley Jones remarked, 'he is never called the evening star'.[7]

At the risk of over-quoting my earliest theological mentor, a man quite literally consumed with the passionate intensity of telling God's story, I close, as I began, by echoing the hard-won optimism and modest certainty of P.T. Forsyth.

> I hope, in these compressed and tense but not unmeaning words of mine, that the Lord in some measure has been transfigured before us. I hope the atmosphere has been luminous even if every thought is not lucid, and that it has been good to be here even if not knowing all we said. The glory of the Lord is something more than lucid when it breaks out upon waiting, watching, praying, bemazed disciples. And there is laid upon us, as we go down from the Mount, the command of silence in the form of incapacity for due speech. We cannot see the glory of that light, and what we do see is as yet beyond a human voice to utter. Still I trust that we have felt some of

the depth of that glory which with unveiled faces we shall one day behold, and rejoicing in it be made like it.

Let us, as we descend, go down with a secret which we cannot perhaps expound but which we cherish, and smile to each other like silent lovers in a crowd, and thus in a true Church of faith-adepts overcome the world. Let us go down to know that there is nothing in all the raging valley – neither the devilry of the world nor the impotence of the Church – that can destroy our confidence, quench our power, or derange our peace. Let us go down to know that the meanest or the most terrible things of life now move beneath the eternal mastery and triumphant composure of an almighty Saviour and a final salvation which is assured in heavenly places in Jesus Christ our Lord.[8]

Notes

[1] Jürgen Moltmann, *The Way of Jesus Christ: Christology in Messianic Dimensions*, 107.

[2] Ibid., 107.

[3] Hauerwas, *Peaceable Kingdom*, 97.

[4] Fackre, *Doctrine of Revelation*, 225.

[5] Ibid., 63.

[6] Ibid.

[7] E. Stanley Jones, *The Unshakable Kingdom and the Unchanging Christ*, 141.

[8] P.T. Forsyth, *The Person and Place of Jesus Christ*, 357.

Bibliography

Achtemeier, E., 'The Canon as the Voice of the Living God' in
    C.E. Braaten & R.W. Jenson (eds.), *Reclaiming the Bible for the
    Church* (Edinburgh: T. & T. Clark, 1995), 119–30

Achtemeier, P. & E., *The Old Testament Roots of Our Faith*
    (London: SPCK, 1962)

Adeney, B., *Strange Virtues: Ethics in a Multicultural World*
    (Leicester: Apollos, 1995)

Anderson, B.W., *Creation Versus Chaos: The Reinterpretation of
    Mythical Symbolism in the Bible* (Philadelphia: Fortress Press,
    1987)

—, *From Creation to New Creation: Old Testament Perspectives*
    (Minneapolis: Fortress Press, 1994)

—, *Contours of Old Testament Theology* (Minneapolis: Fortress
    Press, 1999)

Barth, K., *A Karl Barth Reader* (tr. by G.W. Bromiley, R.G. Erler &
    R. Marquard; Edinburgh: T. & T. Clark, 1986)

—, *Evangelical Theology* (Edinburgh: T. & T. Clark, 1963)

Bauckham, R., *The Theology of the Book of Revelation* (Cambridge:
    Cambridge University Press, 1993)

—, *The Climax of Prophecy* (Edinburgh: T&T Clark, 1993)

Beale, G., 'The Eschatological Conception of New Testament
    Theology', in K.E. Brower and M.W. Elliott (eds.), *The Reader
    Must Understand – Eschatology in Bible and Theology*
    (Leicester: Inter-Varsity Press, 1997), 11–52

Berger, P.L., *A Rumour of Angels: Modern Society and the Rediscov-
    ery of the Supernatural* (Harmondsworth: Penguin Books,
    1973)

Bock, Darrell, 'Scripture and the Realisation of God's Promises' in H.W. Marshall & D. Peterson (eds.), *Witness to the Gospel: The Theology of Acts* (Grand Rapids: Eerdmans, 1998), 41–62

Brown, W.P., *Character in Crisis: A Fresh Approach to the Wisdom Literature of the Old Testament* (Grand Rapids: Eerdmans, 1996)

—, *The Ethos of the Cosmos: The Genesis of Moral Imagination in the Bible* (Grand Rapids: Eerdmans, 1999)

Brueggemann, W., *Genesis* (Interpretation; Atlanta: John Knox Press, 1982)

—, *Hopeful Imagination: Prophetic Voices in Exile* (Minneapolis: Fortress Press, 1987)

—, 'A Shape for Old Testament Theology, 11: Embrace of Pain', in P. Miller (ed.), *Old Testament Theology* (Minneapolis: Fortress Press, 1992)

—, *Theology of the Old Testament: Testimony, Dispute, Advocacy* (Minneapolis: Fortress Press, 1997)

Buechner, F., *The Magnificent Defeat* (San Francisco: Harper-SanFrancisco, 1985 [1966])

—, *The Clown in the Belfry: Writings on Faith and Fiction* (San Francisco: Harper, 1992)

Burge, G.M., 'Territorial Religion, Johannine Christology and the Vineyard of John 15', in J.B. Green & M. Turner (eds.) *Jesus of Nazareth: Lord and Christ* (Grand Rapids/Carlisle: Eerdmans/Paternoster, 1994), 384–96

—, *John* (NIV Application Commentary; Grand Rapids: Zondervan, 2000)

Butterfield, H., *Writings on Christianity and History* (New York: Oxford University Press, 1979)

Caird, G.B., *The Gospel of Luke* (London: A. & C. Black, 1963)

—, *Commentary on the Revelation of St. John the Divine* (London: A. & C. Black, 1966)

—, *New Testament Theology* (Oxford: Clarendon Press, 1994)

Carson, D., 'Matthew' in Frank Gaebelein (ed.), *The Expositors Bible Commentary.* Vol. 8 (Grand Rapids: Zondervan, 1984)

Chesterton, G.K., *The Everlasting Man* (London: Hodder & Stoughton, 1928)

Clowney, E., *Preaching and Biblical Theology* (Grand Rapids: Eerdmans, 1961)

Curtis, B. & J. Eldredge, *The Sacred Romance* (Nashville: Thomas Nelson, 1997)

DeSilva, D.A., *The Hope of Glory: Honor Discourse and New Testament Interpretation* (Collegeville: The Liturgical Press, 1999)

—, *Honor, Patronage, Kinship & Purity* (Downers Grove: Inter-Varsity Press, 2000)

—, *Perseverance and Gratitude: A Socio-Rhetorical Commentary on the Epistle to the Hebrews* (Grand Rapids: Eerdmans, 2000)

Dodd, C.H., *According to the Scriptures: The Sub-structure of New Testament Theology* (London: Fontana, 1965)

—, *The Founder of Christianity* (London: Collins, 1971)

Dudley-Smith, T., *John Stott: The Making of a Leader* (Leicester: Inter-Varsity Press, 1999)

Dumbrell, W.J., *Covenant and Creation: A Theology of the Old Testaments Covenants* (Exeter: Paternoster, 1984)

—, *The End of the Beginning: Revelation 21–22 and the Old Testament* (NSW: Lancer Books, 1985)

Durham, J., *Exodus* (WBC; Waco: Word, 1987)

Dyrness, W.A., *Themes in Old Testament Theology* (Downers Grove/Exeter: InterVarsity Press/Paternoster, 1979)

Ellul, J., *The Presence of the Kingdom* (London: SCM Press, 1951)

Enns, P., *Exodus* (NIVAC; Grand Rapids: Zondervan, 2000)

Evans, C.A., 'Jesus & the Continuing Exile of Israel', in C. Newman (ed.) *Jesus and the Restoration of Israel: A Critical Assessment of N.T. Wright's 'Jesus and the Victory of God'* (Downers Grove/Carlisle: InterVarsity Press/Paternoster, 1999), 76–100

Fackre, D. & G., *Christian Basics: A Primer for Pilgrims* (Grand Rapids: Eerdmans, 1991)

Fackre, G., *The Christian Story: A Pastoral Systematics* (Grand Rapids: Eerdmans, 1978)

—, *The Doctrine of Revelation: A Narrative Interpretation* (Edinburgh: Edinburgh University Press, 1997)

Farrar Capon, R., *The Romance of the Word* (Grand Rapids: Eerdmans, 1995)

Fishbane, M., *Biblical Text and Texture: A Literary Reading of Selected Texts* (Oxford: Oneworld, 1998)

Forsyth, P.T., *Missions in State and Church* (London: Hodder & Stoughton, 1908)

—, *This Life and the Next: The Effect on this Life of Faith in Another* (London: The Macmillan Company, 1918)

—, *The Justification of God: Lectures for Wartime on a Christian Theodicy* (London: The Independent Press, 1948 [1917])

—, *God the Holy Father* (London: The Independent Press, 1957 [1897])

—, *The Person and Place of Jesus Christ* (London: Independent Press, 1961 [1909])

Fowler, J., *Faith Development and Pastoral Care* (Minneapolis: Fortress Press, 1988)

France, R.T., *Matthew – Evangelist and Teacher* (Exeter: Paternoster, 1989)

—, *Jesus and The Old Testament: His Application of Old Testament Passages to Himself and His Mission* (Vancouver: Regent College Publishing, 1998)

Fretheim, T., *Exodus* (Interpretation; Louisville: John Knox Press, 1991)

Gibson, R.J. (ed.), *Interpreting God's Plan: Biblical Theology and the Pastor* (Carlisle: Paternoster, 1998)

Goldingay, J., *Models for Scripture* (Grand Rapids: Eerdmans, 1994)

Gordon, R., *1 and 2 Samuel* (Exeter: Paternoster, 1986)

Gowan D., *Theology in Exodus: Biblical Theology in the Form of a Commentary* (Louisville: Westminster John Knox Press, 1994)

Green, J.B., *The Gospel of Luke* (NICNT; Grand Rapids: Eerdmans, 1997)

Grenz, S., *Theology for the Community of God* (Nashville/Carlisle: Broadman and Holman/Paternoster, 1994)

Guinness, O., *The Call: Finding and Fulfilling the Central Purpose of Your Life* (Nashville: Word, 1998)

Hamilton, V.P., *The Book of Genesis 1–17* (NICOT; Grand Rapids: Eerdmans, 1990)

Harris, M.J. *Colossians and Philemon: Exegetical Guide to the Greek New Testament* (Grand Rapids: Eerdmans, 1991)

Hauerwas, S., *The Peaceable Kingdom: A Primer in Christian Ethics* (London: SCM, 1984)

—, *Truthfulness and Tragedy: Further Investigations in Christian Ethics* (Notre Dame: University of Notre Dame Press, 1985 [1977])

Hauerwas, S., & W. Willimon, *Resident Aliens: A Provocative Christian Assessment of Culture and Ministry for People Who Know That Something is Wrong* (Nashville: Abingdon, 1993 [1989])

—, *Lord, Teach Us: The Lord's Prayer & the Christian Life* (Nashville: Abingdon, 1996)

Hays, R., *The Faith of Jesus Christ: An Investigation of the Narrative Substructure of Galatians 3:1–4:11* (SBLDS 56; Chico: Scholars Press, 1983)

—, *Echoes of Scripture in Paul* (New Haven: Yale University Press, 1989)

—, 'Crucified with Christ': A synthesis of the Theology of 1 and 2 Thessalonians, Philemon, Philippians and Galatians', in Jouette Bassler (ed.) *Pauline Theology* (Vol. 1 – Thessalonians, Philippians, Galatians, Philemon; 4 Vols.; Minneapolis: Fortress Press, 1991–7 [1991]), 227–46

—, 'Adam, Israel, Christ – The Question of Covenant in the Theology of Romans: A Response to Leander E. Keck and N.T. Wright', in David Hay & Elizabeth E. Johnson (eds.), *Pauline Theology* (Vol. 3 – Romans; 4 Vols.; Minneapolis: Fortress Press, 1991–7 [1995]), 68–86

—, *The Moral Vision of the New Testament: Community, Cross, New Creation: A Contemporary Introduction to New Testament Ethics* (Edinburgh: T. & T. Clark, 1997)

Heschel, A., *Man Is Not Alone: A Philosophy of Religion* (New York: The Noonday Press, 1951)

—, *Moral Grandeur and Spiritual Audacity: Essays* (New York: Farrar, Straus and Giroux, 1996)

Holwerda, D.E., *Jesus & Israel: One Covenant or Two?* (Grand Rapids/Leicester: Eerdmans/Apollos, 1995)

Hull, B., *Building High Commitment in a Low Commitment World* (New York: Fleming Revell, 1995)

Jantzen, J.G., *Job* (Interpretation; Atlanta: John Knox Press, 1985)

Jenson, R.W., 'How the world lost its story' *First Things* 36 (1993), 19–24

Johnston, P. & P. Walker (eds.), *The Land of Promise: Biblical, Theological and Contemporary Perspectives* (Leicester: Inter-Varsity Press, 2000)

Jones, Stanley E., *The Unshakable Kingdom and the Unchanging Christ* (Nashville: Abingdon, 1972)

Kaiser Jnr., W.C., *Toward an Old Testament Theology* (Grand Rapids: Zondervan, 1978)

—, *Toward Rediscovering the Old Testament* (Grand Rapids: Zondervan, 1987)

Keesmat, S.C., *Paul and his Story: (Re)interpreting the Exodus Tradition* (JNTS; Sheffield: Sheffield Academic Press, 1999)

Kilne, M.G., *The Structure of Biblical Authority* (Grand Rapids: Eerdmans, 1972)

Knight III, H.H., *A Future for Truth: Evangelical Theology in a Postmodern World* (Nashville: Abingdon, 1997)

König, A., *The Eclipse of Christ in Eschatology* (Grand Rapids: Eerdmans, 1989)

Lewis, C.S. 'The Magicians Nephew' in *The Chronicles of Narnia* (London: Collins, 1998)

Linafelt, T., & T.K. Beal (eds.), *God in the Fray: A Tribute to Walter Brueggemann* (Minneapolis: Fortress Press, 1998)

Lincoln, Λ., *Ephesians* (WBC; Dallas: Word, 1990)

Lints, R., *The Fabric of Theology: A Prolegomenon to Evangelical Theology* (Grand Rapids: Eerdmans, 1993)

Lloyd-Jones, D.M., *God's Ultimate Purpose: An Exposition of Ephesians One* (Edinburgh: The Banner of Truth Trust, 1978)

Longenecker, B.W., 'Covenant Theology', in Richard Longenecker (ed.) *The Road to Damascus: The Impact of Paul's Conversion on His Life, Thought, and Ministry* (Grand Rapids: Eerdmans, 1997), 125–46

—, *The Triumph of Abraham's God: The Transformation of Identity in Galatians* (Edinburgh: T. & T. Clark, 1998)

Lyotard, J.F., *The Postmodern Condition: A Report on Knowledge* (tr. G. Bennington and B. Massumi; Minneapolis: University of Minneapolis Press, 1984)

Mascall, E.L., *Grace and Glory* (London: The Faith Press, 1961)

McClendon, J. Wm., *Systematic Theology* (Vol 1 – *Ethics*; Vol. 2 – *Doctrine*; Nashville: Abingdon, 1986)

McComiskey, T.E., *The Covenants of Promise: A Theology of the Old Testament Covenants* (Nottingham: Inter-Varsity Press, 1985)

McGrath, A.E., *Evangelicalism and the Future of Christianity* (London: Hodder & Stoughton, 1994)

—, *A Passion for Truth: The Intellectual Coherence of Evangelicalism* (Leicester: Apollos, 1996)

McNight, S., *A New Vision for Israel: The Teachings of Jesus in National Context* (Grand Rapids: Eerdmans, 1999)

Mehl, R., *The Ten(der) Commandments* (Oregon: Multnomah, 1998)

Messer, D.E., *Contemporary Images of Christian Ministry* (Nashville: Abingdon Press, 1989)

Meyer, B., *The Aims of Jesus* (London: SCM, 1979)

Middleton, J.R. & B.J. Walsh, 'Facing the Postmodern Scalpel: Can the Christian Faith Withstand Deconstruction', in T.R. Phillips and D.L. Okholm (eds.), *Christian Apologetics in the Postmodern World* (Downers Grove: InterVarsity Press, 1995), 131–54

—, *Truth is Stranger Than It Used To Be: Biblical Faith in a Postmodern Age* (London: SPCK, 1995)

Miller, C., *The Singer* (London: CPAS, 1976)

—, *Spirit, Word and Story: A Philosophy of Preaching* (Dallas: Word, 1989)

—, *Into the Depths of God* (Minneapolis: Bethany House Publishers, 2000)

Moberley, R.W.L., *The Bible, Theology and Faith: A Study of Abraham and Jesus* (Cambridge: Cambridge University Press, 2000)

Moltmann, J., *Theology of Hope: On the Ground and the Implications of a Christian Eschatology* (London: SCM, 1967)

—, *God in Creation: An Ecological Doctrine of Creation: The Gifford Lectures 1984–1985* (London: SCM, 1985)

—, *The Way of Jesus Christ: Christology in Messianic Dimensions* (London: SCM, 1990)

Morris, L., *The Apostolic Preaching of the Cross* (London: Tyndale Press, 1960)

Neuhaus, R.J., *Freedom for Ministry* (Grand Rapids: Eerdmans, 1979)

Newbigin, L., *Truth to Tell: The Gospel as Public Truth* (London: SPCK, 1991)

—, *A Word in Season: Perspectives on Christian World Missions* (Grand Rapids: Eerdmans, 1994)

Owens, V.S., *And The Trees Clap Their Hands: Faith, Perception, and the New Physics* (Grand Rapids: Eerdmans, 1983)

Palmer Robertson, O., *The Christ of the Covenants* (Phillipsburg: Presbyterian & Reformed, 1980)

Perdue, L.G., *Wisdom in Creation: The Theology of Wisdom Literature* (Nashville: Abingdon, 1994)

Peterson, E., 'Eat This Book: The Holy Community at the Table of the Holy Scripture' in *Theology Today* 56.1 (April, 1999), 13–4

Phillips, J.B., *Your God is too Small* (London: Epworth, 1952)

—, *The New Testament in Modern English* (London: Geoffrey Bles, 1958)

Phillips, T.R. & D.L. Okholm (eds.), *Christian Apologetics in the Postmodern World* (Downers Grove: InterVarsity Press, 1995)

Piper, J., *Desiring God: Meditations of a Christian Hedonist* (Oregon: Multnomah Press, 1986)

—, *The Pleasures of God: Meditations on God's Delight in Being God* (Oregon: Multnomah, 1991)

—, *The Purifying Power of Living by Faith in Future Grace* (Leicester/Oregon: Inter-Varsity Press/Multnomah, 1995)

—, *God's Passion for His Glory: Living the Vision of Jonathan Edwards* (Leicester: Inter-Varsity Press, 1998)

Pryor, J.W., *John, Evangelist of the Covenant People: The Narratives and Themes of the Fourth Gospel* (London: Darton, Longman & Todd, 1992)

Ramachandra, V., *The Recovery of Mission: Beyond the Pluralist Paradigm* (Carlisle: Paternoster, 1996)

Richardson, D., *Eternity in their Hearts* (Ventura: Regal Books, 1981)

Scott, J.M., 'For as many as under the works of the Law are under a Curse', in C.A. Evans & J.A. Sanders (eds.), *Paul and the Scriptures of Israel* (JSNT; Sheffield: Sheffield Academic Press, 1993), 187–221

—, 'The Restoration of Israel', in G.F. Hawthorne, R.P. Martin &

D.G. Reid (eds.), *Dictionary of Paul and his Letters* (Downers Grove/Leicester: InterVarsity Press/Inter-Varsity Press, 1993)

Sennett, R., *The Corrosion of Character: The Personal Consequences of Work in the New Capitalism* (New York: W.W. Norton, 1998)

Sereny, G., *Albert Speer: His Battle with Truth* (London: Picador Books, 1996)

Smail, T., *Reflected Glory: The Spirit in Christ and Christians* (London: Hodder, 1975)

Smedes, L., *How Can It Be All Right When Everything Is All Wrong?* (San Fransisco: Harper, 1992)

Squires, J.T., 'The Plan of God' in H.W. Marshall & D. Peterson (eds.), *Witness to the Gospel: The Theology of Acts* (Grand Rapids: Eerdmans, 1998), 19–39

Thielicke, H., *The Silence of God* (Grand Rapids: Eerdmans, 1962)

Tolkien, J.R.R., *The Lord of the Rings* (London: George Allen & Unwin, 1969)

VanGemeren, W.A., *The Progress of Redemption: The Story of Salvation from Creation to the New Jerusalem* (Grand Rapids: Zondervan, 1988)

—, *Interpreting the Prophetic Word: An Introduction to the Prophetic Literature of the Old Testament* (Grand Rapids: Zondervan, 1990)

Vos, G., *Biblical Theology, Old and New Testament* (The Banner of Truth Trust, 1948)

Walker, P.W.L., *Jesus and the Holy City: New Testament Perspectives on Jerusalem* (Grand Rapids: Eerdmans, 1996)

Webb, B., *The Message of Isaiah* (BST; Leicester: Inter-Varsity Press, 1996)

Webb, W.G., *Returning Home: New Covenant and Second Exodus as the Context for 2 Corinthians 6:14–7:1* (JNTS; Sheffield: Sheffield Academic Press, 1993)

Wells, D.F., *No Place for Truth: The Reality of Truth in a World of Fading Dreams* (Grand Rapids: Eerdmans, 1993)

—, *God in the Wasteland: The Reality of Truth in a World of Fading Dreams* (Grand Rapids/Leicester: Eerdmans/Inter-Varsity Press, 1994)

Wells, S., *Transforming Fate into Destiny: The Theological Ethics of Stanley Hauerwas* (Carlisle: Paternoster, 1998)

Wenham, G., *Genesis 1–15* (WBC; Waco: Word, 1987)

Williamson, P.R., 'Promise and Fulfilment: The territorial inheritance', in P. Johnston & P. Walker (eds.) *The Land of Promise: Biblical, Theological and Contemporary Perspectives* (Leicester: Inter-Varsity Press, 2000), 15–34

—, *Abraham, Israel and the Nations: The Patriarchal Promise and its Covenantal Development in Genesis* (Sheffield: Sheffield Academic Press, 2000)

Willimon, W., & S. Hauerwas, *Lord, Teach Us: The Lord's Prayer & the Christian Life* (Nashville: Abingdon, 1996)

Willimon, W.H., *Shaped by the Bible* (Nashville: Abingdon, 1990)

Witherington, B., *The Christology of Jesus* (Minneapolis: Fortress Press, 1990)

—, *Paul's Narrative Thought World: The Tapestry of Tragedy and Triumph* (Louisville: Westminster John Knox Press, 1994)

—, *The Paul Quest: The Renewed Search for the Jew of Tarsus* (Downers Grove: InterVarsity Press, 1998)

Wright, C.J.H., *Knowing Jesus Through the Old Testament: Rediscovering the Roots of Our Faith* (London: Marshall Pickering, 1992)

—, *Walking in the Ways of the Lord: The Ethical Authority of the Old Testament* (Leicester: Apollos, 1995)

—, *Deuteronomy* (NIBC; Peabody/Carlisle: Hendrikson/Paternoster, 1996)

Wright, N.T., 'Jesus', in S.B. Ferguson & D.F. Wright (eds.), *New Dictionary of Theology* (Downers Grove: InterVarsity Press, 1988), 348–51

—, *The Climax of the Covenant: Christ and the Law in Pauline Theology* (Edinburgh: T. & T. Clark, 1991)

—, *The New Testament and the People of God* (London: SPCK, 1992)

—, *Who Was Jesus?* (London: SPCK, 1992)

—, *Jesus and the Victory of God* (London: SPCK, 1996)

—, *The Original Jesus: The Life and Vision of a Revolutionary* (Oxford: Lion, 1996)

—, 'Jesus and the Quest', in D. Armstrong (ed.), *The Truth about Jesus* (Grand Rapids: Eerdmans, 1998), 4–25

—, 'New Exodus, New Inheritance: the Narrative Substructure of Romans 5–8', in S. Soderlund & N.T. Wright (eds.), *Romans and the People of God: Essays in Honour of Gordon Fee on the Occasion of his 65th Birthday* (Grand Rapids: Eerdmans, 1999), 26–35

—, *The Challenge of Jesus: Rediscovering Who Jesus Was and Is* (London: SPCK, 2000)

Yoder, J.H., *The Royal Priesthood* (Grand Rapids: Eerdmans, 1994)

Young, F., & D. Ford, *Meaning and Truth in 2 Corinthians* (London: SPCK, 1987)

Zuck, R., (ed.), *A Biblical Theology of the Old Testament* (Chicago: Moody Press, 1991)